CONTRACTS OF EMPLOYMENT

by Michael Duggan

Employment Law, Practice and Precedents Series

General Editor, Michael Duggan

Published by
EMIS Professional Publishing Ltd
31–33 Stonehills House
Welwyn Garden City
Hertfordshire
AL8 6PU

ISBN 1 85811 239 7

Typeset by Tracey Dabell and Jane Conway

Cover design by Jane Conway
Cover photography by Jon Adams

Printed and bound in the UK by Antony Rowe Ltd, Bumper's Farm, Chippenham, Wiltshire.

For my Mother and Father

CONTENTS

FOREWORD

This book has had a very lengthy gestation period because of the pace of change in employment law over the last twelve months. The volume of legislation has been such that the CBI has asked the Government to enact no more employment legislation, claiming that the burden on employers runs in billions, whilst the Government estimate is an additional £14 million a year. Public Interest Disclosure, new Data Protection and E-mail Statute and Regulations, the Part Time Workers Regulations, developments in the Working Time Regulations, the implementation of the Employment Rights Act 1999, the new ACAS Code on Disciplinary and Grievance procedures, amongst others, have all conspired to repeatedly put back the publication date. Hopefully, the book is the better for being up to date. I am grateful to Andrew Griffin and Jane Cramp of EMIS (formerly CLT) Professional Publishing Ltd for their patience and forbearance as I repeatedly made excuses as to why the proofs were not quite ready.

This book is intended to be a practical working tool for the employment lawyer or human resources manager who needs ready access to contractual terms and conditions, and should appeal to specialist and non specialist alike. The scheme of the book and how to use it is set out in the first chapter. Hopefully, the book will prove useful as an everyday desktop working manual. The emphasis is on the precedents but there is also a running commentary on the legal principles which is meant as guidance rather than to be exhaustive. Suggestions are always welcome and contact numbers have been provided. The book should be read in conjunction with my other titles: *Unfair Dismissal, Law, Practice and Guidance* (February 2000); *Wrongful Dismissal, Law, Practice and Precedents* (forthcoming 2001) and *Re-organisations, Redundancies and Transfers* (forthcoming 2001) all published by EMIS (formerly CLT) Professional Publishing Ltd.

An on-line version of this book will be available in the Spring of 2001. Details of this updated service can be obtained direct from the publishers on 01707 334823 or at publishing@centlaw.com.

As ever my love and thanks go to my wife, Michelle, whose encouragement always keeps me going, and to my sons, Francis, Andrew and Thomas.

The law is stated as at 24th November 2000.

MICHAEL DUGGAN

LITTLETON CHAMBERS
3 KINGS BENCH WALK NORTH
TEMPLE EC4 Y 7HR
TEL: 020 7797 8600
E-MAIL: MDUGG@aol.com1

TABLE OF CASES

TABLE OF STATUTES
AND REGULATIONS

Statutes

Regulations

SECTION ONE
GENERAL PRINCIPLES OF
EMPLOYMENT CONTRACTS

CHAPTER ONE
INTRODUCTION

This book is intended to be a practical working manual for the employment lawyer who needs ready access to precedents on a whole range of employment contracts. Whilst there is a running commentary on the law, this is intended as guidance to illustrate the reasoning behind the precedents and, in a book of this size, should not be taken as comprehensive. There has been much statutory intervention of late which has a fundamental effect on the employees' rights and liabilities — with the commensurate knock on effect as to how contracts of employment should be drafted. The book is divided into four sections:

Part I   covers recruitment, section 1 statements and contracts of employment in general.

Part II   looks at specific types of contracts of employment on an A to Z basis from Agency Workers through to the new extended rights for 'Workers' contained in recent legislation. Particular issues, relevant to the type of work are highlighted and, where appropriate, precedents or part precedents are supplied, or the particular type of employment is cross referenced with the precedents in Part III.

Part III contains a model manual or sets of terms and conditions that may be incorporated into contracts of employment covering all relevant aspects of employment or used as a Manual. The precedents set out in this part are at the heart of this book, and are referred to throughout as the 'Model Terms and Conditions'/'Manual' precedents.

Part IV   deals with Service Agreements of Directors, since the contractual position of directors raises particular issues that are unique to the nature of their employment and company status.

Parliament has been pro-active in recent years in areas which affect how the contract of employment should be drafted. In particular:

- The Working Time Regulations 1998 affect the number of hours that a worker may be required to work, rest periods, breaks, holidays, holiday payments and nightworkers.
- The Public Interest Disclosure Act 1998 incorporates amendments into the Employment Rights Act 1996 relating to 'whistleblowing'.
- The National Minimum Wages Act 1998 came into effect on 1st April 1999.
- The Employment Relations Act 1999 affects maternity rights, introduces time off for parental leave and time off for dependants; affects the manner of representation before disciplinary and grievance hearings; introduces protection for part time workers and extends employment status, removes the ability to contract out for fixed term contracts, and has spawned a considerable body of statutory instruments, including the Maternity and Parental Leave etc Regulations 1999 [1999/3312].
- The draft Part Time Workers (Prevention of Less Favourable Treatment) Regulations 2000 give equal rights to certain part time employees in certain areas.
- The ACAS Code of Practice on Disciplinary and Grievance Procedures was laid before Parliament on 7th June 2000, and has come into force.

There has also been considerable case law that affects how contracts are drafted, notably **CarMichael v National Power PLC** [1999] ICR 1226 (which impacts upon casual workers) and **Cerebus Software Limited v Rowley** [2000] ICR (payments *in lieu*) and these are fully considered in the commentaries that follow.

RELATED PUBLICATIONS

This book has been written, mindful of the fact that *Unfair Dismissal* and *Wrongful Dismissal* cover the substantive law relating to dismissals in detail and there is a considerable overlap with this book. Wherever these publications contain further elucidation of the points made in the commentary, cross reference will be made to them.

A further publication is intended in 2001, namely *Reorganisations, Redundancies and Transfers*. This book will cover in detail employment law relating to re-organisations of a business, redundancies and redundancy procedures and transfer of undertakings as well as providing full precedents for these areas and is intended to be complementary to this book.

WRITTEN CONTRACTS OF EMPLOYMENT

Whilst it is not essential for there to be a written contract of employment it is advisable for the employer to have the duties and obligations of the employee reduced into writing. Protection is provided to the employer whose terms are clear and the employee will know where he stands, particularly in relation to disciplinary matters or employer's policies. If the contract is not in writing or some term has not been included, things said during the recruitment stage may be incorporated into the contract of employment. In **Tayside Regional Council v McIntosh** [1982] IRLR 272, for example, the employee applied for a job as a motor mechanic and was told at his interview that a clean driving licence was essential. His written offer of employment did not refer to a clean driving licence. When he lost his licence three years later he was dismissed. The EAT held that the need for a clean driving licence was an essential and continuing part of his job, so that the dismissal was fair (see further Chapter 2 on recruitment). Clearly if the requirement had been embodied in the written offer the case would not have ended up in the Employment Appeal Tribunal in the first place.

Although employers are obliged to provide a statement of Terms and Conditions under section 1 of the Employment Rights Act 1996 such a document will not necessarily constitute the Terms and Conditions of Employment, although it is a good starting point in considering what terms the parties intended to be in the contract (see further Chapter 3 on section 1 statements).

There are particular requirements relating to directors and they have therefore been dealt with in a separate part of the book. There are also areas of particular interest for specific employment situations and these are dealt with in alphabetical order in Section II, Chapter 5 (for example: Sunday working is a specific issue with betting or shop workers, as are deductions from wages and precedents are required in this respect).

THE KEY TO USING THIS BOOK

Section 1 of the Employment Rights Act 1996 contains a list of 15 matters which must be provided to the employee in written form within two months after the beginning of employment whilst section 3 specifies that a note must be provided which includes five matters where the number of employees in employment were more than twenty at the commencement of the employee's employment. These matters may be seen as the central terms of the employee's employment. If they are not provided the employee will have the right to apply to an Employment Tribunal in order to have them provided or clarified. However, they only provide a partial list of the terms and conditions which the reasonable, and prudent, employer will wish to include in the contractual relationship governing employer and employee. Account should be taken of the additional rights that employees have been given over the years, whether by statute or case law. The prudent employer will have provision relating to equal opportunities including harassment, maternity, paternity, dependants, staff development, health and safety, whistleblowing and the standard to be expected from their employees. The nature of the employment may dictate the necessity for provision relating to the type of employment, deductions from wages, Sunday working, working time and many other specialised matters.

All in all this presents a difficult task for a general book of this nature, that is, how to present precedents which are sufficiently all-encompassing to cover the many employment situations whilst at the same time making it sufficiently user friendly for the user to be able to draft together a contract that will cover the case in mind, a matter perhaps made more complicated by the size and resources of the employer for whom the contract is intended. In the case of the large scale employer a comprehensive Manual may be ideal; with the small employer it may be cumbersome and place impossible requirements on the employer (*i.e.* too detailed disciplinary procedures). I have therefore attempted to write this book on a "mix and match" basis where the drafter should be able to find all the essential clauses provided he follows the scheme set out herein. To explain how to use this book the following stages should be considered.

THE DOCUMENTATION REQUIRED BY THE EMPLOYER

1. The First Alternative

For the most straightforward of contracts the following documentation may suffice:
- The written letter of appointment or offer letter.
- The section 1 statement of Terms and Conditions.

2. The Second Alternative

However, the danger with only providing the documents in (1) is that they do not take into account the many statutory rights that are engrafted on by legislation. It is suggested that, as a minimum, the reasonable employer would be expected to have the following documentation in place:
- The written letter of appointment.

- Section 1 statement of terms and conditions or a contract of employment that contains these essentials but also covers relevant clauses such as duties, restrictive covenants, termination, garden leave and other clauses that are individual to the employee — such as deductions from wages and working time (these are listed in the paragraphs relating to particular areas of employment).
- A maternity and paternity policy (bearing in mind the provisions introduced by the Employment Relations Act 1999).
- Policy on dependants and a statement relating to other reasons for absence.
- Where applicable, a statement relating to employee representation.
- A policy on public interest disclosure (whistleblowing). This is likely to be of increased importance given the provisions introduced by the Public Interest Disclosure Act 1998.
- A clear Disciplinary Procedure.
- A clear Grievance Procedure.
- An Equal Opportunities Policy, including a policy on harassment.
- Health and Safety Policies.

3. The Third Alternative

The above documents may be issued as stand alone policies or be contained in a comprehensive Manual. The advantage of a Manual is that the employee knows precisely where to look and where he stands, particularly as the Manual may be updated from time to time. The documentation will then consist of:

- The offer letter of letter of appointment.
- The section 1 statement or contract of employment.
- The Manual.

> To follow the option you require, use the tables at page 9 to help compile the section 1 statement. Model letters of appointment are at Chapter 2.

Specific matters

Other than the policies and statements already referred to, specific matters may need to be covered such as the provision of a vehicle, restrictive covenants and other matters specific to the type of employment. These may be in a policy, a statement, a Manual or may more appropriately be dealt with in the contract that is specific to the individual.

THE TABLES

The following tables set out:

- The essential terms required by the section 1 statement and the appropriate section in section 3 of the Model terms and conditions/Manual where further clauses relating to these terms may be found.
- The areas relevant to the employment relationship which may be included in stand alone policy document or a manual and the sections of the Model Terms and Conditions/Manual where this stand alone document may be found.
- Specific areas where the employee may wish to include a statement in a policy document or manual but where it is necessary, if such clauses are to be definitively binding between employer and employee, to consider including these clauses in the contract of employment and the sections of the Model Terms and Conditions/Manual where these clauses may be found.

In addition Section 2 of this book deals with specific areas of employment and highlights clauses that should be included in the contracts of those working in these areas. Directors have been given a separate Section 4 as the contractual issues raised in relation to them are different from the other areas of employment.

SUMMARY OF ESSENTIAL TERMS AND CONDITIONS OF EMPLOYMENT

These are the terms and conditions that one would expect to find in the section 1 statement or any contract of employment because they are required by the ERA 1996.

Essential Terms and Conditions	ERA Section	Location of Terms and Conditions
Terms and conditions of employment that must appear in section 1 statements.		Terms and conditions in the Model Terms and Conditions /Manual which further expand upon the requirements of the section 1 statement. *(See also Chapter 4 on s.1 statements.)*
1. Name of employer and employee.	1(3)(a)	
2. Date when employment began.	1(3)(b)	
3. Date when continuous employment began.	1(3)(c)	
4. Scale or rate of remuneration.	1(4)(a)	Part E F
5. Intervals at which remuneration is paid.	1(4)(b)	Part E F
6. Terms and conditions relating to hours of work.	1(4)(c)	Part D
7. Terms and conditions relating to holidays and to holiday pay to enable the employee to precisely calculate entitlement.	1(4)(d)(i)	Part I Note the Working Time Regulations gives rights to holiday and holiday pay. *See the commentary to Part I.*

Essential Terms and Conditions	ERA Section	Location of Terms and Conditions
8. Terms and conditions relating to incapacity for work due to sickness or injury, including any provision for sick pay.	1(4)(d)(ii)	Part J
9. Terms and conditions relating to pensions and pension schemes.	1(4)(d)(iii)	Part F G
10. The length of notice which the employee is obliged to give and entitled to receive.	1(4)(e)	Part V There are statutory rights to minimum periods of notice.
11. The title of the job which the employee is employed to do or a brief description of the work for which he is employed.	1(4)(f)	Part B C Note the possibility of flexibility clauses which the employer may want to include.
12. Where the employment is not intended to be permanent, the period for which it is expected to continue or, if it is for a fixed term, the date when it is to end.	1(4)(g)	Part V See Chapter 5 on fixed term contracts.
13. Either the place of work or, where the employee is required to work or permitted to work at various places, an indication of that and of the address of the employer.	1(4)(h)	Part G Note the possibility of mobility clauses which the employer may wish to include.
14. Any collective agreements which directly affect the terms and conditions of the employment including, where the employer is not a party, the persons by whom they were made.	1(4)(i)	This will normally be referred to in the letter of appointment, section 1 statement or contract but may be incorporated by a policy/manual.

Essential Terms and Conditions	ERA Section	Location of Terms and Conditions
15. Where the employee is required to work outside the United Kingdom for more than one month: i) the period that he is to work outside the United Kingdom; ii) the currency in which he is to be remunerated iii) any additional remuneration and benefits provided by reason of him working outside the United Kingdom iv) any terms and conditions relating to his return to the United Kingdom	1(4)(k)	See Chapter 5 on employment overseas as this raises issues that are specific to the nature of this contract.

Where there are twenty or more employees, a note on disciplinary procedures that sets out the following:

16 Any disciplinary rules applicable to the employee or referring the employee to the provisions of a document specifying such rules which is reasonably accessible to the employee	3(1)(a)	Part R May be freestanding or in manual. Although the section refers to over 20 employees, the employer who does not have a proper procedure is at risk in unfair dismissal proceedings especially given the effect of the Employment Relations Act 1999.
17. By description or otherwise the person to whom the employee can apply if dissatisfied with any disciplinary decision relating to him	3(1)(b)	Part R Free standing or in manual.
18. A person to whom the employee can apply for the purpose of seeking redress of any grievance relating to his employment and the manner in which any such application should be made	3(1)(b)	Part S Free standing or in manual.

Essential Terms and Conditions	ERA Section	Location of Terms and Conditions
19. Where there are further steps consequent on any such application this should be specified (*i.e.* appeals).	3(1)(c)	Part R S
Pensions		
20. Where there are more than twenty persons it is also necessary that there be a note that states whether there is in force a contracting out certificate (issued in accordance with Chapter 1 of Part III of the Pension Schemes Act 1993) or stating that the employment is contracted out employment for the purposes of that Act	3(4)	Part F

The above 20 matters refer to the Particulars of Terms and Conditions that must be contained in the Particulars of Terms and Conditions or the contract of employment if that is what has been issued. In addition to those matters set out above, the reasonable employer will issue the employee with terms and conditions in relation to the following (which may be contained in the contract of employment, be issued as separate policy documents or, if there is a manual be contained in the employment manual).

The following table sets out, in alphabetic order, where these areas may be found in the Model Terms and Conditions/Manual. Careful consideration may need to be given to including these clauses in the contract or a policy statement if there is no manual applicable to the employment.

Terms	Location in Manual
Employee Representation	Part O The Employment Relations Act 1999 introduces new rights to trade union recognition. See the commentary to Part O.
Equal Opportunities	Part T
Harassment	Part T A separate harassment policy a sensible provision in light of recent cases. See the commentary to Part T.
Health and Safety	Part U
Maternity, Paternity and Dependency Leave	Part K Important new rights are introduced by the Employment Relations Act 1999.
Public Interest Disclosure	Part P Employers should have a policy under the new whistleblowing legislation that make it clear that employees have the right to air their concerns and the circumstances in which this is permitted.
Staff Development and Appraisal	Part N

OTHER SPECIFIC ISSUES

The employer may also wish to cover the following specific issues:

Subject	Contract	Policy	Location in model terms / manual
Cars	Mention will usually be made of the provision of the vehicle in the contract.	There should be a policy whether contained in separate document or manual.	Part F9 Stands alone as a policy or in manual.

Conduct and Standard of Work	Different jobs may merit different standards. See commentary to Part M.	Disciplinary procedure and specific policies.	Part M (Should be read together with the disciplinary procedure as breaches may give rise to disciplinary sanctions.)
Deductions from wages	Section 13(2) ERA 1996 requires a clause in the contract that constitutes an agreement in writing from the worker that there may be deductions.	Agreement to deductions must be in contract or in express written agreement. See commentary to F4.	Part F4 Certain provisions must be incorporated into contract or agreed in writing. *See 5.14 on Shop Workers*
Loans	Discretionary? Manual or policy is usually sufficient but may require specific agreement for deductions from wages.		Part F8 May stand alone or be in manual but note that it is sensible that the employee agrees possibility of deductions in writing.
Probationary Periods	Part H sets out requirements that may be in Letter of Appointment. It is sensible that employee knows of requirements before employment commences.		Part H If manual is to be given before or at time of appointment. The other alternative is to provide as a freestanding document.

Restrictions during and after employment	It is particularly important that restrictive covenants especially post termination are tailor made to the position.	A separate document is a good idea as it highlights the existence and important of the provisions.	Part Q Sets out many examples which may be contained in a manual but should also be contained in a separately signed document so that it may be regarded as tailor made to the employee.
Termination	Will be referred to in section 1 statement or disciplinary procedure. Right to require garden leave should be in contract.	Disciplinary Procedures or Policy likely to be relevant document.	Part V Note that grounds for termination may depend on the nature of the contract (*i.e.* a contract for a task or while funding exists).
Time off other than sickness, holiday, maternity, paternity, dependency	There may be a statutory right (*i.e.* public Service) or discretionary. Check Part L to decide whether to include in contract.	Can be stand alone policy.	Part L Sets out specific areas.
Working Time Regulations	Agreement to waive 48 hour week may be agreed with worker. See the chart at pages 216ff.	Exclusion or modification in relation to reference periods, night work, rest breaks, leave may be in collective/ work-force agreement. See the chart at pages 216ff	Part D contains a commentary on the Regulations. Necessary to ensure that agreements have been incorporated by employee's agreement or collective/work-force agreement.

Each section commences, where appropriate, with specific precedents that cover the area. There then follows a commentary on the area of law and upon the specific contents of the precedents or the requirements of the particular employment. It is hoped that practitioners will be able to find a precedent to cover the employment situation with which they are concerned and the structure of the book will enable updates from time to time.

If any readers have any suggestions about further additions to, or improvements that may be made to this book, they would be welcomed by the author, who can be contacted at:

Michael Duggan,
Chambers of Michael Kallipetis QC,
Littleton Chambers,
3 Kings Bench Walk North,
Temple EC4Y 7HR

or

MDUGG@aol.com

In particular, any suggestions for further precedents are welcome.

CHAPTER TWO
RECRUITMENT AND
JOB OFFERS

PRECEDENT 2.1: OFFER OF EMPLOYMENT TO POTENTIAL EMPLOYEE

DATE

Dear

I am writing to you to confirm the offer that was made to you at your interview on .... and to set out the principal terms and conditions that will be applicable to your appointment. As explained to you at the interview, the Terms and Conditions of the Company's manual and the Company's section 1 Statement of Terms and Conditions are incorporated into your contract. Where there is any conflict between this letter and the section 1 statement or Manual then this letter will prevail.

PRE-CONDITIONS

I formally offer you the position of ....

References
This offer of employment is subject to the Company receiving satisfactory references from the [NUMBER] referees that you named upon your application form, and you confirmed by signing that form that you have no objection to the Company writing to your named referees. Please note that this offer of employment is liable to be withdrawn if the references are, for any reason, not satisfactory or your referees do not provide the references.

Ability to accept offer of work

You confirmed at the interview that you are not subject to any restrictive covenants [that your current employer has no objection to you taking up the above post] and that you are required to give .... weeks/days' notice to your employer. This offer is conditional on you taking up employment with the Company by .... though an earlier start will be welcomed. Please advise us if there are any difficulties in this respect.

Work permits

As you are aware, the Company must obtain a work permit to enable it to allow you to work in the United Kingdom. Upon confirmation that you accept this offer an application will be made and this offer is conditional on that application being successful.

Medical examination

The job offer is further dependant upon a medical examination to confirm that you are fit and able to do the work. Please contact Personnel at .... so that an appointment can be arranged.

You confirmed at the interview that you had no disability or other impediment that may affect you in this position. The Company is an Equal Opportunity employer and seeks to accommodate persons with disabilities. If there are any problems you should consult the Personnel Department.

Qualifications

You confirmed that you were qualified as [SET OUT] and had the appropriate qualifications from [SET OUT NATURE AND BODY] and this offer is made subject to your producing written confirmation.

Driving licence

It is a condition of this job offer that you have a valid driving licence and your employment is at all times subject to you being able to continue to drive. It is not Company policy to permit disqualified drivers to use other means of transport.

Covenants

It is a condition of this job offer that you sign and return the Confidentiality/ Covenant agreement contained with this letter. If you do not sign this then your employment will not be confirmed.
[SEE PART Q OF MODEL TERMS FOR DRAFTS.]

Probationary period

The first six months of your employment is a probationary period. However, you may be dismissed at any time during this period if the standard of your work or your conduct is considered to be unsatisfactory. If your employment is considered satisfactory then it will be confirmed at the end of six months. During the probationary period the notice will be one week on either side. If your employment is confirmed it will be [as per the Statement of Terms and Conditions/Manual/Contract of Employment].

Place of work

You will be employed at the Company's [Head Office] at .... but you accept that you are subject to being moved to any office of the Company in the United Kingdom [*ALTERNATIVELY CLAUSES IN PART G OF THE MANUAL*].

Salary and benefits

Your commencing salary will be £....... gross per annum payable monthly in arrears by transfer.

You will be eligible to join the Company's pension scheme once you have completed the necessary qualifying period.

You will be eligible to a Company car being ....

[SEE PART F OF THE MANUAL FOR OTHER ITEMS THAT MAY BE INCLUDED.]

As already stated, all other terms and conditions are contained within the Statement of Terms and Conditions/Contract of Employment [and the Company Manual].

Please sign and return this letter, together with the Confidentiality document.

Yours sincerely,

....

I accept the employment terms set out in this letter and the enclosed particulars of terms and conditions of employment, together with the Manual. I agree that the terms set out herein will constitute the terms and conditions of my employment.

Signed: ....

Dated: ....

COMMENTARY ON OFFER LETTER

This letter contains the basic pre-conditions to the employee taking up employment (see Part H of the Manual for further drafts). In addition to the contents, where there is no company manual consideration may be given to including a job description (Manual Part B), a summary of the scope of the employee's duties (Manual Part C), detailed references to other benefits (Manual Part F), a mobility clause (Manual Part G) and entitlement to holiday and absence due to sickness etc (Manual Parts I to L) and consideration should be given to equal opportunity and other policies, in particular whistleblowing. Disciplinary procedures and other terms will, in any event, have been contained in the section 1 statement (see next chapter).

The following points may be made about Precedent 2.1:

- It is important to make clear which document will prevail in the event of any conflict.
- It should be made clear that the offer may be withdrawn if references are not satisfactory, even if the employee has commenced employment. Similarly, if qualifications are required then it should be made clear that the offer is dependant upon proof or, where they have not yet been obtained, that continued employment depends upon the employee successfully obtaining them (see commentary to Manual Part H).
- A medical examination will often be desirable. Note the way in which the DDA 1995 may affect the employer's duties.
- If a driving licence is needed this must be made very clear (see Manual Part H2).
- Where there is a probationary period the employer will wish to make it clear that the employer can terminate employment at any time **during** the probabtionary period of employment or it may find itself saddled with the probationer for the whole of the probationary period.
- Terms relating to restrictive covenants and to flexibility should be tailor made and the reader is referred to the Model Terms and Conditions/Manual for some ideas in this respect. A confidentiality document may be desirable.

RECRUITMENT: LAW AND PRACTICE

The recruitment process in the United Kingdom is largely free of statutory intervention and parties are, generally, free to agree terms and conditions, subject to legality and the statutory legislation which outlaws discrimination. It is necessary to consider the way in which the recruitment process should be carried out from the stage where the job is advertised to the nature and content of the job offer. In particular, the arrangements made for recruiting may be discriminatory where the employer has evinced an intention to discriminate under the SDA 1975, RRA 1976 or has failed to make a reasonable adjustment under the DDA 1995.

THE CONCEPT OF DISCRIMINATION: A SUMMARY

Race and Sex Discrimination

In order for there to be discrimination under the SDA 1975 and RRA 1976 there must have been direct or indirect discrimination.

- Direct discrimination is treating an individual less favourably than another real or hypothetical comparator on the grounds of sex or race.
- Indirect discrimination takes place where a requirement or condition is applied with which a considerably smaller proportion of the complainant's sex or racial group can comply, and which cannot be justified on grounds irrespective of race or sex.

Disability Discrimination

Discrimination under the Disability Discrimination Act 1995 can occur in two ways.

- Under section 5(1) an employer discriminates against a disabled person if for a reason which relates to the disabled person's disability he treats that disabled person less favourably than he treats or would treat others to whom the reason does not apply, and the employer cannot show the treatment to be justified.
- Under section 5(2) the employer discriminates if he fails to comply with a duty of reasonable adjustment imposed on him by section 6 in relation to the disabled person and the employer cannot show that his failure was justified.

In disability cases a comparison is to be made between the disabled person and persons who were able to carry out the main functions of the job. The tribunal then moves on to consider the question of justification (see **Clark v TDG Limited (t/a Novacold** [1999] *Discrimination Law Reports* Issue 2 Page 240).

Arrangements

It is necessary for there to have been discrimination within the meaning of the above concepts before a claim may succeed. The Acts then set out various 'employment sanctions' whereby there may be discrimination in the employment field. In the area of recruitment it is unlawful for a person, in relation to employment, to discriminate:

> "in the arrangements he makes for the purpose of determining who should be offered that employment"
> (SDA 1975 s 6(1)(a); RRA 1976 s 4(1)(a); DDA 1995 s 4(1)(a)).

The word "arrangements" has a wide meaning. The Disability Discrimination Code of Practice refers to "specifying the job, advertising the job, and the process of selection, including the location and timing of interviews, assessment techniques, interviewing and selection criteria".

It is important to note that a different approach must be taken under the RRA 1976 and SDA 1975 to that under the DDA 1995. Whereas in race and sex discrimination cases the emphasis is on treating all candidates equally without reference to their sex or race, in disability related cases the individual circumstances must be considered and such consideration is in fact crucial in order to avoid discrimination.

Employers will have to reconsider their recruitment policies in order to meet the demands of the disability legislation; in particular the duty to make reasonable adjustments is a new concept to discrimination law and may require positive steps to be taken by employers. It does not matter that there is no intention to discriminate if that is the effect. There has been a spate of cases under the DDA 1995 since its implementation which offers guidance upon the circumstances in which a reasonable adjustment is appropriate.

Section 6 of the DDA 1995 contains provisions relating to the duty to make reasonable adjustments. This requires the employer in certain circumstances to take positive steps to accommodate the requirements of individual disabled persons. The duty to make reasonable adjustments is one of the central pivots of the Act because the manner in which the non disabled world structures employment and the workplace largely causes the difficulties that exist for disabled persons.

By section 6(1) where:

- any arrangements made by or on behalf of an employer, or
- any physical feature of premises occupied by the employer

place the disabled person concerned at a substantial disadvantage in comparison with persons who are not disabled, it is the duty of the employer to take such steps as it is reasonable in all the circumstances of the case for him to have to take in order to prevent the arrangements or feature having that effect.

A failure to comply with section 6 is not actionable in itself. The importance of section 6 is that it is unlawful discrimination to fail without justification to make a reasonable adjustment by section 5(2). This means that if there is a breach under section 4 and an employer has failed to make a reasonable adjustment then the employer will not be able to justify the discrimination.

There is no general duty to make reasonable adjustments to facilitate the employment of disabled people if the employer does not know and cannot reasonably be expected to know that a disabled person is an applicant or has a disability and is placed under a substantial disadvantage (section 6(6), DDA 1995). The knowledge of employees or agents are imputed to the employer (4.62 Code of Practice). (See **O'Neill v Symm & Co Limited** [1999] Disc LR 59; **Radiate v TC Group** [1999] Disc LR 9 for two cases where the employer was not aware of the disability.)

The adjustments may relate to arrangements or to the physical features of premises. Physical features of premises is defined in the Disability Discrimination (Employment) Regulations 1996 (SI 1996/1456) Regulation 9 as being:

- any feature arising from the design or construction of a building on the premises;
- any feature on the premises of any approach to, exit, from, or access to such building;
- fixtures, fittings, furnishings, furniture, equipment or materials on the premises;
- physical element of quality of any land on the premises.

The duty applies to premises occupied by the employer (section 6(1) DDA 1995). Section 16 may make deemed changes to a lease where the premises are occupied by way of a tenancy. There are various exceptions depending on the application of the Building Regulations and Listed Buildings which are outside the scope of this book.

Section 6(3) of the DDA 1995 sets out a list of examples of steps that may be taken. These are only examples and the Code of Practice sets out further examples. The Act refers to 12 matters:

(1)   making adjustments to premises;
(2)   allocating some of the disabled person's duties to other persons;
(3)   transferring the disabled person to fill an existing vacancy;
(4)   altering the disabled person's working hours;
(5)   assigning the disabled person to a different place of work;
(6)   allowing the person to be absent during working hours for rehabilitation assessment or treatment;
(7)   giving the disabled person or arranging for him or her to be given training;
(8)   acquiring or modifying equipment;
(9)   modifying instruction or reference manuals;
(10)   modifying procedures for testing or assessment;
(11)   providing a reader or interpreter;
(12)   providing supervision.

The Act is predicated on a cost/benefit basis in this respect. The Government can introduce a cap on the amount that employers must spend (s.6(9) DDA 1995) but this has not yet happened. Section 6(10) sets out a number of factors that will be taken into account in deciding whether it is necessary to take a particular step to comply:

(1)   the extent to which taking the step would prevent the effect in question;
(2)   the extent to which it is practicable to take the step;
(3)   the financial and other costs which will be incurred by the employer and the extent to which it would disrupt the employer's activities;
(4)   the employer's financial and other resources;
(5)   the availability of financial or other assistance.

If an employer should make a reasonable adjustment and there has been discrimination under section 4 then it will be liable. Failure to make a reasonable adjustment may be justified *if the reason for the failure is material to the circumstances of the particular case and substantial.*

The Disability Discrimination (Employment) Regulations Act 1996 covers performance related pay and pension schemes. In relation to performance related pay Regulation 3(2) provides that adjustments do not apply where the pay is wholly or partly dependant on the person's performance and the provisions apply to all employees or class of employees which includes the disabled person.

ARRANGEMENTS FOR RECRUITING

Arrangements for recruiting include:

(1)   Advertisements
(2)   Methods of recruitment
(3)   The role of Job Descriptions or specifications
(4)   Application forms and letters applying for employment, including the use of photographs
(5)   Selection criteria
(6)   Qualifications
(7)   Interviews and interview techniques
(8)   Work permits

Advertisements

The approach taken under the SDA 1975 and RRA 1976 to advertisements is different to that under the DDA 1995. Under the former two Acts, the Equal Opportunities Commission and the Commission for Racial Equality have primary responsibility in relation to advertisements that indicate an intention to discriminate. By section 38(1) of the SDA, section 29(1) of the RRA:

> "It is unlawful to publish or cause to be published an advertisement which indicates, or might reasonably be understood as indicating, an intention by a person to do any act which is or might be unlawful..."

within the meaning of the Acts.

The definition of advertisement is extremely wide under both Acts and includes:

> "...every form of advertisement, whether to the public or not, and whether in a newspaper or other publication, by television or radio, by display of notices, signs, labels, showcards or goods, by distribution of samples, circulars, catalogues, price lists or other material by exhibition of pictures, models or films, or in any other way, and references to publishing of advertisements shall be construed accordingly."
> (SDA 1975 s 82(1); RRA 1976 78(1)).

Employers should in practical terms make it clear that applicants will not be excluded because of their race, sex, marital status or disability. This will involve care in wording of adverts so that they cannot be taken as indicating an intention to discriminate against a particular group.

Section 38(3) of the SDA 1975 states that the use of a job description with a sexual connotation — *e.g.* waiter, salesgirl, postman or stewardess — shall be taken to indicate an intention to discriminate unless the advertisement contains an indication to the contrary. In **EOC v Robertson & Ors** [1980] IRLR 44 a tribunal considered this issue and provided a number of examples of advertised job descriptions that would be discriminatory because they had a sexual connotation:

- craftsman
- ex policeman or similar
- manageress had a sexual connotation but manager did not
- carpenter/handyman had a sexual connotation whereas carpenter did not
- an advertisement for a 'bloke'.

An advertisement for a head waiter was held to be unlawful in **EOC v Masser and Carriages Leisure Centre** [COIT 13013/90].

An advertisement for a secretary headed the 'Secretary's prayer' and consisting of a poem seeking a secretary 'willing to listen to her master's voice on eternal tapes' was held to be unlawful in **EOC v Eldridge McFarlane Watts** [COIT 17256/90].

The overall impact of an advertisement is also important. The EOC Code of Practice recommends that advertising literature be reviewed to ensure that it does not present men and women in stereotyped roles; for example showing just men carrying out the particular job. Nor should adverts contain requirements or conditions that could constitute indirect discrimination (see below) such as age limits, physical attributes and qualifications that are not justifiable in terms of the job on offer.

An advert is unlawful where it indicates or might reasonably be understood as indicating an intention to discriminate on the part of the employer. It does not matter that the employer does not intend to discriminate. In **Race Relations Board v Associated Newspapers Group** [1978] 3 All ER 419 Lord Denning stated that it is necessary to consider

> "what is the natural or ordinary meaning of the words? On this question no evidence is admissible to show what was intended by the words by the person who inserted the advertisement or published it; nor is evidence admissible to show what the readers of the advertisement understood by them. The question is one for the Tribunal of fact; what would an ordinary reasonable man or woman understand by the words?"

Some advertisements can be lawful even though they indicate an intention to discriminate. In particular where the job is one where a genuine occupational qualification applies under section 7 of the Sex Discrimination Act 1975 so that it may be offered to one sex only and reference should be made to the exceptions in that section.

Proceedings for enforcement can only be brought by the EOC or the CRE, the remedy being a declaration from a tribunal that the advert is unlawful. These bodies may also seek an injunction or carry out an investigation. However, although an individual cannot bring proceedings in the same manner as the EOC or CRE, it may be that the advertisement forms part of the arrangements for recruitment. If the individual is affected, a claim may be brought under section 6 of the SDA 1975 or section 4 of the RRA 1976, as in **Brindley v Tayside Health Board** [1976] IRLR 364 where the tribunal found there was such an arrangement. However, if the complainant has not applied for the job but merely objects to the content of the advertisement this will not be enough to found a cause of action (**Cardiff Women's Aid v Hartup** [1994] IRLR 390).

The provisions under the DDA 1995 are different. There is no provision that makes discriminatory advertisements unlawful. Instead section 11 of the Act provides that if the conditions contained therein are satisfied a presumption of discrimination may arise. The requirements are that:

- a disabled person has applied for employment with an employer;
- the employer has refused to offer or has deliberately not offered him the job;
- the disabled person has presented a complaint of discrimination;
- the employer has advertised the job whether before or after the disabled person applied for it;
- the advertisement indicated or might reasonably be understood to have indicated that any application would or might be determined **to any extent** by reference to the successful applicant not having any disability or category of disability that includes the applicant's disability or the employer's reluctance to make reasonable adjustments.

An advertisement under the DDA 1995 is defined as every form of advertisement whether to the public or not. The Disability Code of Practice gives the example of an advert that states:

"Sorry but gaining access to our building can be difficult for some people" [Paragraph 5.7]

(NB: The Code states that an employer may state that it welcomes applications from disabled people.)

Section 11(2) provides that the tribunal 'shall assume' unless the contrary is shown that the employer's reason for refusing to offer or deliberately not offering employment was related to the complainant's disability.

It may be a reasonable adjustment for an employer to provide information about jobs in a different format. The Disability Code provides an example of the employer who knows a person to be disabled providing information in a different medium *e.g.* braille, tape or computer disc (paragraph 5.9).

Different methods of recruitment

Certain methods of recruitment may have the effect of excluding classes of individuals as, by their very nature, they are limited in scope and may be indirectly discriminatory. Methods of recruitment include the following:

- *Recruitment by word of mouth*
  Where news of a vacancy is passed on by word of mouth in a white dominated workplace such vacancies may never come to the attention of other racial groups thus perpetuating racial imbalance.
- *Informal*
  Recruitment through the grapevine by word of mouth is potentially discriminatory. The CRE Code of Practice at paragraph 1.10 recommends that procedures should be avoided where recruitment takes place through the recommendation of employees if the skills set of workforce does not represent that of the labour market at large.
- *Employment Agencies*
  Recruiting through employment agencies where certain groups are not fully represented may constitute indirect discrimination (**Hussein v Saints Complete Home Furniture** [1979] IRLR 337).
- *Unsolicited letters*
  Care must be taken that unsolicited letters are not in reality recruitment 'through the grapevine'.
- *Internal appointments*
  Such appointments will often be justified by the needs of the business but care must be taken that appointments in this manner are justifiable if there is a racial or sexual imbalance in the workforce.

Job descriptions and specifications

Employers must be astute to avoid the implication of discrimination in the way that a job description is described. Recruitment literature must also be carefully vetted to ensure that there is nothing within it that may present the image of an all white/all male workforce or that disabled persons will not be welcome *e.g.* 'The company prides itself on being thoroughly British'.

In the field of discrimination, job specifications may have a particular impact in deterring disabled persons from applying for jobs. It is essential to check that job specifications are drawn up in a way that relates to the needs of the job and that it does not contain requirements or statements that may exclude disabled persons and not be justifiable as necessary for the job. Paragraph 5.3-4 of the Disability Code of Practice sets out examples of unnecessary or marginal requirements that may amount to discrimination:

- The employer stipulates that the employee must be 'energetic' when in fact the job in question is largely sedentary in nature.
- A driving licence is required when the job involves limited travelling.

Blanket exclusions may also lead to discrimination; for example excluding people with epilepsy or stipulating that candidates must not have a history of mental illness (paragraph 5.4 of the Code). Health requirements may be stipulated if they are needed for the job (Code paragraph 5.5). Employers may prefer a certain type of person but this may be discriminatory if it is not necessary for the job; *i.e.* a certain level of educational qualification which is not needed for the job and excludes a person with a learning disability.

Application forms and letters
With regard to race and sex discrimination, the employer must careful to ensure that application forms are so worded that they only ask questions that are relevant to the job. For example an employer must consider carefully whether it is necessary to include questions relating to the matrimonial status or domestic obligations of applicants as such questions may lead to an inference that women may be less favourably treated if they are married or have children. Application forms should all be processed in the same way and care should be taken to ensure that the same criteria and method of selection is applied to all applications. For example, separate lists based upon sex or racial groups must not be made. It should also be noted that the use of application forms or letters from applicants to form a view about the applicant's abilities may in itself be discriminatory if reading or writing English is not part of the job: **Isa & Rashid v BL Cars Limited** [COIT 1103/125]. The CRE Code of Practice states at paragraph 1.13 that the ability to complete a form should only be used as a means of assessment where it is a valid test of the standard of English necessary for the safe and effective performance of the job. Such use is also liable to be in breach of the DDA

1995 where it excludes people with learning disabilities and the requirements are not necessary for the job.

The application form is likely to be the first contact that an employer has with the applicant. An important issue for employers is whether they should ask about disabilities on the form. There is no duty to make reasonable adjustments until the employer knows that a particular disabled person is or may be applying for a job and is likely to be substantially disadvantaged by the employer's premises or arrangements (section 6(6)). Once the employer knows he may have to make reasonable adjustments. The Disability Code states at paragraph 4.57 that an employer should take all steps that he could reasonably be expected to in order to find out whether someone has a disability which may put him under a substantial disadvantage. The Disability Code of Practice at paragraph 5.11 suggests that an employer may also wish to ask whether the individual might need a reasonable adjustment.

Selection criteria

The way in which selection criteria is drawn up and applied may result in direct or indirect discrimination. Employers should be careful to ensure that any selection criteria that are drawn up are both relevant and objective or they may be liable for direct discrimination. Subjective criteria may lead to the danger of unconscious or conscious discriminatory assumptions on the part of employers and thus to a finding of direct discrimination. Selection criteria based on 'hunches', 'gut feeling' and subjective appraisal may be discriminatory (**Noone v North West Thames Regional Health Authority** [1988] IRLR 195). The CRE and EOC Codes of Practice states that selection criteria should be related to the job and should be aimed at measuring an individual's actual or inherent ability to do that job. The Code adds that the criteria should be reviewed on a regular basis to ensure that the criteria remain relevant and free from unjustifiable bias. Selection criteria should be applied in a way that does not amount to discrimination (see (**Gilby v Chesterfield Borough Council** [COIT 1800/146]). Random selection should generally be avoided.

Requirements or conditions that are imposed as part of the selection criteria may amount to indirect discrimination, though in order to fit within the concept of indirect discrimination the requirement or condition must generally be in the nature of an imperative: **Perera v Civil Service Commission** [1983] IRLR 166. However, requirements or conditions that have a disproportionate effect on one sex or racial group will be discriminatory unless they can be justified (**Price v Civil Service Commission** [1977] IRLR 291; **Hurley v Mustoe** [1981] IRLR 208).

It has already been noted above that selection criteria should be drawn up in such a way that they relate to the needs of the job and do not place disabled persons under a substantial disadvantage without justification. The Disability Code notes that it is not unlawful to carry out aptitude or other tests in the recruitment process but notes that in cases where tests substantially disadvantage disabled persons, the tests may need to be assessed to take account of the disabled persons "except where the nature and the form of the test were necessary to assess a matter relevant to the job". A lower pass rate or longer interview may be appropriate:

- where a numeracy test is set that is not related to the job and a person with learning difficulties does not achieve the level required;
- a short oral test is set and a disabled person who has a stammer when under stress is disadvantaged by the interview.

Qualifications

The qualifications that are required by an applicant should relate to the needs of the job. A requirement of GCSE's or A' levels for a manual job where such academic qualifications are utterly unrelated to the job may be discriminatory of certain racial groups. The employer should therefore be astute to ensure that its requirements do relate to the needs of the job functions. The EOC Code of Practice recommends that when recruiting the employer should:

- treat each individual according to his or her ability to carry out a job and not make assumptions based on sex;
- ensure that the qualifications or requirements for a job which may inhibit applications from one sex are justifiable;
- retain age limits for jobs only if they are necessary and justifiable.

On the other hand it may be evidence of direct discrimination that the person who was best qualified was passed over for the job, though in **McCormack v University of Reading** [COIT 886/231] a tribunal stated that "there is nothing in law which says that the best qualified person should get the job". Nevertheless, tribunals have found discrimination where the better qualified candidate has been passed over without any explanation that amounts to a sufficient justification (**Whittle v South Tyneside Metropolitan Borough Council** [COIT 1420/102]; **Dickinson v Durham County Council** [COIT 1537/22]). A difficult area is delineating between personality and qualifications since conclusions based on personality (*i.e.* the face does not fit) may be inherently discriminatory (**Staffordshire County Council v Bennett** [EAT 67/94]).

In the field of disability the Code notes that employers can specify that applicants must have certain qualifications. However, the employer will have to justify the requirement if a person is rejected due to a requirement that relates to his disability. The Code gives two examples:

- An administrative post requires a level NVQ 4 qualification and the disabled person has only reached level 3 because of his disability. If level 4 reflects the complexity and needs of the job and these aspects of the job cannot reasonably be altered by way of a reasonable adjustment then the employer will be able to justify rejecting the disabled person;

- Two GCSE's are specified as necessary simply to show that a candidate has the general level of ability required. A disabled person with dyslexia does not have the qualification but can show that she has the skill and intelligence required. The qualifications are therefore not justified.

Interviews and interview techniques

The way in which an interview is conducted may be of fundamental importance since the nature of the questions asked may indicate stereotyped assumptions about an applicant's sex/racial group/disability and may amount to less favourable treatment. Asking different questions may lead to an inference that there was discrimination. In **Saunders v Richmond upon Thames London Borough Council** [1978] ICR 75 it was said that putting certain questions to one sex and different questions to another sex was not in itself discriminatory but was likely to go some way to convincing a tribunal that the employer's final choice was in fact discriminatory. Questions that may indicate racial stereotyping are likely to be found to be discriminatory (**Adams v Strathclyde Regional Council** [EAT 456/88]; **Karimjee v University of Newcastle upon Tyne** [EAT 545/84]; **Virdee v EEC Quarries Limited** [1978] IRLR 295). The type of work that is involved may determine whether or not questions that are asked are discriminatory. In **Wedhead v West Yorkshire Police** [EAT 285/89] sustained questioning about domestic arrangements were held not to be discriminatory in the context of the special nature and demands of police work.

Questions relating to whether the applicant will be able to get on/be compatible with/be able to instruct and order work colleagues may indicate direct discrimination. For example: in **Makiya v London Borough of Haringey** [COIT 03023/89] asking a female how she would deal with reactionary male teachers was discriminatory where no male applicants were asked the question (see also **Simon v Brimham Associates** [1987] IRLR

307). The EAT has stated that words of discouragement at an interview may be part of the arrangements made for offering employment (**Tower Hamlets London Borough Council v Rabin** [1989] ICR 693), so that there may be discrimination in such a context.

Paragraphs 5.15 to 5.17 of the Disability Code deals with an employer's arrangements for an interview. 5.15 notes that giving applicants the chance to state any disability, and to suggest any reasonable adjustments, may help to avoid discrimination, whilst paragraph 5.16 notes that the employer may nevertheless be under a duty to make any reasonable adjustment from the time that it is discovered the applicant has a disability. A number of reasonable adjustments with regard to the interviewing process are outlined:

- rearranging the time of interview;
- carrying out the interview in such manner that the disabled person is not disadvantaged;
- paying travel expenses for a taxi rather than bus or train;
- holding the interview in a room that is accessible to a wheelchair;
- allowing a friend to be present;
- allowing longer for an interview where there is sign language or an interpreter.

In **Radiate v TC Group** [1999] IRLR 8 it was held that there was no duty to change the arrangements for an interview where the applicant alleged she was disadvantaged because she suffered from a rare form of epilepsy that meant the lighting at the interview affected her. No reasonable employer would have been expected to know about this without being told in terms by the applicant. Where the disability is an unusual one or requires an adjustment that may not be obvious to an employer it is important for individuals who consider an adjustment can be made to state this in the clearest possible terms.

The Act does not prohibit questions being asked about a person's disability and, indeed, the Disability Code at 5.20 states that an employer should only ask about a disability if it is relevant to a person's ability to do the job, after a reasonable adjustment if necessary. The Code gives the example of asking about changes that are needed in the workplace to accommodate the disability.

Work permits

An employer who improperly distinguishes between people on the basis of their real or assumed permit holding status runs the risk of a finding of discrimination. In **Grampian Health Board v Cole** [EAT 470/85] the

Respondents were found to have discriminated when they jumped to the conclusion that the applicant was a person who needed a work permit (see also **Karimjee v University of Newcastle Upon Tyne** [EAT 545/84]). However, it was held in **Dhatt v McDonalds Hamburgers Limited** [1991] IRLR 130 that there had not been discrimination when the employer asked the applicant to produce proof of entitlement to work on the basis that nationality was a relevant circumstance for differentiating between the two groups of job applicants.

The Asylum and Immigration Act 1998 creates a criminal offence to employ someone who has no permission to work in the UK. By section 8 it is a criminal offence to employ a person who has attained the age of 16 where the employee has not been granted leave to enter or to remain in the United Kingdom or the leave is not valid and subsisting or is subject to a condition precluding him from taking up employment. By section 8(2) it is a defence to prove that:

- before the employment began there was produced to the employer a document which appeared to him to relate to the employee and to be of a description specified in an order made by the Secretary of State; and
- either the document was retained by the employer or a copy or other record was made in a manner specified in the order.

The defence is, however, not available where the employer knew that the employment of the employee would constitute an offence under the section. A person is liable to a fine on scale 5 for a breach of this section and it may apply to a director, manager, secretary or other similar officer or any person who was purporting to act in such capacity where the offence has been committed by a body corporate and the offence has been committed with the consent or connivance of the individual or to be attributable to any neglect on the part of the individual.

TERMS ON WHICH EMPLOYMENT IS OFFERED

In this section two areas are considered:

(1) Discrimination in the terms of employment offered to the employee.
(2) Particular legal pitfalls that may apply in concluding the contract of employment with the employee.

Discrimination

The Acts provide that it unlawful to discriminate in the terms of which employment is offered to the complainant. There is again a departure between the RRA 1976, SDA 1975 and the DDA 1995 in respect of the terms on which employment is offered since the DDA 1995 *does* permit less favourable terms to be offered to disabled persons in certain circumstances whereas the other Acts outlaw such less favourable treatment. Applications under this head are relatively rare since by far the most common discrimination that occurs is by simply not offering the applicant the job. There is a 'pitfall' for complainants who have not reached the stage of being offered employment. In **Ogilview v Harchills Conservative Club** [EAT 449/92] the complainant walked out of an interview when she felt that she was being discriminated against. The EAT found that she would have been offered the job so that it could be said that there was discrimination in the arrangements for recruitment and as she had not yet been offered the job it could not be said there was discrimination in relation to the terms on which she was offered employment.

Section 4(1)(b) of the DDA 1995 makes it unlawful to discriminate in the terms on which the employment is offered to a disabled person. This means that the employer must consider whether any reasonable adjustments are necessary to be made in the terms and conditions, *e.g.* a change of hours where an applicant has difficulty using transport during rush hour. An employer may be able to offer a less favourable contract to a disabled person in certain circumstances. The Disability Code gives the example of a person's disability meaning that she has a significantly lower output of work but at the same quality as others. The employer would be able to pay less in proportion to the lower output.

Concluding the contract

The contract of employment is no different from any other contract in many respects, though there may be specific rules for certain types of employment. It is necessary for the parties to intend to create legal relations, for there to be an offer and acceptance of terms that are sufficiently certain and for there to be consideration.

Offer and acceptance

The terms that are offered must be sufficiently certain to be capable of acceptance. It is likely that the offer will contain certain pre-conditions — as with Precedent 2.1 — which must be satisfied before the employment of the individual is confirmed. There is however, a distinction between pre-conditions (such as a satisfactory medical reference or possession of a clean driving licence) and a statement from which it is clear that the parties are continuing to negotiate. This was the position in **Polymer Products Limited v Power** [EAT 599/80] where the employees' contract stated that on a relocation he would be offered new duties, relocation allowance and salary "as to be mutually agreed." The EAT held that this was not an offer capable of acceptance but merely an agreement to agree. This may be compared with **National Coal Board v Galley** [1958] 1 WLR 16 where a provision that deputies were to work such periods as reasonably required was held to be enforceable. Where the employer intends the offer of employment to be subject to a precondition this should be made clear as otherwise the employer may find itself stuck with an employee who has not complied with conditions that were intended but not incorporated (see **Stubbes v Trower, Still & Keeling** [1987] IRLR 321).

The employer should be careful not to induce the employee to give up any current employment until it is satisfied with the pre-conditions as there may otherwise be a collateral contract whereby in consideration for leaving employment, the employee is entitled to claim a period of employment (**Gill v Cape Contracts Limited** [1985] IRLR 499).

The terms of the contract

We have seen that the terms may be contained in the offer letter, the section 1 statement or other documents. Difficulties sometimes arise where the employer has made a statement in the advert or at interview and the employer must be careful to make it clear that it is the documentation that amounts to the terms of the contract. This occurred in **Joseph Steinfeld & Co v Reypert** [EAT 550/78] where there was a constructive dismissal because the job did not match up to what had been stated in the advert. Similarly, in **Holliday Concrete (Testing) Limited v Woods** [1979] IRLR 310 there was an unfair dismissal where the advert had stated that the job would last for 15 months and it finished prematurely. In **Pedersen v London Borough of Camden** [1981] IRLR 173 it was stated that a Tribunal can look at all the circumstances, including the advert, in deciding the terms of the contract. This will also apply to the employee, so, for example where the advert stated that a driving licence was required the EAT held that this could be looked at even though it was not mentioned in the contract (**Tayside Regional Council v McIntosh** [1982] IRLR 272).

Statements or promises made at the interview may be regarded as binding where they amount to an offer (**D H Russell (London) Limited v Magee** [EAT 201/78]). Thus, there were breaches in **Wilson-Undy v Instrument and Control Limited** [1976] ICR 508 and **Hawker Siddeley Power Engineering Limited v Rump** [1979] IRLR 425 where there were oral promises that the employees would not have to move sites and the employers then required them to move. It is clear that care is required as to what is said during the interview process so that the employee is not given a false expectation as to what the job entails.

REFUSING OR OMITTING TO OFFER EMPLOYMENT

Again, two specific areas of difficulty arise:

(1)   Discrimination by refusing or failing to offer employment;

(2)   The position where the employer or employee changes his mind.

Discrimination

It is necessary for the applicant to show that but for the discrimination the applicant would have got the job (or that there was a percentage chance that the applicant would have got the job). It was stated in **Callery v Leeds Metropolitan District Council** [COIT 867/181] that:

> "Discrimination always takes place against unsuccessful candidates. They are always treated 'less favourably' than the person who succeeds because, unfortunately in this life, not everybody can be appointed to the same job."

Nevertheless such 'discrimination' must not be on the ground of race, sex or disability and appointing a person with inferior qualifications to the complainant may lead to an inference of direct discrimination. The tribunal will examine all of the circumstances of the recruitment process to consider whether it has been tainted and may infer discrimination where the primary facts are consistent with a finding of discrimination and in the absence of any explanation on the part of the employer. One common scenario is for the complainant to be told that the job has gone only to see it advertised at a later date and an inference may be drawn in these circumstances. Similarly, with disability it is discrimination to refuse or deliberately omit to offer the job on account of disability. All of the above factors will be taken into account including whether a reasonable adjustment could have been made.

Change of heart

The employee may not turn up or the employer changes its mind about the employee's employability after having offered the job. Where there are pre-conditions there may not be a difficulty. Where the employee simply does not turn up there may be a breach of contract on his part but as the remedy will only sound in damages, is probably not worthwhile because of its quantum as the employer cannot compel the employee to work (section 236 Trade Union and Labour Relations (Consolidation) Act 1992). If there is a restrictive covenant the employer may be able to prevent the individual going to work elsewhere. If additional costs are involved in re-advertising a post then these may be claimed.

Where the employment has been offered and accepted and the employer then changes its mind it will be in breach and liable for damages for wrongful dismissal. In certain limited circumstances (where there is no breakdown in trust and confidence) an injunction may be granted (see further, Duggan on *Wrongful Dismissal, Law Practice and Precedents*).

CHAPTER THREE
RIGHT TO STATEMENT OF EMPLOYMENT PARTICULARS

PRECEDENT 3.1: STATEMENT OF INITIAL EMPLOYMENT PARTICULARS

These particulars are given to you in accordance with the requirements of section 1 of the Employment Rights Act 1996 which sets out certain minimal entitlements to particulars.

Your job title is .... and your supervisor is .... You should have been issued with a job description at the time of your employment.

STATEMENT OF TERMS AND CONDITIONS UNDER SECTION 1

1. Name and address of employer	Your employer is .... of ....
Name of employee	To..
2. Date when employment began	Your employment began on .... [DATE].
3. Date when continuous employment began	Your period of continuous employment began on .... No employment with a previous employer counts as continuous employment.

	[*ALTERNATIVELY*: Your employment with .... from .... counts as part of your continuous employment.]
4. Scale or rate of remuneration	Your scale or rate of remuneration is £...... per hour [*OR*] £...... per week [*OR*] £...... per month.
5. Intervals at which remuneration is paid	You will be paid [*WEEKLY/MONTHLY*] in arrears and your salary shall accrue from day to day. Payment will be made into your bank account on the .... day of each [*WEEK/MONTH*]. Salary increases are at the discretion of the employer.
6. Terms and conditions relating to hours of work	Your normal hours of work are from ..... am to ..... pm, Mondays to Fridays with .... for lunch. You must ensure that you can carry out your duties and it may be necessary to exceed your hours in accordance with the Working Time Regulations. Overtime may be payable *[SET OUT HOW - SEE PART E OF MANUAL]*. *[IT WOULD ALSO BE SENSIBLE TO STATE IF THERE ARE ANY EXCLUSIONS UNDER THE WORKING TIME REGULATIONS.]*
7. Holiday	(1) You are entitled to statutory holidays being New Year's Day, Good Friday, Easter Monday, May Day, Spring Bank Holiday, Late Summer Bank Holiday, Christmas Day and Boxing Day, or holiday *in lieu* if you work on those days. (2) In addition you are entitled to ...... days' holiday a year to be taken at times agreed with .... (3) The holiday year runs from ..... to....... .

	(4) You may not carry over holiday without permission which should be obtained from .... (5) You will be paid during the period that you take your holidays. (6) If your employment terminates and you have outstanding entitlement you will be paid your basic salary representing the number of days outstanding.
8. Absence due to sickness etc.	(1) If you are going to be absent from work for any reason you or someone on your behalf must contact your supervisor to inform them on the first day of absence and of the reason for absence. (2) You must complete a record form within 7 days from the commencement of your absence. (3) If you are absent for more than 7 days you must provide a medical certificate signed by your doctor that should be sent to your supervisor. (4) You will be entitled to your basic salary during absences up to ...... days per year. (5) You will not be entitled to payment if you are absent without authorisation or have not complied with the above procedure. *[NOTE ALTERNATIVE PROCEDURES IN THE MANUAL.]*
9. Pensions	There is no pension scheme applicable to your employment. [You are entitled to join the contributory pension scheme and may obtain details from ....]

10. Notice	You are entitled to the following notice: (1) Any time during the first six months' probationary period: 1 week. (2) If your employment is confirmed: — one week's notice up to two years' service. — one week's notice for each completed year of service up to a maximum of 12 weeks. Your employment may be terminated summarily in the event of breach by you that warrants summary termination. *[SEE THE MANUAL FOR FURTHER PROVISIONS.]*
11. Job title	As set out above.
12. Temporary or fixed term contracts	*[SEE PART V OF THE MANUAL AND CHAPTER 5.6 ON FIXED TERM CONTRACTS]*
13. Place of work	Your normal place of work is as set out above. You may be required to travel anywhere in the United Kingdom in the performance of your duties. *[SEE PART G OF THE MANUAL FOR ALTERNATIVE MOBILITY CLAUSES.]*
14. Collective agreements	There are no collective agreements affecting your employment.
15. Overseas employment	*[SEE CHAPTER 4 ON EMPLOYMENT OVERSEAS AS THIS RAISES ISSUES THAT ARE SPECIFIC TO THE NATURE OF THIS CONTRACT.]*

16. Disciplinary procedures	The disciplinary procedures are attached. They are not part of your contract of employment and the employer may alter them from time to time. *[SEE PART R OF THE MANUAL]*
17. If you are not satisfied with any disciplinary decision	If you are not satisfied with any disciplinary decision relating to your employment you may appeal in accordance with the terms of the disciplinary procedure. The appeal will be heard by *[SET OUT]*.
18. Grievances	You may raise any grievance that you may have in accordance with the terms of the grievance procedure.
19. Further steps	Any further steps that you may take consequent upon any disciplinary procedure or grievance are set out in the procedures.
20. Contracting out	A contracting out certificate pursuant to the Pension Scheme Act is [not] in force.

Your normal retirement age will be 65 and you will retire at the end of the month in which you attain that age.

I accept the above particulars of terms and conditions.

[OR]

I accept the terms and conditions as forming part of my contract of employment, subject to my letter of appointment and [the staff Manual].

....

SIGNED

COMMENTARY ON THE SECTION 1 STATEMENT

The following comments should be noted in relation to Precedent 3.1:

1. *The employer*
   Where the statement identifies a party as its employer and the employee acts in such a way that a reasonable man would rely on it, then it has been held that the party may be estopped from denying that they were the employer (**Smith v Blandford Gee Cementation Limited** [1970] 3 All ER 154).

4. *Scale or rate of remuneration*
   The statement must give the scale or rate of remuneration or the method of calculating it and the intervals at which it is paid. This may include bonuses (**Mole Mining Limited v Jenkins** [1972] ICR 282) or expenses (**S & U Stores Limited v Lee** [1969] 1 WLR 626) but does not include *e.g.* tips from a third party (**Palmanor Limited v Cedron** [1978] ICR 1008).

7. It is possible for there to be a situation where no accrued holiday pay is payable on termination of employment (**Morley v Heritage Tile** [1993] IRLR 400). It is important to note that the Working Time Regulations 1998 may affect the legality of holiday paid on an accrued monthly basis (see the commentary to Part I Model Terms and Conditions/Manual).

14. Where there are collective agreements which are incorporated into the statement then this will be stated. The issue of new terms and conditions which omit a statement that the Employer's General Instructions or collective agreements are included, which appeared in earlier statements may lead to the conclusion that such agreements and instructions are no longer incorporated (**Lee v GEC Plessey Telecommunications** (Unreported 19.1.1993 Connell J).

Note that many of the particulars need to be expanded upon by reference to other documents or more detailed terms. Where necessary this has been referred to.

The above section 1 statement contains the basic terms and conditions as required by section 1 of the Employment Rights Act 1996 and adopts the format in Chapter 1 so that it can be cross referred to the model terms/manual for ease of reference. The Model Terms and Conditions/ Manual provides a number of variants on these particulars which should cover most situations. In addition to these terms consideration should be given to the policies referred to in Chapter 1 as being necessary documents. Chapter 5 also contains provisions that are specific to particular employment and these can be incorporated into the section 1 statement. A comprehensive set of terms can by produced to cover the particular situation. Section 1 was amended to comply with the EC Proof of Employment Relationships Directive (91/533) (and see **Kampelmann & Ors v Landschaftsverband Westfalen-Lippe** [1998] IRLR 333, ECJ) for the requirements of the Member States to comply with the Directive. It is not possible to contract out.

The contract

The particulars may or may not be the contract of employment depending upon the intent and agreement of the parties. However, unless there is evidence to the contrary the statement will not normally be the contract. It was stated by Lord Parker in **Turriff Construction Limited v Bryant** [1967] KIR 659 that the statement "is not the contract; it is not even conclusive evidence of the terms of the contract". This approach was adopted in **System Floors (UK) Limited v Daniel** [1982] ICR 54. Daniel received a statement that provided he had started work on 19th November 1979 when in fact he had started on 26th November 1979. He was dismissed on 14th November 1980. He had signed an acknowledgement of receipt of the statement. The EAT held that the statement was not the contract and he did not have continuity. Whilst a statement may be strong *prima facie* evidence it does not constitute the written contract between the parties. The case of **Gascol Conversions Limited v Mercer** [1974] ITR 420 was distinguished. In that case Mr Mercer had signed a statement that provided:

> "I confirm receipt of a new contract of employment ...which sets out ...the terms and conditions of my employment."

The EAT held that this was clearly a binding contract and being reduced to writing was the sole evidence that it was permissible of the contract and its terms. Precedent 3.1 contains alternatives provisions for the end of the contract depending on whether it is intended to make the statement the contract of employment. A statement cannot be used as evidence of the written terms and conditions contained in the contract of employment (**Robertson v British Gas Corporation** [1983] ICR 351).

Timing

By section 1(2) of the ERA 1996 the written particulars must be given within two months of the commencement of employment and may be given in instalments, though particulars (numbered as above) 1 to 7, 11 and 13 shall be included in a single document (section 2(4) ERA 1996). A statement posted on a staff noticeboard is not sufficient (**Green v Moyses Stevens Limited** [1974] IRLR 274).

Changes

By section 4 a statement of changes to the particulars should be given at the earliest opportunity and in any event within one month after the change in question or, where the change results from the employer being required to work outside the United Kingdom, the time when he leaves the United Kingdom in order to begin work, whichever is the earliest. The statement of change may refer some other document that is reasonably accessible to the employee for a change in any of the matters mentioned (as numbered above) in 1, 3, 7 and 8. It has been held that a failure to give a statement which refers to a variation does not affect its validity if it was a proper contractual variation (**Parkes Classic Confectionery Limited v Ashcroft** [1973] 7 ITR 43). On the other hand a statutory statement cannot of itself effect a contractual variation where it has not been accepted by the employee or where he has stayed silent but worked on under the new statutory statement. Where the variation does not take immediate effect, such as a new mobility clause, the courts will be cautious before they find that there has been an implied agreement to any change (**Jones v Associated Tunnelling Co Limited** [1981] IRLR 477).

Where the employer may provide particulars by reference to a document that is reasonably accessible, by section 6 this is taken to be reference to a document or collective agreement that the employee has reasonably opportunities of reading in the course of his employment or it has been made reasonably accessible in some other way.

By section 11(1) an employee may make a reference to a tribunal where he is not given a statement or because it does not comply with what is required and the tribunal may determine what particulars ought to have been included or referred to in a statement so as to comply with the requirement of section 1 or 4.

Where a statement purporting to be a statement under section 1 or 4 or a pay statement or a standing statement of fixed deductions is given and a question arises as to the particulars that ought to have been included or referred to in the statement the employer or employee may require the question to be referred to and determined by the tribunal (section 11(2)). The right to an itemised pay statement and to a statement relating to fixed deductions is contained in sections 8 and 9 of the ERA 1996.

Where the tribunal makes a determination under section 11(1) the employer shall be deemed to have given a statement that included the particulars as specified by the tribunal (section 12(1)). On reference under 11(2) the tribunal may confirm the particulars, amend them or substitute other particulars as it determines and the particulars will be deemed to include such particulars. However, the courts will not invent a term merely because they think it reasonable to do so (**Eagland v British Telecomm-unications PLC** [1992] IRLR 323) though the tribunal will have to make a finding where a mandatory term has been excluded from the statement (**Mears v Safecar Security Limited** [1982] ICR 626; IRLR 183). The tribunal's jurisdiction is to ensure that the statutory statement accurately records what has been agreed (**Construction Industry Training Board v Leighton** [1978] IRLR 60; cf. **Boothferry Borough Council v Boyle** [EAT 322/84]).

CHAPTER FOUR
SOURCES OF THE
CONTRACT OF
EMPLOYMENT

INTRODUCTION

This chapter will consider general principles relating to the terms of employment. Aside from those general considerations that have already been outlined in earlier chapters, and the provisions contained in the Model Terms and Conditions/Manual, there are employment specific conditions that must be looked at depending upon the nature of the job functions and these are considered in the next chapter. The commencement point in considering what terms should be included are the Particulars at Chapter 3.

SOURCES OF EMPLOYMENT TERMS

The sources of the contract of employment include:

Express terms

The express terms agreed between the parties. Where the express terms are agreed between the parties and the meaning of the agreement is clear it will be a matter of simply looking at the wording of the agreement and the factual situation will have little or no bearing on construction. However, where the agreement is ambiguous the court is entitled to look at the surrounding circumstances to decide how the contract should be construed (see **Adams v British Airways PLC** [1996] IRLR 574).

Express terms incorporated into the contract of employment

Express terms are frequently incorporated into contracts of employment from collective agreements or from terms and conditions that have been agreed by representatives of the workforce. The following points may be made in relation to express incorporation of terms through collective agreements.

- Where it is made clear that the employment relationship is regulated by any national and local collective agreements and the workforce work under such terms they will be bound by them (**NCB v Galley** [1958] 1 WLR 16 — written contract stating "regulated by the national agreement ... for the time being in force"; **The Council of the City of Cardiff v Conde** [1978] IRLR 218 — Letter of Appointment stating "subject to the National Scheme of Conditions and Service..."). The agreement may be contained in a letter passing between employer and the union (**Burke v Royal Liverpool University Hospital NHS Trust** [1997] ICR 730) and does not have to be formally expressed as a collective agreement. They may be incorporated by a section 1 statement (**Camden Exhibition and Display Limited v Lynott** [1966] 1 QB 555).

- Employers are entitled to assume that their employees are aware of the terms of an agreement that has been negotiated on their behalf by a union where they are union members. In **Gray Dunn & Co v Edwards** [1980] IRLR 23 the union agreed that being drunk at work would incur summary dismissal. The employee was dismissed three weeks later for this offence. The EAT stated that "Where employers negotiate a detailed agreement with a recognised union they are entitled to assume that all members of the union know of and are bound by its provisions." Once a clause has been incorporated it does not matter if the employee later resigns from the union (**Burroughs Machines Limited v Timmoney** [1977] IRLR 404) though strict proof that the employee has accepted that terms will be incorporated will be necessary if he is not a member or has resigned before terms have been agreed (**Singh v British Steel Corporation** [1974] IRLR 131).

- The union must have some form of authority to negotiate (**The Burton Group v Smith** [1977] IRLR 351; **Hulse v Embrey Limited** [EAT 400/77]).

- Where a term has been incorporated by a collective agreement it will remain in force for the contract of employment even if the collective agreement comes to an end (**Gibbons v Associated British Ports**

[1985] IRLR 376; **Robertson v British Gas Corporation** [1983] ICR 351).

- It is possible for local agreements to amend or displace national agreements and this is a question of construction (**Saxton v NCB** [1970] ITR 196; **Barratt v NCB** [1978] ICR 1101) though a local agreement expressed to be 'binding in honour only' could not override a national agreement (**Gascol Conversions Limited v Mercer** [1974] ICR 420).

- A collective agreement cannot oust statutory rights (**Tocher v General Motors Scotland Limited** [1981] IRLR 55).

- Some terms are not susceptible to incorporation, such as the machinery for collective bargaining (**NCB v NUM** [1986] ICR 736; IRLR 439), or policy matters (**British Leyland (UK) Limited v McQuilken** [1978] IRLR 245) and certain terms may not be appropriate (**Young v Canadian Northern Railway Company** [131] AC 83).

- Where it is arguable that a term has been incorporated the court may grant a restraining order (interim injunction), as in **Anderson v Pringle of Scotland Limited** [1998] IRLR 64 where a LIFO agreement had been negotiated for redundancies (See further Duggan on *Wrongful Dismissal, Law, Practice and Precedents*).

- The consideration for an improvement in terms and conditions by the employee will be the employee continuing to work or desisting from making any claim for further or greater improvements to terms and conditions (**Lee v GEC Plessey Communications Limited** Unreported 19.1.1993,Connell J).

This book is intended to be a manual of terms and conditions for contracts of employment and will therefore cover express terms as dictated by implied terms. However, even where there is an express term in a contract of employment the employer may be under a duty to operate the term in a manner that is reasonable and does not destroy the relationship of trust and confidence that should exist between the parties. Where the express term is quite clear, however, there will be no reason to imply into the contract a term that limits the scope of the term: see **Nelson v British Broadcasting Corporation** [1977] ICR 469 where the Court of Appeal could see no reason to imply any limitation into a clear flexibility clause. *Nelson* may be compared with the cases set out in the commentary to Model Terms and Conditions/Manual Parts C and G.

Implied Terms

(For a full exposition on this see Duggan, *Wrongful Dismissal, Law, Practice and Precedents*.) A term will only be implied if it is necessary to give business efficacy to the contract or if the parties had directed their minds to it then both would have said that it formed part of the contract (**Reigate v Union Manufacuring Co Limited** [1918] 1 KB 592) or where it was so obvious that it would go without saying (the 'officious bystander test': see **Shirlaw v Southern Foundries Limited and Federated Foundries Limited** [1939] 2 All ER 113). Where one party would have agreed to a term but the other only have agreed if he realised there would be no contract otherwise, then the court may imply a term. In **Mears v Safecar Security Limited** [1982] IRLR 183; ICR 626, the Court of Appeal stated:

> "We can treat as an agreed term a term which would not have been at once assented to by both parties when they made the contract *e.g.* where one party would at once have assented to it and the other would have done so after it had been made clear to him that unless he did so there would be no contract..."

The Court thought that the employee in this case would have taken the job once he realised that unless he accepted that there was no sick pay he would not be given the post; so that he was not entitled to sick pay.

A term may be implied by custom and practice where it is reasonable, certain and notorious (**Sagar v Ridehalgh & Son Limited** [1931] 1 Ch 310).

Where it is not possible to rely on the orthodox tests of custom and practice or business efficacy the court may look at the conduct of the parties after the contract was entered into and infer the appropriate terms from this conduct (**Wilson v Maynard Shipbuilding Consultants Limited** [1977] IRLR 491; ICR 376; see also *Mears*).

A list of possible implied terms are considered in *Wrongful Dismissal*. For the purpose of drafting employment contracts there are three implied terms that are likely to be of particular relevance to the drafter:

(1)   *A duty on the part of the employer to inform the employee of a particular contractual benefit*
It was held by the House of Lords in **Scally v Southern Health and Social Services Board** [1991] ICR 771; IRLR 522 that where an employee cannot be expected to be aware of a right that is exercisable under his contract unless the employer draws it to his attention, it is right to imply a term that the employer bring it to the

employee's attention. The employees had a right to enhance their pension but could not be aware of this unless it was drawn to their attention and a term, therefore, had to be implied by necessity in order to render the benefit efficacious. Lord Bridge stated that a term may be implied if defined with sufficient precision as being where the following circumstances apply:

> "(i) the terms of the contract of employment have not been negotiated with the individual employee but result from negotiation with a representative body or are otherwise incorporated by reference; (ii) a particular term of the contract makes available to the employee a valuable right contingent upon action being taken by him to avail himself of its benefit; (iii) the employee cannot, in all the circumstances, reasonably be expected to be aware of the term unless it is drawn to his attention. I fully appreciate that the criterion to justify an implication of this kind is necessity, not reasonableness."

However, it was held in **University of Nottingham v (1) Eyett (2) The Pensions Ombudsman** [1999] IRLR 87 that where an employee agreed to take early retirement there was no duty on the part of the employer to advise him that if he had waited until the following month the pension would have been higher as it would have depended upon the annual salary rise. Mr Eyett knew about his early retirement rights and the court were of the view that he could have worked out the benefit to him of waiting a further month before retirement. *Scally* was not authority for the proposition that the implied duty of trust and confidence meant there was a positive obligation to give employees advice but was only applicable where the employee had no means of discovering the existence of a benefit unless told by the employer.

(2) *The duty of trust and confidence that should exist between the parties*
This is more fully considered in *Wrongful Dismissal*. It has been recognised for some time that an employer is under a duty to conduct itself in such manner that does not destroy trust and confidence between the parties. This was acknowledged by the House of Lords in **Malik v Bank of Credit and Commerce International** [1997] ICR 606 where the operation of a business in a corrupt of dishonest manner amounted to a breach of the term, though it was not directed to the employee. Lord Steyn stated that he regarded the emergence of the implied term of mutual trust and confidence as a sound development. Examples of such conduct would include inducing an employee to resign and take up

employment with a new company with the sole intent of evading unfair dismissal claims (**Sword v Ashley Vinters** [EAT 731/81] or requiring an employee to undergo a medical examination in a way which is fundamental and repudiatory (**Bliss v South East Thames Regional Health Authority** [1987] ICR 700; 1985 IRLR 308).

(3) *There will be an implied term that the employer does not conduct itself in such manner that amounts to intolerable conduct on the part of the employer.* The employer may be in breach of this implied term even though it is acting within the terms of the contract. The following are examples of such a term:

- In **Giblin v Seismograph Services (England) Limited** [EAT 305/78] the employee was employed as an 'accounts assistant'. One third of her job was concerned with cashier's duties whilst two thirds were concerned with purchase ledgers. Her job was restructured whilst she was absent so that the cashier's duties were taken away. However, when she objected she was allowed to share these duties. The EAT held that there had not been breach of the implied term because the employer had attempted to redress the situation and so had not behaved intolerably.

- However, in **Fyfe & McGrouther Limited v Burns** [1977] IRLR 29 there was a breach when the employer called in police on flimsy evidence and there was evidence of animosity against the employee from the employer. The EAT said that "...by adopting this attitude in a situation for which he was not responsible they had destroyed any basis of confidence that could ever exist between them and him in the future."

Clearly these implied terms will need to be borne in mind by the employer in drafting and implementing the terms of the contract of employment.

SECTION TWO
A-Z OF DIFFERENT
TYPES OF EMPLOYMENT

CHAPTER FIVE
A-Z OF DIFFERENT TYPES OF
EMPLOYMENT

There are a wide range of types of employment where specific provisions apply, as well as the more general provisions mentioned in the earlier chapters, or where the contract is tailor made to the particular circumstances. This section will consider particular issues that are relevant to staff and, where it is considered appropriate, a precedent will be supplied in respect of those particular employees.

1. AGENCY WORKERS

PRECEDENT 5.1
AGREEMENT BETWEEN AGENCY AND AGENCY WORKER

This Agreement between . . . . ('the Agency') who agree to engage you as a Worker from time to time, as and when required, in order to supply to the Customers of the Agency. By signing this document you agree to be bound by the terms and conditions that follow.

STATEMENT OF TERMS AND CONDITIONS RELATING TO THE AGENCY AND THE WORKER

1. Name and address of Agency	The full name of the Agency is . . . . and its address is . . . .
Name of Worker	To: . . . .
2. Engagement of the Worker	The Agency will offer you engagements from time to time with Clients of the Agency on the terms and conditions contained in this Agreement. A Client of the Agency is a Company, Firm, Person or other entity that has contracted with the Agency for the supply of Workers of particular skills as and when the Client requires such Workers.
3. Continuous Employment	There is no period of continuous employment. You agree that:

3. Continuous Employment (continued):

1. The Agency will from time to time offer you an engagement to supply you to Clients and, if you accept, you will work for the Client to the Client's instructions, as provided for in the terms and conditions set out hereafter.

2. The Agency has no obligation to offer you an engagement with any Client and you are under no obligation to accept an engagement with a Client.

3. Any period during which you are not working does not count in calculating continuity with the Agency so that any gaps in engagements whereby you are supplied to Clients will break continuity of service if the same does, otherwise, in any event, exist.

4. Scale or rate of remuneration	You will normally be paid at an hourly rate of . . . . . . which may be altered from time to time. However, the hourly rate that you are paid for any engagement with a particular Client is at the absolute discretion of the Agency which will offer you the hourly rate it considers appropriate for the particular engagement. The Agency is under no obligation to offer you an engagement at any particular rate and you are under no obligation to accept.
5. Intervals at which remuneration is paid	You will be normally be paid [WEEKLY][MONTHLY] in arrears but this is subject to (1) submission of time sheets to the Agency by you (2) and the time sheets having been verified and agreed between the Agency and the Client (3) and payment made by the Client to the Agency in respect of your engagement for the period covering the time sheet. You should note that you are under an obligation to submit the time sheets to the Agency as instructed and non-submission may result in you not being paid.
6. Terms and conditions relating to hours of work	The number of hours that you work for a particular Client will be agreed between yourself and the Agency beforehand, subject to the Agency agreeing hours with the Client. They will normally be not more than [37] hours per week. Where it is agreed that overtime will be worked you must inform the Agency on your time sheet that such overtime has been agreed between yourself and the Client.

You should note that your engagement may be subject to the Working Time Regulations and, whilst the Agency will take all reasonable steps to ensure that they are complied with, you should inform the Agency immediately if you have any concern about instructions given by the Client to you in respect of your hours of work. |
| 7. Holiday | You have certain rights to holiday under the Working Time Regulations if you work for a continuous period of more than 13 weeks and the Agency will inform you of these rights if you are likely to be engaged to work for a Client for a continuous period of 13 weeks or more. |

8. Absence due to sickness, *etc.*	1. You are working for the Client who will have certain rules relating to absences. You are under a duty to acquaint yourself with the Client's rules. Any breach of these rules may be regarded as a breach of the terms of your engagement with the Agency.
	2. You must inform the Agency immediately if you are likely to absent form work with the Client as this is likely to affect the Agency's relationship or right to be paid by the Client or, alternatively, the Agency may be able to provide a replacement in your absence. Failure to inform the Agency without good excuse will normally be regarded as a fundamental breach of this Agreement and is likely to lead to its termination.
	3. You will not normally be entitled to be paid for absences, unless there is an express agreement in writing to the contrary in respect of a specific engagement.
9. Pensions	The Agency does not operate a pension scheme.
10. Termination of engagement	You accept that you are expressly engaged to provide services to particular Clients and that your engagement may be terminated by the Agency immediately upon the Client no longer requiring your services. The Agency will try to ensure that you are given the longest possible notice but cannot make any guarantees in this respect and notice will normally be for one week where possible.
11. Your services	You are on the Agency's books and may be engaged from time to time to provide the services of a [COMPUTER PROGRAMMER ETC] to the requirements of the Client. You will be advised of the requirements of the Client before you agree to take on the engagement. By agreeing to the engagement, you agree, represent and warrant:
	1. That you have all the relevant skills in order to carry out the services required by the Client.
	2. That you will at all times provide your services to the Client to the standard of a reasonably qualified person and, in so far as special skills are

11. Your services (cont.)	required, that you will carry out your services to the relevant standard.

3. That you have the requisite qualifications to carry out the services required by the Client.

4. That you know of no reason why you cannot work for the particular Client or provide the services.

5. That if for any reason you are unable to carry out the services required by the Client you will immediately inform the Agency.

12. Obligations of the Worker, Client and Agency	You are aware that you will be working for different Clients from time to time and, as such, there are rights duties and obligations on the part of yourself, the Agency and the Client. In particular:

Your obligations:

1. You are under a duty to comply with all reasonable instructions given by the Client whilst you are working for the Client.

2. You must acquaint yourself with all of the relevant policies of the Client, including any policies relating to Equal Opportunities, standard of care, Disciplinary or Grievance Procedures or other relevant policies.

3. Whilst you are working for a particular Client you will be subject to the disciplinary and other procedures of that Client and you accept that you will abide by such policies and procedures.

4. You should immediately inform the Agency if you have any concerns about your particular engagement.

Client

1. Since you are working to the instructions of the Client and at the Client's premises, the Client owes duties to you, in particular in respect of your safety at work and other legislation, including anti-discrimination legislation.

2. You should first seek to deal with any concerns that you may have directly with the Client but may at any time raise any concerns with the Agency.

12. Obligations of the Worker, Client and Agency (cont.)	*Agency* 1. The Agency is committed to ensuring that all relevant legislation is complied with in relation to the work that you carry out.
13. Place of work	You will work for a particular Client at the place(s) agreed prior to your particular engagement
14. Collective agreements	There are no collective agreements.
15. Covenants	You agree with the Agency that you will not accept or take up employment, whether as an employee, self employed, or a consultant or otherwise howsoever, and whether directly or indirectly, with any Client for whom you have carried out work within a period of [6/12] months prior to carrying out any work for that Client by way of an engagement through the Agency. If you intend to take up any such position you will immediately inform the Agency, which may, subject to appropriate payment, agree at its absolute discretion to you taking up the position.
16. Disciplinary procedures	You will be subject to the Client's disciplinary procedures whilst you work for a particular Client and it is your duty to acquaint yourself with the procedures. The Agency may terminate your engagement if you are in breach of any such procedure or if: 1. Your are guilty of neglect or negligence in relation to the position for which you were engaged. 2. You do anything that is likely to cause harm to the Agency or place it in disrepute.
17. If you are not satisfied with any disciplinary decision	If you are not satisfied with any complaint or alleged breach of discipline or procedure you may speak to . . . . of the Agency who will consider your concerns in accordance with the Agency's procedures.

18. Grievances	You may raise any grievance that you may have about any engagement or Client by speaking to . . . . who will consider your concerns.
SIGNED ON BEHALF OF AGENCY:	. . . .
SIGNATURE OF WORKER:	. . . .

AGENCY WORKERS: COMMENTARY

In the case of individuals who carry out work through an agency, the common set up is that the individual works under a contract with the agency who supply him to a client. The client will utilise the services of the agency and this may be on a temporary basis or with the intention that the worker will become employed by the agency on a full time basis, in which case, the agency is often paid an additional lump sum to reflect this. From the point of view of the employment relationship, the following issues are likely to be of relevance.

The Employer

Where the individual is supplied by the agency to a client on a temporary basis, but is subject to the control of the client, the identify of the employer may on the face of it be a matter in issue. The nature of the relationship was considered in **McMeechan v Secretary of State for Employment** [1997] IRLR 353. It was held that a temporary worker was entitled to be treated as an employee of an employment agency for the purposes of the specific contract governing the engagement in respect of which payment was owed to him. A temporary worker can have the status of employee of the employment agency in respect of each assignment actually worked, notwithstanding that the same worker may not be entitled to employee status under his general terms of engagement. In determining whether a temporary worker is to be treated as an employee, in a case where the money claimed is related to a single stint served for one individual client, it is logical to relate the claim to employment status to the particular job in respect of which payment is being sought. In **Serco Limited v Blair & Ors** [EAT 345/98] it was held that a tribunal had erred when it found that there was an employment relationship between the worker and the company to whom he was supplied. The contract of employment was with the agency. However, where the worker becomes permanently employed by the company then the relationship will be with the company. Precedent 5.1.1 deals with temporary workers and it can be seen that clauses 1 and 2 deal with the relationship.

Provisions governing the employment relationship

Where the individual is subject to the control, instructions and disciplinary or other procedures of the client it is necessary to consider what provision should be contained in the contract between worker and agency and between agency and client should a dismissal situation or other particular issue arise. Where the worker falls below the standards that are required by the client, there must be some provision to cover standards of work and termination (in this respect see Clauses 11 and 12 of the precedent). It should be noted that where a third party insists that it will no longer deal with particular individuals the termination of the engagement by the agency may be fair for SOSR (see **Dobie v Burns International Security Services (UK) Limited** [1984] ICR 812 and Duggan on *Unfair Dismissal* at page 282). However, the worker would need to have qualifying service in the first place and this may not be so with a temporary worker. Clause 3 covers the issue of continuous employment.

Liabilities

The liability of the agency for the acts of the worker and the liability of the client for acts committed on its property need to be considered. The agency will need to make it clear to the client that it is not liable for acts or defaults of the worker. This is a separate issue to the agreement with the worker and may need to be catered for by insurance. Since the worker is the agency's employee it will need to consider the issue of its vicarious liability for the employee's defaults. The question of indemnities may also needs to be considered in the contract between agency and client. It should be noted, however, that where the client controls the activities of the worker it may be liable for claims for personal injury (**Mersey Docks and Harbour Board v Coggins & Griffith (Liverpool) Limited** [1947] AC 1, but probably not for unfair dismissal or personal injuries where the agency is the primary employer (**Cross v Redpath Dorman Long (Contractors) Limited** [1978] ICR 730).

Restrictive covenants

The issue of restrictive covenants or other provisions restricting the acts of the worker after he leaves the agency, if he desires to be supplied through another agency or if he desires to work for the client need to be catered for: see Clause 15 of the precedent.

Holiday and other entitlements

Liability for holiday entitlement or other entitlement where there is a statutory right will be that of the agency. This will include liability under the Working Time Regulations. (In particular — on holidays — see the cases at **Manual Part I.**)

Indemnities

The issue of whether indemnities should be supplied may become a live issue. Since the client has control of the worker the agency will wish to seek an indemnity against any claims that may be made due to defaults on the part of the work, arising out of instructions from the client. Again, this is an issue between client and agent rather than worker and agent.

Statutory intervention

The law relating to agency workers has been fundamentally affected by the Employment Relations Act 1999 and the Act and Regulations can be summarised as follows:

- Under Schedule 7.2.(2) of the Act, Regulations may be made that restrict the services that may be provided by agencies, regulating the way in which and the terms on which services may be provided and restricted or regulating the charging of fees.
- Schedule 7.3 now makes it clear that it is absolutely prohibited to take any form of fee from any person for providing services (whether this simply be in relation to the provision of information or otherwise).
- Regulations are to be brought into force to implement and set out a detailed scheme under these sections.

2. BETTING WORKERS

PRECEDENT 5.2.1
NOTICE UNDER SECTION 42(5) OF THE ERA 1996

STATUTORY RIGHTS IN RELATION TO
SUNDAY BETTING WORK

You have become employed under a contract of employment under which you are or can be required to do Sunday betting work, that it to say, work at a track on a Sunday on which your employer is taking bets at the track, or in a licensed betting office on a Sunday which is open for business.

However, if you wish, you can give a notice as described in the next section to your employer and you will then have the right not to do Sunday betting work once three months have passed from the date on which you gave the notice.

Your notice must:
- be in writing;
- be signed and dated by you;
- say that you object to doing Sunday betting work.

For three months after you give the notice, your employer can still require you do to all the Sunday betting work your contract provides for. After the three months has ended, you have the right to complain to an employment tribunal if, because of your refusal to do Sunday betting work, your employer:
- dismisses you; or
- does something else detrimental to you, for example, failing to promote you.

Once you have the rights described, you can surrender them only by giving your employer a further notice, signed and dated by you saying that you wish to do Sunday betting work or that you do not object to doing Sunday betting work and then agreeing with your employer to do such work on Sundays or a particular Sunday.

PRECEDENT 5.2.2
STATEMENT OF INITIAL EMPLOYMENT PARTICULARS
VARIATIONS FOR BETTING WORKERS
(IN ADDITION TO TERMS DESCRIBED IN PRECEDENT 2.1)

These particulars are given to you in accordance with the requirements of section 1 of the Employment Rights Act 1996 which sets out certain minimal entitlements to particulars.

Your Job Title is . . . . and your immediate supervisor is . . . . You should have been issued with a job description at the time of your employment. Your position is such that you are a betting worker within the meaning of section 233 of the Employment Rights Act 1996.

1. Intervals at which remuneration is paid	You will be paid [*WEEKLY*][*MONTHLY*] in arrears and your salary shall accrue from day to day. Payment will be made into your bank account on the . . . . . day of each [*WEEK*][*MONTH*]. Salary increases are at the discretion of the Employer.
	You have expressly agreed that deductions may be made from your salary as follows:
	1. In respect of any cash shortage which may occur from time to time and for which you were responsible, by deduction in accordance with the provisions of Part II of the Employment Rights Act 1996. The Employer will not deduct more than ten percent of your gross salary on any one pay day.
	2. You have agreed that you will pay upon prior demand made to you prior to any pay day up to ten percent of your gross salary.
	3. The Employer shall be entitled to deduct monies in respect of such shortages or deficiencies from your final salary on termination of your employment to the extent necessary to cover such shortages.
2. Terms and conditions relating to hours of work	Your normal hours of work are: . . . . You have agreed to work on a Sunday and you were served with the requisite statutory notice at the time that you entered into this agreement. Your attention is drawn to the contents of that notice.

3. Place of work	Your normal place of work is . . . . but you may be required to work at any of the Employer's betting shops or sites within a radius of . . . . . miles from . . . . . .

Additional clause

Your attention is drawn to the dress code applicable to the terms of your employment. This is strictly enforced and any breach of it will be regarded as a disciplinary matter.

BETTING WORKERS: COMMENTARY

The following issues are likely to arise.

1. SUNDAY WORKING

Apart from the standard terms and conditions to be included in the contract as set out above, the specific area for concern with betting workers (and indeed shop workers) relates to the requirements that the employer may have for Sunday working. Part IV of the Employment Rights Act 1996 contains provisions to protect betting and shopworkers who do not wish to work on Sundays. There are also prescribed forms, contained in section 42 of the ERA 1996, as set out above, whereby the employer may give notice requiring the betting or shop worker to work on a Sunday and informing the betting or shop worker of the right to refuse to so work.

Betting workers

Section 233 defines a betting worker as an employee who under this contract of employment may be required to do betting work, being:

- work at a track in England and Wales for a bookmaker on a day on which the bookmaker acts at the track, which consists of or includes dealings with betting transactions and work in a licensed betting office on a day when the office is open for such transactions; and
- a betting transaction includes the collection and payment of winnings on a bet and any transaction in which one or more of the parties is acting as a bookmaker;
- a bookmaker being a person who whether on his own account, or as a servant or agent to any other person, carries on the business of receiving or negotiating bets or conducting pool betting operations or by way of business holds himself out or permits himself to be a person who receive or negotiate bets or conducts such operations.

Protected status of betting and shop workers

By section 36(1) of the ERA a shop worker or betting worker is protected if sections 36(2) or (2) applies.

Section 36(2) applies where:

- in the case of a shop worker he was employed before 26th August 1994 and in the case of a betting worker was employed before 3rd January 1995 but not to do work only on Sunday;
- he has been continuously employed between that date and the effective date of termination;
- throughout the period he was subject to a contract of employment as a betting worker or shop worker. Section 36(4) deems an employee to be a protected worker even if the employment had ceased before the relevant commencement date where continuity was preserved under section 212(2) or 212(3) or section 219 and when the employment relationship ceased the employee was a betting or shop worker not employed to work on Sunday.

Section 36(3) applies where the shop worker or betting worker cannot be required to work on Sunday and could not be required even if the provisions of Part IV relating to betting and shop workers were disregarded.

Where the betting or shop worker is protected then any agreement that he work on a Sunday is unenforceable (section 37) unless an opting in notice has been given (37(3) ERA 1996). Where the protected worker has ceased to work on a Sunday and the employer was required to provide a specified number of hours the employer will not be required to make up those hours lost on the Sunday by providing employment during the week (section 38 ERA 1996).

OPTING OUT

Opted out status for shop and betting workers

Under section 40 of the ERA a betting or shop worker may at any time give his employer written notice, signed and dated, that he objects to Sunday working where the contract requires him to work on Sunday and he is not employed to work only on Sunday. The shop or betting worker will be regarded as opted out where:

- he has given his employer an opting out notice;
- he has been continuously employed during the period beginning with the date when the opting out notice was given and the effective date of termination;
- three months have expired after the opting out notice was served.

In these circumstances the employee will be entitled to refuse to work on a Sunday and any dismissal will be unfair.

Duty of Employer
Where the shop or betting worker may be required to work on Sundays and that is not the only day that he works, the employer is under a duty to give a notice in the prescribed form in accordance with section 42 (see Precedent 5.2.1) which sets out the employee's right to serve an opting out notice. If the statement has not been given within a period of two months from the date that the employee becomes a shop or betting worker then the three month period to opt out is reduced to one month (section 42(2) ERA 1996).

Effect of opting out notice
The effect of the opting out notice will be that the contract under which he was required to work on a Sunday will become unenforceable after a three month period and any agreement to the contrary will be unenforceable (section 43 ERA 1996).

Opting in notice
The betting or shop worker ceases to be protected if an opting in notice is given and after giving the notice the employee expressly agrees to do shop or betting work on a Sunday or a particular Sunday (section 36(5)). Such an opting in notice must be in writing, signed and dated by the employee and it must state that he wishes to work on Sunday and does not object to Sunday working. The contract of employment will then be regarded as varied to give effect to such notice.

Remedies
By section 101 ERA 1996 dismissal of a betting worker or shop worker because he sought to exercise rights under Part IV will be automatically unfair. (See Duggan, *Unfair Dismissal, Law, Guidance and Practice*.) By section 45 the employee has the right not to be subjected to a detriment.

2. OTHER ISSUES

Other specific clauses that are likely to be of special relevance include:

- deductions from salary on account of shortfall of takings;
- dress and appearance.

These are considered further under shop workers, below and precedents are contained in the Model Terms and Conditions Manual at D6, F4 and M.

3. CASUAL STAFF, OCCASIONAL AND TEMPORARY STAFF

PRECEDENT 5.3.1
CONTRACT FOR CASUAL WORKERS ON THE BASIS THAT THEY ARE NOT EMPLOYEES

AGREEMENT BETWEEN . . . . AND . . . . FOR THE PROVISION OF CASUAL LABOUR

NATURE OF SERVICES/LABOUR TO BE PROVIDED . . . .
[I.E. WAITER, COMPUTER PROGRAMMER, ETC. WHERE APPROPRIATE ADD A FURTHER DESCRIPTION]

1. Name of Company	. . . . whose address is	
Name of Casual Worker	. . . . whose contactable address is	
2. Provision of Services/Labour	From time to time the Company has a requirement for casual/occasional or temporary workers to provide services or labour.	
	By this Agreement you have stated to the Company that you may make yourself available to provide Services/your labour to the Company. You are under no obligation to accept any work if it is offered to you by the Company.	
	The Company is under no obligation to offer or provide work to you but may in its absolute discretion offer work as and when it sees fit.	
3. Self Employment	During any period that you are working for the Company you provide your services on a self employed basis and you are responsible for the payment of all taxes and any other statutory payments that may be applicable to you as a self employed person. Where you are registered for VAT you must take the necessary steps to comply with all statutory provisions and you should provide to the Company your VAT Registration number and such documentation as is necessary.	

3. Self Employment (cont.)	For the avoidance of doubt you have no continuity with the Company so that, for periods when you are not working, these cannot count towards continuity for any statutory purpose.
4. Payment	You will be paid [ON AN HOURLY BASIS] [FOR THE PARTICULAR SESSION] [ON A DAILY BASIS] as agreed between the Company and yourself prior to the provision of your Services for a particular engagement. [CONSIDER WHETHER THERE ARE ANY OTHER APPROPRIATE MEANS OF REMUNERATION I.E. COMMISSION ONLY, BONUS, ETC.] You are responsible for paying all taxes or other statutory payments.
5. Hours of Work	The hours that you work will be agreed with you beforehand if the company does offer you work which you decide to accept.
6. Holiday	Since you are providing your services on a casual, as and when required basis, there is no holiday entitlement save as any legislation may provide otherwise.
7. Sickness, etc.	You are not entitled to any payments for sickness or any other absence. In the event that you are unable to provide your service/labour for any reason, including sickness, you must immediately inform the Company. You will not be paid for any absences save as any legislation may provide otherwise.
8. Pension	For the avoidance of doubt, there is no pension scheme and you are responsible for any arrangements that you may see fit to make.
9. Your Services	If you decide to accept any offer of work from the Company you have agreed to provide these services as set at the beginning of this Agreement [OR IN ANY DESCRIPTION THAT HAS BEEN AGREED BETWEEN YOURSELF AND THE COMPANY]. In agreeing that you may provide your labour/these services, you agree, represent and warrant: 1. That you have all the relevant skills in order to carry out the services including any necessary professional qualifications.

9. Your Services (cont.)	2. That you will at all times provide your services/labour to the standard of a reasonably qualified and competent person providing their services/labour and that where special skills are required that you possess these skills and will provide your services/labour to that standard.
	3. That you have the requisite qualifications to carry out the services.
	4. That you know of no reason why you cannot work for the Company or provide particular services to the Company.
	5. That if for any reason you are unable to carry out the services or provide labour to the Company you will immediately inform the Company (*i.e.* Ill health or because you cease to have the necessary qualifications).
10. Standard of work *etc.*	You agree that you have the ability to provide your services/work to the standard as set out above. During the course of providing your services/labour to the Company:
	1. You are under a duty to comply with all reasonable instructions given to you that fall within the scope of the services or work that you are carrying out. You agree that there is a certain amount of flexibility so that the Company may, if it considers it necessary and for the better operation of its business, require you to carry out functions that do not fit within the description set out above but which are of a comparable nature.
	2. You must acquaint yourself with all policies of the Company, including any policies relating to Equal Opportunities, standard of care or other policies that are relevant the provision of your services/labour. (In particular there may be standards of dress, appearance or behaviour that apply to you).
	3. You should acquaint yourself with the Company's disciplinary procedure so far as it sets out what it regards as misconduct or gross misconduct as these matters are applicable to you in the provision of your services/labour (*i.e.* fighting at work will merit summary dismissal, *etc.*). Since you are self employed the Company's disciplinary procedure is not appropriate but before

10. Standard of Work *etc.* (cont.)	terminating your services for misconduct the Company will: a) satisfy itself that you are in breach of contract; b) make such inquiries and investigation as it considers in its absolute discretion to be appropriate in the circumstances. *[CONSIDER WHETHER IT IS SENSIBLE TO APPEND A LIST OF ITEMS THAT WOULD BE REGARDED AS BREACH OF CONTRACT SUFFICIENT TO JUSTIFY DISMISSAL]*
11. Place of work	At the time you are offered work you will be advised where that work is to be carried out. There is no set place of work and the Company shall be entitled to move you as it considers fit during any time that you are providing your services/labour. You will be advised of any proposed move and are under no obligation to accept the same but, once you have moved you can only terminate your contract by giving the appropriate notice.
12. Notice	The Company recognises that once you have agreed to accept work that it has offered you may miss the opportunity to work for other sources. Accordingly, as a matter of contract it is agreed that the Company will not terminate any agreed engagement before giving the following notice: *[THIS NEEDS TO BE TAILOR MADE DEPENDING UPON HOW THE SERVICES/LABOUR IS PROVIDED]* or You provide your Services on a session by session *[PARTICULAR TASK/ENGAGEMENT]* basis and your contract with the Company comes to an end at the end of that session/task or *[IF MORE LONG TERM — 1 WEEK'S NOTICE?]* You recognise that once you have agreed to accept work that the Company has offered you have entered into a contractual commitment to provide your services/labour in relation to that work. Accordingly, you must give the Company the following notice: *[AGAIN THIS NEED TO BE TAILOR MADE AND THE EXAMPLES ABOVE MAY BE ADAPTED]*

13. Covenants

You are under no obligation to provide your service/labour to the Company and the Company is under no obligation to offer you work. Accordingly you are free to accept work from other parties provided that you are not undertaking this work during the time that you have agreed to provide your services/labour to the Company or that such work does not detrimentally affect your ability to provide your services/labour to the Company. **However**:

1. Working for Competitors whilst you are providing your Services/Labour to the Company:

   You recognise that the Company has a legitimate interest in protecting its business interests and you therefore agree that at no time whilst you are providing your services/labour to the Company will you provide any services or carry out any work, whether directly or indirectly, for any company, firm, person or other entity that is or is likely to be in competition with the Company or which is likely to or may place you in a position of a conflict of interest. Provided that, where you are concerned that this may be the position you may notify . . . . [*MANAGING DIRECTOR?*] in writing and the Company may agree in writing that they have no objection to the provision of your services/labour to that party. You recognise that it is a fundamental breach of contract for you to work for such a party whilst you are providing services/labour to the Company.

2. Working for Competitors at other times:

   You recognise and agree that, whilst you may work for competitors at other times, the Company has a legitimate interest in protecting its business so that you will not make use of, disclose or otherwise utilise any methods of working, procedures, business methods or other processes that you learned whilst working for the Company **provided** that you are always entitled to use the skills and knowledge that may be regarded as your own.

[ADD IN CONFIDENTIALITY CLAUSE OR CONSIDER SEPARATE AGREEMENT — SEE MANUAL PART Q.]

13. Whole Agreement	This contract contains the whole agreement between yourself and the Company together with any other documents that may be incorporated, which for the avoidance of doubt include:
	
	[*1. DESCRIPTION OF NATURE OF SERVICES.*
	
	  2. POLICIES OF THE COMPANY RELATING TO: [LIST I.E. EQUAL OPPORTUNITIES ETC]
	
	  3. LIST ANY OTHER DOCUMENTS]

SIGNED ON BEHALF OF THE COMPANY	. . . .
SIGNED BY CASUAL WORKER	. . . .

PRECEDENT 5.3.2
STATEMENT OF INITIAL EMPLOYMENT PARTICULARS/
CONTRACT FOR CASUAL STAFF ON THE BASIS THAT THEY
ARE EMPLOYEES

This Agreement is made between . . . . ['*THE COMPANY'/EMPLOYER*] and . . . . and constitutes the whole agreement between the parties.

The Company recognises that whilst working for it you are regarded as an employee. This document therefore also provides particulars in accordance with the requirements of section 1 of the Employment Rights Act 1996 which sets out certain minimal entitlements to particulars.

You may be engaged by the Company on a casual/temporary/occasional basis from time to time, in which case the terms and conditions set out in this Agreement will be applicable. By signing this document you agree to be bound by the terms and conditions that follow.

Nature of the Services/Labour to be provided . . . .
[*WHERE APPROPRIATE ADD A FURTHER DESCRIPTION*]

TERMS AND CONDITIONS OF ENGAGEMENT AND STATEMENT OF TERMS AND CONDITIONS UNDER SECTION 1

1. Name of Employer	Your Employer is . . . . of . . . .
Name of Employee	To . . . .
2. Date when employment began	Since there is no period of continuous employment, your employment will commence on each date during a period when you first began to provide your services/labour to the Employer.
3. Date when continuous employment began	You are engaged from time to time by the Employer as and when there is a need for your services.
	You are under no obligation to accept work and may refuse any work that is offered to you.
	The Employer is under no obligation to offer you work.

(cont.)

3. Date when continuous employment began (cont.)	There is no period of continuous employment. You agree that: 1. The Employer may from time to time offer you work and, if you accept, you will work for the Employer to the Employer's instructions, as provided for in the terms and conditions set out hereafter. 2. Any period during which you are not working does not count in calculating continuity with the Employer so that gaps in work will break continuity of employment.
4. Scale or rate of remuneration	Your scale or rate of remuneration is: [£ .... PER HOUR] [£ .... PER WEEK] [£ ..... PER MONTH]. However, the hourly rate that you are paid for any particular work offered by the Company is in the absolute discretion of the Company which will offer you the hourly rate it considers appropriate for the particular work. The Company is under no obligation to offer you work at any particular rate and you are under no obligation to accept. The fact that you have been paid a particular rate for work for one period does not mean that you are entitled to the same rate for any other period.
5. Intervals at which remuneration is paid	You will be paid [WEEKLY][MONTHLY] in arrears and your salary shall accrue from day to day. Payment will be made into your bank account on the . . . . . day of each [WEEK][MONTH]. Salary increases are at the discretion of the Employer. [TAILOR MAKE THIS TO THE TYPE OF WORK I.E. PAYMENT BY SESSION, ETC.]
6. Terms and conditions relating to hours of work	Your normal hours of work are from . . . . . a.m. to . . . . . p.m., Mondays to Fridays with . . . . . . for lunch. You must ensure that you can carry out your duties and it may be necessary to exceed your hours in accordance with the Working Time Regulations. Overtime may be payable. [TAILOR MAKE TO THE NATURE OF THE WORK]

7. Holiday	1. If you have sufficient continuity of employment as provided for by the Working Time Regulations you may be entitled to paid holiday. Details should be obtained from . . . . 2. The holiday year runs from . . . . . to . . . . . 3. You may not carry over holiday without permission which should be obtained from . . . . 4. You will be paid during the period that you take your holidays in accordance with statutory requirements. 5. If your employment terminates and you have outstanding entitlement you will be paid your basic salary representing the number of days outstanding. 6. You are under a statutory obligation to give notice when you want to take holiday and the Company may serve a counter notice on you. Details of this may be obtained from . . . .
8. Absence due to sickness, *etc.*	1. If you are going to be absent from work for any reason you or someone on your behalf must contact your supervisor to inform them on the first day of absence and of the reason for absence. 2. If appropriate, you must complete a record form within 7 days from the commencement of your absence. 3. If you are absent for more than 7 days you must provide a medical certificate signed by your doctor that should be sent to your supervisor. 4. You are not entitled to be paid during sickness absence save as provided for by legislation. 5. You will not be entitled to payment if you are absent without authorisation or have not complied with the above procedure. *[THIS PROVISION WILL HAVE TO BE TAILOR MADE FOR THE PARTICULAR NATURE OF THE CASUAL WORK]*
9. Pensions	There is no pension scheme applicable to your employment.

10. Notice	The Company recognises that once you have agreed to accept work that it has offered you may miss the opportunity to work for other sources. Accordingly, as a matter of contract it is agreed that the Company will not terminate any agreed engagement before giving the following notice:
	[THIS NEEDS TO BE TAILOR MADE DEPENDING UPON HOW THE SERVICE/LABOUR IS PROVIDED]
	or
	You provide your Services on a session by session *[PARTICULAR TASK/ENGAGEMENT]* basis and your contract with the Company comes to an end at the end of that session/task
	or
	[IF MORE LONG TERM - 1 WEEK'S NOTICE?]
	You recognise that once you have agreed to accept work that the Company has offered you have entered into a contractual commitment to provide your services/labour in relation to that work. Accordingly, you must give the Company the following notice:
	[AGAIN THIS NEEDS TO BE TAILOR MADE AND THE EXAMPLES ABOVE MAY BE ADAPTED]
	[NOTE THAT SINCE THE INDIVIDUAL IS AN EMPLOYEE 1 WEEK'S NOTICE MAY BE REQUIRED. IF THE WORK IS FOR A PARTICULAR TASK THEN THE PROVISIONS REFERRED TO IN CHAPTER 5.15 SHOULD BE INCORPORATED SO THAT NOTICE IS NOT NECESSARY.]
11. Job title/services to be provided	You have no specific job title but if you decide to accept any offer of work from the Company you have agreed to provide the services as set at the beginning of this Agreement (or in any description that has been agreed between yourself and the Company). In agreeing that you may provide your labour/these services, you agree, represent and warrant:
	1. That you have all the relevant skills in order to carry out the services including any necessary professional qualifications.
	2. That you will at all times provide your services/labour to the standard of a reasonably qualified and competent person providing their services/labour and that where special skills are

11. Job title/services to be provided (cont.)	required that you possess these skills and will provide your services/labour to that standard.
	3. That you have the requisite qualifications to carry out the services.
	4. That you know of no reason why you cannot work for the Company or provide particular services to the Company.
	5. That if for any reason you are unable to carry out the services or provide labour to the Company you will immediately inform the Company (*i.e.* Ill health or because you cease to have the necessary qualifications).
12. Temporary or fixed term contracts	*NOT APPLICABLE SAVE AS ALREADY PROVIDED FOR*
13. Place of work	You have no normal place of work. At the time you are offered work you will be advised where that work is to be carried out. There is no set place of work and the Company shall be entitled to move you as it considers fit during any time that you are providing your services/labour. You will be advised of any proposed move and are under no obligation to accept the same but, once you have moved you can only terminate your contract by giving the appropriate notice.
14. Collective Agreements	There are no collective agreements affecting your employment.
15. Overseas employment	*[SEE CHAPTER 5.10 ON EMPLOYMENT OVERSEAS AS THIS RAISES ISSUES THAT ARE SPECIFIC TO THE NATURE OF THIS CONTRACT BUT NOT LIKELY TO BE RELEVANT IN THE CONTEXT OF CASUAL STAFF.]*
16. Disciplinary procedures	The disciplinary procedures are attached. They are not part of your contract of employment and the employer may alter them from time to time. **[SEE PART R OF THE MANUAL.]**
17. If you are not satisfied with any disciplinary decision	If you are not satisfied with any disciplinary decision relating to your employment you may appeal in accordance with the terms of the disciplinary procedure. The appeal will be heard by *[SET OUT].*

18. Grievances	You may raise any grievance that you may have in accordance with the terms of the Grievance Procedure.
19. Further steps	Any further steps that you may take consequent upon any disciplinary procedure or grievance are set out in the procedures.
20. Contracting out	A contracting out certificate pursuant to the Pension Scheme Act is [not] in force.
21. Covenants	You are under no obligation to provide your services/labour to the Company and the Company is under no obligation to offer you work. Accordingly you are free to accept work from other parties provided that you are not undertaking this work during the time that you have agreed to provide your services/labour to the Company or that such work does not detrimentally affect your ability to provide your services/labour to the Company. **However:**

1. Working for Competitors whilst you are providing your services/labour to the Company:

   You recognise that the Company has a legitimate interest in protecting its business interests and you therefore agree that at no time whilst you are providing your services/labour to the Company will you provide any services or carry out any work, whether directly or indirectly, for any company, firm, person or other entity that is or is likely to be in competition with the Company or which is likely to or may place you in a position of a conflict of interest. Provided that, where you are concerned that this may be the position you may notify .... [*MANAGING DIRECTOR?*] in writing and the Company may agree in writing that they have no objection to the provision of your services/labour to that party. You recognise that it is a fundamental breach of contract for you to work for such a party whilst you are providing services/labour to the Company.

2. Working for Competitors at other times:

   You recognise and agree that, whilst you may work for competitors at other times, the Company has a legitimate interest in protecting its business so that you will not make use of, disclose or otherwise

21. Covenants (cont.)	utilise any methods of working, procedures, business methods or other processes that you learned whilst working for the Company **provided** that you are always entitled to use the skills and knowledge that may be regarded as your own. *[ADD IN CONFIDENTIALITY CLAUSE OR CONSIDER SEPARATE AGREEMENT — SEE PART Q.]*
22. Whole Agreement	This contract contains the whole agreement between yourself and the Company together with any other documents that may be incorporated, which for the avoidance of doubt include: *[1. DESCRIPTION OF NATURE OF SERVICES.* *2. POLICIES OF THE COMPANY RELATING TO: [LIST I.E. EQUAL OPPORTUNITIES ETC]* *3. LIST ANY OTHER DOCUMENTS]*
SIGNED ON BEHALF OF THE COMPANY	. . . .
SIGNED BY CASUAL WORKER	. . . .

CASUAL STAFF: COMMENTARY

There are certain areas of industry where employers only require staff on an 'as and when' required basis. In particular the hotel and catering sector and sporting events may only require staff to cover certain functions. However, the employer obviously will have requirements in respect of reliability. Such staff will be subject to the usual provision relating to conduct and standard of work, uniforms and appearance and there will be agreed remuneration which may be on a daily basis or by the event. However, the casual employee may not have the benefit of sickness provisions, holiday pay and other benefits that the full time or permanent employee enjoys. This may of course suit the employee who does not wish to enter into a formalised contract. Moreover, the casual member of staff will still have the benefit of the anti discrimination legislation as the employer found to its cost in **Burton v De Vere Hotels** [1996] IRLR 596.

The House of Lords has recently considered the status of casual workers in the important case of **CarMichael v National Power PLC** [1998] ICR 1167; IRLR 301. The applicants acted as guides, taking parties on tours of power stations. After interviews they received letters which stated that they were to be employed on a casual as required basis and they were asked to write back on a standard letter to confirm this. The applicants performed the work as and when it arose. They were paid only for the hours that they worked and tax and national insurance were deducted. They were not obliged to take work and the company did not guarantee them work. They requested a statement of terms and conditions under section 1 which the company refused to provide. The House of Lords held that, as a matter of construction, the letters meant that there was no obligation to provide work or for the applicants to take it. There was an absence of the irreducible mutuality of obligation necessary to create a contract of service. However, the House of Lords also noted that it was only appropriate to determine the issue solely by reference to documents where it appeared from the terms, or from what the parties had said and done, that the documents were intended to be an exclusive record of the parties' agreement. A determination on documents is a matter of law with which the higher courts could interfere. The tribunal had in this case decided that the letters were not the exclusive record but had looked at the surrounding circumstances which was a matter of fact. The tribunal was entitled to find as a matter of fact that the individuals were not employees and this was not a matter that the higher courts could interfere with (for a further consideration of the status of casual staff see Duggan on *Unfair Dismissal, Law, Practice and Guidance*).

Thus, the starting point may be whether or not the casual staff are employees at all. However, it should be noted that considerable protection is now extended to workers in a number of areas (see 5.16 — Workers) so that casual staff will not be wholly without protection though they will not get many of the benefits of the Employment Rights Act 1996 (*i.e.* unfair dismissal, *etc.* or redundancy payments, *etc.*). Moreover, *CarMichael* did not decide that casual, temporary or intermittent staff could not be employees.

However, the following issues are likely to be of some significance, even in relation to casual staff:

Self employment
There may be an issue as to whether or not the casual is self employed or is in reality an employee (as to which see **O'Kelly v Trusthouse Forte PLC** [1983] ICR 728; IRLR 269 and the cases cited in *CarMichael*).

The 48 hour week
Where the casual worker is an employee and the hours of work may be over 48 per week the provision of the Working Time Regulations must be considered (See **Manual at Part D**).

Continuity

Where staff are employed on a regular basis but there are breaks in employment these may amount to a temporary cessation of employment under Part XIV of the Employment Rights Act 1996. Even where there is no contract of employment continuity may be retained where there is a temporary cessation of work (**Ford v Warwickshire CC** [1983] IRLR 126; **Byrne v City of Birmingham MDC** [1988] ICR 480 and cf. **Hellyer Brothers Limited v McLeod** [1987] ICR 526). (See further Duggan, *Unfair Dismissal* Chapter One). Where the gaps are regular and foreseeable, continuity may not be broken though the relationship between the parties was not covered by a contract of employment at that stage.

Holiday

It should be noted that casuals (if they are employees) and those on temporary contracts may be given rights under the Working Time Regulations 1998 if they have accrued the requisite number of weeks during which the contract has been in existence (See Model Terms and Conditions/Manual **Part I**). This may cause particular problems for employers since the entitlement will be to the whole of the four weeks and the casual/temp will be entitled to payment. For some instances of how employers have sought to deal with this problems see the discussion of the tribunal cases at **Part I**.

Standard of work

Provisions relating to place of work and standard of work should be included. Where the employee is a casual worker he may, nevertheless, claim unfair dismissal if there is sufficient continuity.

The Precedents are otherwise self explanatory and cross reference should be made to the provisions of the Model Terms and Conditions/Manual for specific comment on legal matters.

4. CONSULTANTS

The following precedent sets out in short form the terms that once would expect to see in a consultancy agreement.

PRECEDENT 5.4
CONSULTANCY AGREEMENT

THIS AGREEMENT dated .... is made between .... Limited (hereafter called the Company) and Mr .... of .... (hereafter called the Consultant)

PREAMBLE

1. The Company wishes to procure the benefit of the services and the skills of the Consultant and the Consultant has agreed to provide his time and service to the Company as agreed in this Consultancy Agreement (which services may be provided through a Limited Company).

2. It is agreed and recognised between parties that the Consultant is and will remain at all times an independent contractor who will provide its services for the period of this Agreement and there will be no employment relationship between the Consultant and the Company.

IT IS AGREED THAT

1. The Consultant has been engaged under the terms of this Agreement to provide:
   (1) Advice and consulting services to the Company and any Company within the Group as may be required;
   (2) Freelance [SET OUT] services to the Company and any Company within the Group as may be required;
   (3) Project and Management advice to the Company and any Company in the Group as may be required;
   (4) [SET OUT ANYTHING MORE SPECIFIC]

[THIS ABOVE CLAUSE MAY BE AS SPECIFIC OR GENERALISED AS REQUIRED.]

2. The above services shall be provided by the Consultant to the Company unless and until terminated as follows:
   (1) By the Company giving ..... days' notice to the Consultant or the Consultant giving ..... days' notice to the Company.
   (2) By the Company paying the equivalent to the Consultant of the period of notice set out in 2(1).
   (3) In accordance with any of the provisions of this Agreement which entitle the Company to terminate the Agreement.

3. The Consultant shall:
    (1) Submit invoices on a [*STATE PERIOD*] basis setting out the hours that he
         has worked for the Company. The Company will pay invoices (which
         shall include VAT) within ..... days of being rendered. If the Company
         has any query about an invoice it will raise this with the Consultant
         within 7 days of its being rendered.
    (2) Submit invoices for approved disbursements (meaning disbursements
         approved in writing by the Chairman of the Company) which shall
         become payable within ..... days after being submitted.

4. The Consultant may accept and perform engagements from other
    companies, firms or persons which do not place him in a conflict of interest
    with the Company and which will not be detrimental to the Company's
    business. The Consultant agrees that he will not accept any position,
    employment or engagement from any person, firm or company which is or
    may be in competition with the Company or its Group within the express
    written permission of the Company's Managing Director.

5. The Consultant agrees that:
    (1) He will be available at all times on reasonable notice to provide such
         assistance or information as the Company may require.
    (2) He will be available on such days as the Company requires.
    (3) He will not hold himself as having any authority to do or say anything
         on behalf of the Company without the express agreement in writing of
         the Chairman of the Company.
    (4) He will not incur any expenditure or disbursement without the express
         agreement in writing of the Chairman of the Company.

6. The Consultant shall be available to provide such information regarding his
    services or any acts taken by him in the provision of the services under this
    Agreement to anyone authorised by the Board, including the directors
    employees or any third parties to request such information.

7. The Consultant warrants and represents to the Company that he is an
    independent contractor.

8. The Consultant will be responsible for the payment of tax and national
    insurance contributions which may be payable and he will indemnify the
    Company in respect of all and any income taxes or other payments which
    may be found due from the Company in respect of such taxes or insurance.
    The Consultant will register for VAT and pay all such sums as may be due
    and shall indemnify the Company against any claims.

9. The Consultant agrees that
    (1) The Consultant will not disclose to any third party, whether by himself
         directly or indirectly, or through any other company, firm or person, or
         otherwise procure cause of facilitate the disclosure of any confidential
         information or trade secrets belonging to the Company or any of the
         Company's Group or any of their customers or clients, which shall include
         information relating to the business, financial or other affairs of the
         Company or the Group or customers or clients save as required by law.

(2) All information and material whether held on disk, tape or any other medium and all computer discs, correspondence, documents, memos and all other records obtained or used by the Consultant during his engagement or connected thereto or prepared by the Consultant for the purposes of carrying out his duties under the terms of the Agreement shall be and remain the property of the Company. Upon lapse, expiry or termination of this Agreement the Consultant will forthwith deliver up all material, as aforesaid to the Company. Insofar as delivery up is not possible (*i.e.* information held on hard disc) the Consultant will if required confirm in writing that it has been destroyed.

(3) *[CONSIDER WHETHER POST TERMINATION RESTRICTIVE COVENANTS ARE APPROPRIATE: SEE MODEL CONDITIONS/ MANUAL PART Q5.]*

(4) *[CONSIDER WHETHER A CLAUSE RELATING TO INTELLECTUAL PROPERTY IS APPROPRIATE.]*

10. If the Consultant has agreed that his services will be provided through any third party, company, employees or other persons this agreement will terminate automatically in the event of unavailability for a period of ...... days. The agreement will terminate automatically if the reason is the Consultant's death, disability, dismissal, insolvency or any reason that is incompatible with this Agreement remaining in force.

11. The Company may terminate this Agreement forthwith and without the payment of any compensation or other monies if the Consultant:

(1) has failed, refused or otherwise proved incapable of providing the services agreed in this Agreement after having been given written notice by the Company that his services are required to be provided in not less than ..... days;

(2) has acted in breach of the Agreement and, where the breach is capable of remedy, has failed to remedy within ..... of being required in writing to remedy the breach;

(3) has been guilty of any act which may reasonably be regarded by the Company as an act of gross misconduct or negligence or which may bring the Company or Consultant into disrepute;

(4) is made bankrupt or insolvent.

12. This Agreement is personal to the Consultant and may not be assigned by the Consultant, nor may any of his duties, rights or liabilities be assigned or transferred without the prior written consent of the Board of the Company. The terms herein contain the entire agreement between the parties and may not be changes, varied or substituted by any oral agreement but only by the written agreement of the parties.

SIGNED . . . .   *FOR THE COMPANY*

POSITION . . . .

[CONSIDER WHETHER REQUIRED AS A DEED]

CONSULTANTS: COMMENTARY

There has been an increasing tendency for senior staff to be employed on consultancy agreements. This may be because they work for a number of companies, as in **Hall (Inspector of Taxes) v Lorimer** [1994] ICR 218; IRLR 171 and wish to have the benefit of not being restricted to one employer. The consultant will also have the benefit of being able to claim expenses whilst the company will pay a flat fee and not have to concern itself with tax and national insurance. It is also quite a common occurrence for the vendor of a business to remain on as a consultant for a period of time, which brings with it the benefit of continuity until goodwill can be transferred and may prevent the consultant from going off and setting up in competition. Alternatively, the consultant may be retained for a specific project. The consultant is likely to be engaged as an independent contractor and although this book is primarily concerned with employment contracts it was felt appropriate to include such a contract because of its increasing popularity.

Precedent 5.4.1 is intended to achieve the following objectives:
• The consultant is engaged to provide the benefit of his services. Note that if an individual is engaged in relation to sales there is always the possibility that the Commercial Agents (Council Directive) Regulations 1993 may be applicable (as to which see *Chitty on Contracts* (28th Edition) at Chapter 32).
• The Agreement emphasises that the consultant is an independent contractor. To this end he pays his own taxes, he is free to work for other parties but should be available when he is reasonable needed by the company. He submits invoices and is paid approved disbursements. There is a warranty that he is an independent contractor. Whilst none of these *indicia* will guarantee a finding that the individual was not an employee they are all a pointer to the same.
• The company will wish to agree standards of services that must be provided and make for provision for termination of the engagement in the event of certain breaches.
• Restrictive covenants will need to be tailor made and Clause 9 contains some suggestions. References should further be made to the Model Terms and Conditions/Manual **Part Q** in relation to restrictive covenants.

A consultancy agreement may be a particularly attractive option where it is intended to retain the benefit the skills of an individual, and to facilitate the transfer of goodwill, after the sale of a business.

5. FACTORY STAFF AND SHIFTWORKERS: SPECIFIC PROVISIONS

PRECEDENTS

The precedent in respect of factory and shiftworkers is covered by the section 1 statement and the precedents contained in the Manual which can be adapted as appropriate.

FACTORY STAFF AND SHIFTWORKERS: COMMENTARY

As well as consideration of the standard terms and conditions there are certain terms and conditions that are likely to be of particular relevance to factory staff, particularly in the manufacturing industry. The process may require the factory to work for 24 hours a day seven days a week with provision for complete shutdown when plant is to be maintained or repaired. There may also be a need for the employer to have the power to lay members of staff off during quiet periods or where there is a shortage of orders or material to be able to so that the factory has to temporarily stop manufacturing. The following clauses are likely to be of particular relevance to factory workers.

Timekeeping
See the Model Terms and Conditions/Manual: **Parts D4 and D7.2 and the commentaries thereto**.

Many factories will operate clocking procedures. It will be important for employees to be fully aware of their obligations with regard to clocking procedures and be aware of the disciplinary penalties for abuse of the system. See the Model Terms and Conditions/Manual **Part D7**.

Shift Working
See the Model Terms and Conditions/Manual: **Parts D5 and D7.1 and the commentaries thereto**. Where there is shift working then the Working Time Regulations are almost certain to impinge upon the contracts of employment of factory workers and reference is made to Part D for a full commentary on the effect of the Regulations. Specific provision will, be made for shift working (**D5** and **D7.1**) and overtime is likely to be paid on an increased hourly rate (Part **D2.4**).

Shutdown and Layoff

See the Model Terms and Conditions/Manual: **Parts D7.3 and D7.4 and I.3 and commentaries thereto**. It is common for there to be shutdown periods with regard to factories and staff will not work during this period. Where there is a shutdown period then employees may be required to take some of their holiday entitlement during this period. Employers will wish to have the right to instruct staff to take the holiday and specific provision should be included to this effect (See **D7.3** and **I.3.**). It should be noted that the Working Time Regulations 1998 assist the Employer in this respect as they permit the employer to instruct the worker when time must be taken off.

A power to lay off should also be included (**D7.4**) which will be subject to the restrictions contained in the Employment Rights Act 1996 (see the commentary to **D7.4**).

Health and Safety

See the Model Terms and Conditions/Manual: **Part U and the commentaries thereto**. Since the factory workplace is likely to contain dangerous machinery it is important that employees are fully aware of their requirements under the Heath and Safety Act 1974 and other legislation. It is beyond the scope of this book to consider health and safety in detail but reference is made to the brief commentary at **Part U** for some of the more relevant issues. A policy against alcohol may be of particular importance (see Model Terms and Conditions/Manual **Part M3**) and there may be a non smoking policy (see **Part M2**).

The Working Time Regulations

Consideration is likely to be given to whether the Regulations are to be excluded or modified and there may be a Workforce Agreement in place (see **Part D8 and the commentary to D on Working Time**).

6. FIXED TERM CONTRACTS

PRECEDENT 5.6
MODIFICATIONS TO SECTION 1 STATEMENT TO MAKE IT
CLEAR THERE IS A FIXED TERM CONTRACT

The section 1 statement contained in Chapter 2 will be modified to make it clear that there is a fixed term contract.

1. Notice	Your employment is for a fixed term as set out in clause 2. However, it may be terminated earlier by the Employer giving not less than ..... days'/weeks' notice [notice as provided for in this document].
2. Temporary or fixed term contract	Subject to the Employer's right to terminate your contract earlier your employment is for a fixed term of ..... months staring on ..... and ending on ....
3. Conduct	Your employment may be summarily terminated where you are guilty of gross misconduct or commit a serious breach of this Agreement.

FIXED TERM WORKERS: COMMENTARY

Where the employee accepts a payment for non renewal of the contract there will still have been a dismissal (**Thames Television Limited v Wallis** [1979] IRLR 136).

Where a fixed term contract provides that it is terminable on earlier notice this can still remain a fixed term contract (**Dixon v BBC** [1979] ICR 281; IRLR 114). Although expiry of a fixed term will normally be a dismissal there may be cases where the employment terminates by mutual agreement, as where the employees wish to go to work for another party (**Manson v University of Strathclyde & Automated Microcopy Systems Limited** [EAT 356/87]).

The power to exclude unfair dismissal and other rights has been fundamentally affected by the Employment Relations Act 1999 which now, by section 18, prevents any opting out of the unfair dismissal provisions and makes it clear that any attempt to do so will be invalid.

From the employee's point of view the fixed term contract will provide security for a certain period of time since, if it is prematurely terminated, the measure of damages will be the damages to compensate him for the lost period of employment (See **Re Joint English Stock Board, Yelland's Case** (1867) LR Eq 350) and Duggan on *Wrongful Dismissal*). Where the employee breaches the contract the measure of damages is likely to be the cost of obtaining an alternative employee (**National Coal Board v Galley** [1958] 1 All ER 91).

7. HOMEWORKERS

PRECEDENT 5.7
HOMEWORKERS TERMS AND PARTICULARS

These particulars are given to you in accordance with the requirements of section 1 of the Employment Rights Act 1996 which sets out certain minimal entitlements to particulars.

Your Job Title is .... and you report, in the first instance, to ....

You will be advised of the reporting procedures that are applicable.

You will work from home but will be required to attend the office of the Employer from time to time as set out herein.

1.	Name and address of Employer	Your Employer is . . . . of . . . .
	Name of Employee	To . . . .
2.	Date when employment began	Your employment began on . . . . [date].
3.	Date when continuous employment began	Your period of continuous employment began on . . . . No employment with a previous employer counts as continuous employment. *ALTERNATIVELY:* Your employment with . . . . from . . . . counts as part of your continuous employment.
4.	Scale or rate of remuneration	Your scale or rate of remuneration is: [£ .... PER HOUR] [£ ..... PER WEEK] [£ ..... PER MONTH]. In addition you will be provided with equipment and you are also entitled to expenses as set out below.
5.	Intervals at which remuneration is paid	You will be paid [WEEKLY] [MONTHLY] in arrears and your salary shall accrue from day to day. Payment will be made into your bank account on the . . . . . day of each [WEEK][MONTH]. Salary increases are at the discretion of the Employer.

6. Terms and conditions relating to hours of work	Since you work from home you will be expected to manage your time and work such hours as are necessary for the performance of your duties. Your normal hours will be not less than . . . . . per week. You are expected to be available at home [*TIMES*] or to be readily contactable. You will not be paid overtime unless agreed.
7. Holiday	1. You are entitled to statutory holidays being New Year's Day, Good Friday, Easter Monday, May Day, Spring Bank Holiday, Late Summer Bank Holiday, Christmas Day and Boxing Day, or holiday *in lieu* if you work on those days. 2. In addition you are entitled to . . . . days' holiday a year to be taken at times agreed with . . . . 3. The holiday year runs from . . . . . to . . . . . . 4. You may not carry over holiday without permission which should be obtained from . . . . 5. You will be paid during the period that you take your holidays. 6 If your employment terminates and you have outstanding entitlement you will be paid your basic salary representing the number of days outstanding.
8. Sickness	1. If you are sick or otherwise incapacitated you or someone on your behalf must contact . . . . . [*SET OUT WHO*] to inform them on the first day of sickness of the reason for your sickness. 2. You must complete a record form within 7 days from the commencement of your sickness. 3. If you are absent for more than 7 days you must provide a medical certificate signed by your doctor that should be sent to . . . . 4. You will be entitled to your basic salary during absences up to . . . . . days per year. 5. You will not be entitled to payment if you have not complied with the above procedure.
9. Pensions	There is no pension scheme applicable to your employment. [You are entitled to join the contributory pension scheme and may obtain details from . . . .]

10. Notice	You are entitled to the following notice:
	1. Any time during the first six month's probationary period: 1 week.
	2. If your employment is confirmed: • one week's notice up to two years service. • one week's notice for each completed year of service up to a maximum of 12 weeks.
	Your employment may be terminated summarily in the event of breach by you that warrants summary termination.
11. Job Title	As set out above.
12. Temporary or Fixed Term Contracts	Not applicable
13. Place of Work	Your normal place of work will be your home address at . . . .
	You may be required to attend the Head Office, as set out at 1, above, as and when necessary. You may also be required to make visits to other offices, customers or suppliers in the United Kingdom as and when instructed.
	You may also be required to attend courses or marketing functions from time to time in order to carry out your duties.
14. Collective Agreements	There are no collective agreements affecting your employment.
15. Overseas Employment	Not applicable
16. Disciplinary Procedures	The disciplinary procedures are attached. They are not part of your contract of employment and the employer may alter them from time to time.
	Given that the Company is permitting you to work from home you should, in particular, note the following disciplinary offences that relate to your employment:
	1. Any act that may invalidate the policy of insurance relating to the equipment or your employment.

16. Disciplinary Procedures (cont.)	2. Any falsification of records or other false statement to the Company relating to you employment or otherwise directly or indirectly connected with the Company's business.
	3. Failure to attend at the Company's premises when required in breach of an express instruction.
	4. Failing to be available at your place of work (*i.e.* your home) without authorisation.
	5. Using the equipment provided by the Company for purposes other than for which it was provided without first obtaining the express written permission of the Company.
17. If you are not satisfied with any disciplinary decision	If you are not satisfied with any disciplinary decision relating to your employment you may appeal in accordance with the terms of the disciplinary procedure.
18. Grievances	You may raise any grievance that you may have in accordance with the terms of the disciplinary procedure.
19. Further steps	Any further steps that you may take consequent upon any disciplinary procedure or grievance are set out in the procedures.
20. Contracting out	A contracting out certificate pursuant to the Pension Scheme Act is [not] in force.
21. Provision of equipment	In order to enable you to carry out your duties you have been provided with the equipment listed in the schedule attached hereto. You agreed that:
	1. The equipment was provided to you in good operating condition.
	2. The Company may install, service, maintain and update such equipment from time to time as it considers appropriate.
	3. You will be responsible for the equipment in respect of any damage to the same, fair wear and tear being excepted.
	4. You will insure the equipment and shall provide a copy of the insurance policy to the Employer. You will not do anything that may invalidate the insurance policy.

21. Provision of Equipment (cont.)	5. Upon termination of your employment for whatever reason you agree that you will forthwith deliver up all equipment provided to you by the Company. You also agree that you will deliver up all computer discs, documents, papers or other confidential information in whatever medium that is the property of the Company or relates to the Company's clients or customers. In so far as it is not possible to deliver up (*i.e.* information on hard disc) you will confirm in writing that it has been destroyed.
22. Entry onto Premises	You agree that the Company or its employees may enter onto the premises at . . . . . . during working hours (being . . . . . to . . . . .) In order to: 1. install or service equipment and, for these purposes, in order to inspect the equipment to ascertain its condition; 2. upon termination of employment, recover the property of the Company. 3. in so far as may be necessary in order to comply with duties relating to health and safety.
23. Expenses	You will be reimbursed your reasonable travel expenses and the expenses of working at home, including telephone charges, a proportion of electricity or other bills attributable to your work and an allowance towards maintaining an office at home. You must submit [*SET OUT PROCEDURE*].
24. Obligations during and after employment	By virtue of the work that you carry out you have access to confidential information belong to the Company. A great deal of trust is given to you since you work from home and you therefore agree and accept that: 1. You have a duty not to disclose confidential information to any party other than has been agreed in the normal course of your employment or without express written permission. Where the permission is uncertain you should first clear it with . . . . . . 2. You agree that you will at no time disclose any confidential information whether before or after your employment and you have agreed to enter

24. Obligations during and after employment (cont.)	into a separate agreement that you agree is entirely reasonable relating to the protection of confidential information and to other interests that the Company is reasonably entitled to protect.

Your normal retirement age will be 65 and you will retire at the end of the month in which you attain that age.

I accept the above particulars of terms and conditions.

or

I accept the terms and conditions as forming part of my contract of employment, subject to my letter of appointment and [the staff Manual].

. . . .

SIGNED

HOMEWORKERS COMMENTARY

Where the individual is employed to work from home there may be a relationship of employer and employee depending on the nature of the services provided by the homeworker. This is apparent from **Airfix Footwear Limited v Cope** [1978] ICR 1210; IRLR 396. Cope worked at home, making heels for shoes manufactured by the appellants. They provided her with tools, materials and patterns and she worked according to instructions. She was paid on a piecemeal basis without any deduction for tax and national insurance and generally worked five days a week. It was held that she was an employee of the company. For seven years, generally five days a week she had delivered similar quantities of heels per day. It is apparent from the cases that a regular routine may harden into the existence of mutuality between the parties that creates a contract of employment.

Where the homeworker is an employee then there may be continuity of employment, even though there are a succession of engagements (see Casual Workers at 5.3). It must also be borne in mind that, if the homeworker is providing similar services to that provided by employees who work from the employer's premises there may be issues of discrimination if the homeworker receives less favourable remuneration or other benefits. Nevertheless, home working is becoming an increasing attractive option, particularly with developments in technology.

The Precedent assumes that the homeworker is an employee and has been drafted on this basis. Particular points to note are:

- Consideration needs to be given to the issue of continuity (Clause 3). Is the engagement such that continuity of employment will be broken between particular tasks, assignments or engagements? Where there is a pattern to the work then there is likely to be continuity of employment.

- In determining the scale or rate of remuneration and other benefits (Clause 4) it will be prudent to make some comparison with office based staff if they are involved in the same or similar positions as there is a danger of claims of discrimination being made and potential claims under the Equal Pay legislation. Homeworkers may also lose out on certain benefits such as canteen facilities, and in using their own home they are providing a resource. This should all be considered in deciding the level of pay.

- The precedent provides for a salary to be paid at regular intervals. Remuneration may of course depend upon piece rates or payment for the completion of a specific job.

- For many, the attraction of home working is that the individual can manage his or her hours. The contract should therefore be sufficiently flexible to reflect this but the employer may wish to stipulate a minimum number of hours as in Clause 6.

- If the homeworker is an employee the Working Time Regulations will give minimum holiday entitlement when there is sufficient continuity. This is reflected in Clause 7 and see Manual **Part I** for commentary.

- The place of work will be the employee's home but provision should be made for the employee to be required to attend the employer's premises, as necessary, as provided for in Clause 13. It is also important to check that the employee is not prevented from using his premises for business premises by, for example, a covenant in the mortgage.

- Since the employee is working from home there are obvious difficulties in monitoring performance. The disciplinary procedure should, however, be tailor made to provide for disciplinary matters that are relevant to the homeworker, as in Clause 16. The quality of the particular kind of work may be of importance and some provision that sets out expected standards may be included.

- It is likely that the employer will have provided some equipment and is paying for the cost of maintenance, *etc.* A provision relating to the equipment should be contained in the contract and the homeworker should be under an obligation to keep it to a certain standard, as in the Clause 'Provision of Equipment'. There should also be a provision that permits entry to the premises to recover any such equipment.

- It is possible that the homeworker will be given access to confidential information and a restrictive covenant in this respect is advisable, as in the Precedent.

8. MANAGERIAL STAFF

PRECEDENT 5.8.1
CONTRACT FOR MANAGER WHERE THERE IS NO COMPANY GROUP

SERVICE AGREEMENT BETWEEN . . . . ('THE COMPANY') AND THE EMPLOYEE ('THE EXECUTIVE MANAGER'/TITLE)

1. Employer and Employee [Executive/ Manager, *etc.*]	The Employer is . . . . of . . . . Company Registration No . . . . The Employee [*EXECUTIVE/MANAGER, ETC.*] is . . . . of . . . .
2. Date employment began, continuous employment and hours of work	The Employee [*EXECUTIVE/MANAGER, ETC.*]'s employment began on . . . . and the Employee [*EXECUTIVE/MANAGER, ETC.*]'s date of continuous employment began on . . . . The Employee [*EXECUTIVE/MANAGER, ETC.*]'s employment is subject to the probationary period and other conditions set out in the Letter of Appointment/ Offer Letter. OR [The Employee [*EXECUTIVE/MANAGER, ETC.*]'s employment began on . . . . and will continue for a [. . .] year fixed period. The employment may be terminated during the fixed period as provided for hereafter, and, subject to termination as set out hereafter, at any time after the end of the fixed period by the giving of [. . . .] months' notice. [*SEE DUGGAN ON WRONGFUL DISMISSAL FOR THE LAW RELATING TO THESE CLAUSES*]. *Hours of work* The Employee [*EXECUTIVE/MANAGER, ETC.*]'s normal hours of work are . . . . a.m. to . . . . p.m. However, the nature of the Employee [*EXECUTIVE/ MANAGER, ETC.*]'s position is such that he must [will be expected] to work such hours as are necessary in order that he can fully carry out his duties and this may entail the Employee [*EXECUTIVE/MANAGER, ETC.*] spending time travelling or away from the place of work or his home on business. The Employee [*EXECUTIVE/MANAGER, ETC.*] is not entitled to

2. Date employment began, *etc*.(cont)	additional remuneration for such time spent save as has been agreed with the Company.
3. Job title and duties	The Employee [*EXECUTIVE/MANAGER, ETC.*] will be employed as [*SENIOR MANAGER/SENIOR MARKETING MANAGER/FINANCE DIRECTOR, ETC.*] from the date his employment began. The Company may change the Employee [*EXECUTIVE/MANAGER, ETC.*]'s job title in its absolute discretion and as it considers necessary and may appoint an Employee [*EXECUTIVE/MANAGER, ETC.*] to act in a joint capacity if it considers it necessary.

Description
The Employee [*EXECUTIVE/MANAGER, ETC.*]'s job description [*WAS PROVIDED WITH THE LETTER OF APPOINTMENT*] [*IS APPENDED TO THIS CONTRACT*].

Duties and flexibility
During the period of his Employment:

1. The Employee [*EXECUTIVE/MANAGER, ETC.*] will well and faithfully serve the Company and will do all in his powers to promote the interests of the Company.

2. The Employee [*EXECUTIVE/MANAGER, ETC.*] will not accept or take up any employment during the hours that he has agreed to work for the Company nor will he accept, whether indirectly or directly, any form of paid or unpaid Consultative or other work [*WITHOUT THE PRIOR PERMISSION IN WRITING OF THE MANAGING DIRECTOR OF THE COMPANY, WHICH WILL NOT BE UNREASONABLY WITHHELD*].

3. The Employee [*EXECUTIVE/MANAGER, ETC.*] agrees that he will carry out such duties as may from time to time be assigned to him by the Company, or instructed by [. . . . . . .], whether or not those duties fall within the job title or description, provided that they are consistent with his status and position with the Company.

4. The Company is part of the . . . . Group and the Employee [*EXECUTIVE/MANAGER, ETC.*] agrees that he will carry out duties for other Companies in the Group if so instructed [*PROVIDED THAT HIS COMPANY WILL REMAIN AS SET OUT IN THIS AGREEMENT*].

4. Remuneration and other benefits	*Salary*

Salary

1. The Employee [*EXECUTIVE/MANAGER, ETC.*] will be paid the sum of £[. . . . .] per annum.

2. The Salary will be calculated and accrue on a daily basis and will be paid by credit transfer on the [. . .] day of each month, provided that the Employee [*EXECUTIVE/MANAGER, ETC.*] acknowledges that the salary may be paid at a later date if, for reasons beyond the control of the Company, salary was not paid on the above date and such late payment shall not be regarded as any breach of this Agreement. Salary will be paid once the Employee [*EXECUTIVE/MANAGER, ETC.*] has provided details of the bank to which it is to be transferred.

3. The salary will be reviewed by [*THE MANAGING DIRECTOR/ BOARD/ REMUNERATION COMMITTEE, ETC.*] on. . . . or by end of the [. . . .] month of each year and a salary rise may be awarded in the absolute discretion of the [*THE MANAGING DIRECTOR/ BOARD/ REMUNERATION COMMITTEE, ETC.*]. There is no guarantee of any salary rise [*BUT THE SALARY WILL NOT BE ADJUSTED DOWN-WARDS*].

Bonus

4. The Company may award a bonus at the [*SET OUT WHEN*]. The bonus is based upon [*SET OUT HOW — E.G. PROFITABILITY OF THE GROUP, DIVISION, TURNOVER BROUGHT IN BY THE EMPLOYEE [EXECUTIVE/MANAGER, ETC.]*]. The bonus is paid at the absolute discretion of the Company [*AND THE EMPLOYEE [EXECUTIVE /MANAGER, ETC.] ACKNOWLEDGES THAT HE HAS NO SET EXPECTATION THAT HE WILL BE PAID A BONUS*].

Commission

5. Commission is paid as follows:
[*SET OUT HOW IT IS CALCULATED*]

6. Where commission is paid in advance and employment terminates the Company may offset any commission or other remuneration that would be otherwise payable against such advance commission.

5. Share options	The Company operates a Share Option Scheme. If the Employee [*EXECUTIVE/MANAGER, ETC.*] is entitled to participate in the Scheme he will have been advised in his Letter of Appointment. The Options are subject to the Rules of the Scheme to which reference should be made.
6. Company car	1. The Employee [*EXECUTIVE/MANAGER, ETC.*] will be provided with a Company car, which shall be not less than [*SET OUT . . . .*]/[*SUITABLE FOR THE EMPLOYEE [EXECUTIVE/MANAGER, ETC.]'S DUTIES AND STATUS*]. The Company will tax and insure the car and pay for maintenance and repairs [*PROVIDED THEY WERE NOT CAUSED BY THE COMPANY'S NEGLIGENCE*]. 2. The car may be replaced when the Company considers it appropriate. 3. The car may be used for private purposes as well as Company business. The Company will pay for petrol used for business purposes which may be claimed as part of expenses. The Employee [*EXECUTIVE/MANAGER, ETC.*] is responsible for petrol for private mileage and for any income tax payable in respect of this benefit. 4. The Employee [*EXECUTIVE/MANAGER, ETC.*] warrants he has a clean driving licence and he will bring to the attention of the Company any matter that may affect his continued ability to drive the car. 5. The Employee [*EXECUTIVE/MANAGER, ETC.*] agrees that he will not do anything that may invalidate the insurance policy. 6. Upon termination of this Agreement, for whatever reason, the Employee [*EXECUTIVE/ MANAGER, ETC.*] agrees that he will immediately deliver up the car or make it available for collection [*AND ACKNOWLEDGES THAT HE WILL NO LONGER BE INSURED TO DRIVE THE CAR FROM THE DATE OF TERMINATION*]. *ALTERNATIVELY —* [*THE COMPANY OPERATES A CAR POLICY WHICH THE EMPLOYEE [EXECUTIVE/MANAGER, ETC.] AGREES HE HAS READ AND SIGNED —* **see MANUAL PRECEDENT F10.**]

7. Pension	The Employee [*EXECUTIVE/MANAGER, ETC.*] is entitled to join the Company's Pension Scheme and the terms of the Scheme are incorporated into this Agreement. There is [*IS NOT*] a contracting out certificate in relation to the Pension Scheme.
8. Expenses	The Employer will reimburse the Employee [*EXECUTIVE/MANAGER, ETC.*]'s expenses incurred in the course of his employment which were incurred in the furtherance of his duties. The Employee [*EXECUTIVE/MANAGER, ETC.*] should acquaint himself with the procedure for reclaiming expenses.
9. Holidays and other absences	*Holiday* 1. The Employee [*EXECUTIVE/MANAGER, ETC.*] is entitled to [. . . . .] days' holiday per year on full salary, in addition to the normal statutory holidays. 2. The Employee [*EXECUTIVE/MANAGER, ETC.*] must agree holiday in advance with [. . . . .] by giving at least twice the number of working days' notice of the number of days he intends to take on holiday and this will be subject to the Agreement of the Company. The Company may stipulate the days that the Employee [*EXECUTIVE/MANAGER, ETC.*] must take as paid holiday. 3. Holidays not taken in the calendar year which runs from [. . . . .] to [. . . . .] cannot be carried over [save with the written agreement of . . . . .]. 4. For the purposes of termination of employment, holidays accrue on a daily basis and the Employee [*EXECUTIVE/MANAGER, ETC.*] will be entitled to any accrued holiday pay on the termination of his employment. *Other absences* The Company operates a maternity and paternity policy to which reference should be made. **[SEE MANUAL PRECEDENT K1]**
10. Sickness absences and benefits	<u>Sickness</u> 1. Where the Employee [*EXECUTIVE/MANAGER, ETC.*] is absent due to sickness he must, as soon as is possible, inform or cause to be informed

| 10. Sickness absences and benefits (cont.) | [STIPULATE WHO — *e.g.* THE MANAGING DIRECTOR] of the Company. |

2. Self certificates must be provided for periods of up to 7 days and medical certificates must be provided for any longer periods.

3. The Company will continue to pay full salary whilst the Employee is absent due to sickness for a period of [. . .] days. However, the Company has the right not to pay salary where:
   (1) The Employee [*EXECUTIVE/MANAGER, ETC.*] is absent for more than [. . .] days in any one period or [. . .] days during the calendar year.
   (2) The Employee [*EXECUTIVE/MANAGER, ETC.*] does not provide certificates as required.
   (3) The Employee [*EXECUTIVE/MANAGER, ETC.*] fails to respond to any reasonable request from the Company about his condition and prognosis.
   (4) The Employee [*EXECUTIVE/MANAGER, ETC.*] has repeated spells of short absence that cumulatively amount to [. . .] days in any six month period.

4. The Employee [*EXECUTIVE/MANAGER, ETC.*] will give credit for any statutory or other benefits he receives arising out of his absence due to sickness and which do not arise out of any private insurance taken out by the Employee [*EXECUTIVE/MANAGER, ETC.*].

5. The Employee [*EXECUTIVE/MANAGER, ETC.*]'s employment may be terminated for sickness in the circumstances set out herein.

Medical examination
The Company may require the Employee [*EXECUTIVE/MANAGER, ETC.*] to undergo a medical examination and refusal to do so may result in non payment of salary or in dismissal.

[SEE MANUAL AT J FOR FURTHER EXAMPLES OF THE ABOVE PRECEDENTS]

Private Health Insurance
The Employee [*EXECUTIVE/MANAGER, ETC.*] [and his family which shall consist of spouse or partner and children] are entitled to membership of the

10. Sickness absences and benefits (cont.)	Company's private health insurance scheme, on the terms that may from time to time exist. If the Employee [EXECUTIVE/MANAGER, ETC.] chooses not to join the Scheme he is not entitled to any sums by way alternative remuneration.
	Third Parties
	Where the Employee [EXECUTIVE/MANAGER, ETC.]'s absences arise out of the actions of a third party which entitle him to claim damages, the Employee [EXECUTIVE/MANAGER, ETC.] agrees that any sums advanced to him by way of salary will be regarded as sums that must be refunded out of any damages recovered for loss of earnings.
	[SEE ALSO MANUAL PRECEDENT F11]
11. Place of work	The Employee [EXECUTIVE/MANAGER, ETC.]'s place of work will be as set out above [OR SET OUT ADDRESS, ETC]. However, the Employee [EXECUTIVE/MANAGER, ETC.] agrees:
	1. Should the Company decide to relocate, he may be required to move to anywhere within the United Kingdom, upon such relocation, provided that the Employer will pay the reasonable costs of removal and other incidental expenses to be agreed beforehand.
	2. The Employee [EXECUTIVE/MANAGER, ETC.] will be required, as part of his duties, to travel in the United Kingdom and abroad (for which he confirms he has a valid passport) and the Company may so instruct him in the proper furtherance of his duties **provided** that he will not have to spend time abroad for more than [. . .] days at any one time without prior mutual agreement. The Employee [EXECUTIVE/ MANAGER, ETC.] can claim expenses in relation to such travel as provided for herein.
	[FOR AN OVERSEAS CONTRACT SEE 5.10]
	[FOR A RESIDENTIAL REQUIREMENT SEE 5.12]
12. Disciplinary and other procedures	The Employee [EXECUTIVE/MANAGER, ETC.]'s attention is drawn to the Company's Disciplinary and Grievance Procedures which are applicable to him. They do not form part of this contract.

12. Disciplinary and other procedures (cont.)	For the purposes of any disciplinary matter, the following persons are responsible: • Warnings: . . . . • Dismissal: . . . . • Appeals against warnings: . . . . • Appeals against dismissal: . . . . For the purposes of the Grievance procedure, the following individuals: • Initial informal grievance: . . . . • Formal grievance: . . . . • Further complaint where not satisfied with outcome: . . . . **[SEE MANUAL PARTS R AND S FOR FURTHER DETAIL]**
13. Standard of work and other duties during employment	The Employee *[EXECUTIVE/MANAGER, ETC.]* acknowledges that his title, position and the nature of his work require a high standard and breach may cause the Company *[IRREMEDIABLE]* harm. He therefore warrants that he has the requisite qualifications and abilities to perform the full functions of his job and will drawn to the attention of the Employer any matter that may affect his ability to carry out his job. Because of the nature of his Employment, the Employee *[EXECUTIVE/MANAGER, ETC.]* recognises that, in addition to those matters set out in the Disciplinary Policy as constituting grounds for dismissal, any act of negligence or act that may bring the Company into disrepute or that undermines the trust and confidence of the Company may lead to summary dismissal. The Employee *[EXECUTIVE/MANAGER, ETC.]* also expressly acknowledges that he will draw to the attention of the Company any act by an employee or third party that is a breach on their part or may harm the interests of the Company. *ALTERNATIVELY:* The Employee *[EXECUTIVE/MANAGER, ETC.]* undertakes that he will disclose to the Company, forthwith upon it coming to his knowledge, any of the following information or matters: • Any activities on the part of other employees that may be harmful to the interests of the Company, including but not limited to:

13. Standard of work and other duties during employment (cont.)	(1) any plans of employees to leave the Company or to join a Competitor or to take any steps to set up or establish a business that is or may be in competition; (2) any steps taken by employees to carry out such plans; (3) any use of confidential information or other property or assets of the Company by employees for the furtherance of such plans; (4) any other matters that may adversely affect the business of the Company. **[SEE MANUAL PART P ON PUBLIC INTEREST DISCLOSURE]**
14. Scope of duties	*Whole Employment* The nature of the Employee [*EXECUTIVE/MANAGER, ETC.*]'s employment is such that the Employee [*EXECUTIVE/MANAGER, ETC.*] cannot be engaged in any activity that may mean he cannot give his full attention to his duties with the Company or which may place him in a position of conflict. The Employee [*EXECUTIVE/MANAGER, ETC.*] therefore agrees that he will not accept or take up any employment during the hours that he has agreed to work for the Company nor will he accept, whether indirectly or directly, any form of paid or unpaid Consultative or other work [without the prior permission in writing of the Managing Director of the Company, which will not be unreasonably withheld.] The Employee [*EXECUTIVE/ MANAGER, ETC.*] may however, purchase shares in [*SET OUT THE EXTENT OF THE INTERESTS THAT MAY BE PERMISSIBLE*]. *Implied Duties* The Employee [*EXECUTIVE/MANAGER, ETC.*] further acknowledges that the nature of his employment creates implied fiduciary duties and duties of fidelity and any and all covenants herein are subject to those implied duties where they be wider.
15. Covenants during employment	*Co Employees* The Employee [*EXECUTIVE/MANAGER, ETC.*] will not at any time during his employment solicit or seek to recruit any current employees of the Company to be engaged or work for the Employee [*EXECUTIVE/*

15. Covenants during employment (cont.)	*MANAGER, ETC.*] or any other person, firm, company or organisation and will not make any comment, representation or statement that may facilitate, induce, persuade procure, or howsoever cause any employee to leave the employment of the Company. *ALTERNATIVELY:* The Employee [*EXECUTIVE/MANAGER, ETC.*] shall not at any time during his employment with the Company, whether directly or indirectly, and for his own behalf or that of any company, firm, person or other third party seek to encourage or entice any employee of the Company to leave the employment of the Company. *Other activities* The Employee [*EXECUTIVE/MANAGER, ETC.*] will not during the period that he is employed by the Company: 1. During the Employee [*EXECUTIVE/MANAGER, ETC.*]'s working hours take any steps to seek work with any competitor; 2. Canvass solicit or otherwise make any representation or statement to any customer or supplier which may cause harm or adversely affect the Company's business or entertain any offers from customers or suppliers, and in the event of the latter shall immediately inform the Company of any offers. *Secret Profits* The Employee [*EXECUTIVE/MANAGER, ETC.*] agrees that he will not take any money or other benefit from any client of the Company and will immediately advise the Company if any such money or other benefit is offered to the Company. **[SEE ALSO MANUAL PRECEDENT Q5]**
16. Intellectual property	*[SHORT FORM CLAUSE]* The Employee [*EXECUTIVE/MANAGER, ETC.*]'s duties will involve him in formulating and dealing with [*LIST E.G. MARKETING, ETC*]. These duties will involve the production of designs, manufacturing methods, plans, processes or techniques in which any copyright or other intellectual property rights will subsist. The

16. Intellectual property (cont.)	Employee [*EXECUTIVE/MANAGER, ETC.*] agrees that any such rights vest absolutely in the Company and he will take all steps and carry out all acts that may be necessary to ensure that the intellectual property is lawfully vested in the Company, including signing all applications and any other documents that may be necessary to apply for any Patent rights or other form of application in the United Kingdom and Worldwide, and that this obligation will continue to exist when the Employee [*EXECUTIVE/MANAGER, ETC.*]'s employment has ended. *ALTERNATIVELY:* Because of the nature of the employment the Employee [*EXECUTIVE/MANAGER, ETC.*] has signed an Intellectual Property Agreement [*OR:* it is a condition of employment that the Employee [*EXECUTIVE/MANAGER, ETC.*] signs the Company's Intellectual Property Agreement]. **[SEE MANUAL Q PRECEDENT Q4 FOR AN AGREEMENT AND Q5 FOR A FURTHER CLAUSE]**
17. Confidentiality	The Employee [*EXECUTIVE/MANAGER, ETC.*] agrees that he will not at any time during his Employment and after the termination of his employment without restriction in time communicate, disclose or divulge to any third person or in any way make use of the Company's Confidential Information or Trade Secrets [which, without prejudice to the generality of the foregoing include [*LIST*]] relating to the Company, its customers or Suppliers **provided** that once the Employee [*EXECUTIVE/MANAGER, ETC.*] has left the employment with the Company this restriction shall not apply where such information has been ordered to be disclosed by a court or otherwise by law and the Employee [*EXECUTIVE/MANAGER, ETC.*] shall not be prevented from using his own skills and experience. **[FOR MORE DETAILED PROVISIONS SEE MANUAL Q PRECEDENTS Q2 AND Q5]**
18. Post termination covenants: non solicitation, non dealing and non poaching	The Employee [*EXECUTIVE/MANAGER, ETC.*] agrees that for a period of [. . . . .] months from the termination of his Employment he will not: 1. Canvass, solicit or otherwise in any way seek to procure, the business or business opportunities from any customer or client of the Company,

18. Post termination covenants: non solicitation, non dealing and non poaching (cont.)

where the customer or client of the Company has been a customer or client [. . . . .] months immediately preceding the termination of employment of the Employee [Executive/ Manager, *etc.*] and with whom the Employee [*EXECUTIVE/MANAGER, ETC.*] has had business dealings within the previous [. . . . .] months.

2. Canvass, solicit or otherwise in any way seek to procure, orders from any supplier of the Company where the supplier has supplied the Company within the previous [. . . . .] months and the Employee has had dealings with the supplier or is aware of any agreement between supplier and the Company.

3. Deal with any customer or client of the Company, where the customer or client of the Company has been a customer or client within [. . . . .] months immediately preceding the termination of employment of the Employee [*EXECUTIVE/MANAGER, ETC.*] and with whom the Employee [*EXECUTIVE/MANAGER, ETC.*] has had business dealings within the previous [. . . . .] months.

4. Deal with any supplier of the Company where the supplier has supplied the Company within the previous [. . . . .] months and the Employee [*EXECUTIVE/MANAGER, ETC.*] has had dealings with the supplier or is aware of any agreement between supplier and the Company.

5. Seek to persuade or solicit or provide work, whether directly or indirectly, or by self employment or consultancy, to any person who was an employee of the Company [. . . . .] years prior to the termination of the Employee [*EXECUTIVE/MANAGER, ETC.*]'s employment, or was engaged in any capacity, and who would be in a position to harm the business of the Company were he to accept any employment or engagement.

6. Accept any orders, whether through himself or a third party, indirectly or indirectly and whether of his own or a third party's benefit any orders for any products or services with which the Employee [*EXECUTIVE/MANAGER, ETC.*] was concerned

18. Post termination covenants: non solicitation, non dealing and non poaching (cont.)	whilst he was working for the Company and which the Company would have been in a position to supply. **[SEE MANUAL PRECEDENT Q5 FOR A MORE DETAILED COVENANT]**
19. Post termination: working for competitors (cont.)	The Employee [*EXECUTIVE/MANAGER, ETC.*] agrees that for a period of [. . . . .] months from the termination of his Employment he will not: 1. Hold any material interest in any business which is or is likely to be in competition with the Company. 2. Hold any material interest in any business which may require or might reasonably be considered by the Employer to require the disclosure of confidential information belonging to the Company in order to property discharge his functions in such business. 3. Accept employment or take any engagement, whether self employed or otherwise and whether directly or indirectly, from any competitor of the Company which is likely to adversely affect the business of the Company. **[SEE MANUAL PRECEDENT Q5 FOR A MORE DETAILED CLAUSE]** **[SEE SALESMAN AT 5.13 FOR A TERRITORIAL COVENANT]**
20. Employer's property	Upon the termination of the Employee [*EXECUTIVE/ MANAGER, ETC.*]'s contract for whatever reason, the Employee [*EXECUTIVE/MANAGER, ETC.*] shall immediately return to the Company all property that belongs to the Company, including: 1. Any computer, printer or other such equipment, and all computer discs and other software. If the Employee [*EXECUTIVE/MANAGER, ETC.*] has a password on any computer the detail of the password. 2. All documents in whatever form, including any copies or summaries of the same and including the Employee [*EXECUTIVE/MANAGER, ETC.*]'s working notes.

20. Employer's property	3. The Company car and keys. For the purpose of this Agreement the Employee [*EXECUTIVE/MANAGER, ETC.*] irrevocably gives the Company the right to enter any property where the Company's property is held and remove the same.
21. Severability of covenants	The Employee [*EXECUTIVE/MANAGER, ETC.*] agrees that the each of the covenants contained in this Agreement are reasonable and are necessary for the protection of the Company's business. However, each provision of this Agreement is independent and severable and if any of them should be found by a Court of Law to be unenforceable or ineffective for whatever reason that shall not affect the validity of the separate covenants. If any covenants would become valid if any wording was deleted then the covenant shall be deemed to be applicable with such deletions and shall apply as so amended as to make the same enforceable.
22. Termination of contract	*Notice* Save as set out below, the Company must give the Employee [*EXECUTIVE/MANAGER, ETC.*] [. . . . .] months' notice to terminate this Agreement and the Employee [*EXECUTIVE/MANAGER, ETC.*] must give [. . . . .] months' notice. *Payment in lieu* **[FOR PAYMENT *IN LIEU* CLAUSES SEE MANUAL AT PRECEDENT V.2]** *Earlier Termination* The notice period is subject to the Company's rights to dismiss the Employee [*EXECUTIVE/MANAGER, ETC.*] without notice if: 1. He is guilty of misconduct set out in the Company's Disciplinary Procedures which warrant dismissal without notice. 2. He commits any act of negligence, neglect of duty which is serious, or does any act which causes the Company to lose trust and confidence and which justifies dismissal without notice. 3. He is in serious or repudiatory breach of this agreement.

22. Termination of contract (cont.)	4. He commits any act outside his employment which is liable to bring the Company into disrepute.
	5. He is declared bankrupt or otherwise enters into any arrangement with his creditors.
	6. He is convicted of a criminal offence and in the case of a motoring offence this results in disqualification or imprisonment.
	7. He suffers from mental disorder.
	8. He is persistently absent from work for a period of [. . . . .] days in any [. . . . .] months.
	9. He is guilty of any serious or repudiatory breach of this Agreement.
23. Garden leave	Where notice has been given by either side to this Agreement, or the Employee [Executive\Manager etc] purports to leave the employment in breach of the notice that he is required to give:
	The Company:
	1. Shall no longer be under any duty to provide work to the Employee [*EXECUTIVE/MANAGER, ETC.*] and the Employee [*EXECUTIVE/MANAGER, ETC.*] shall have no right to carry out any work or services for the Company [but the Employee [*EXECUTIVE/MANAGER, ETC.*] may be required to make himself available during normal working hours should the Company require his services].
	2. May direct that the Employee [*EXECUTIVE/ MANAGER, ETC.*] cease all contact with any customers or suppliers or employees of the Company.
	3. Shall be entitled to exclude the Employee [*EXECUTIVE/MANAGER, ETC.*] from the Company's premises.
	PROVIDED THAT
	4. The Company shall continue to have the right to suspend the Employee [*EXECUTIVE/MANAGER, ETC.*] in the circumstances provided for in the Disciplinary Policy.
	5. During the notice period the Employee [Executive/ Manager, *etc.*] will continue to receive all his contractual benefits.

24. Whole Agreement	This Agreement forms the Whole Agreement between the parties, save that it is subject to any further terms contained in the Letter of Appointment and the Employee [*EXECUTIVE/MANAGER, ETC.*] acknowledges that he has read the Letter, this Agreement and any Company Policies that are referred to in the Letter of Appointment. [*CONSIDER WHETHER EXPRESS REFERENCE SHOULD BE MADE I.E. TO EQUAL OPPORTUNITY POLICIES, ETC.*]
SIGNATURES	[*CONSIDER WHETHER THE DOCUMENT SHOULD BE SIGNED AS A DEED*]

PRECEDENT 5.8.2
CONTRACT FOR MANAGER WHERE THERE IS A COMPANY GROUP

1. Employer and Employee [Executive/ Manager, *etc.*]	The Employer is . . . . of . . . . Company Registration No . . . . The Company is part of the . . . . . Group of Companies and for the purpose of this Agreement the expression Group Company shall mean any Company which is an Associated Company or subsidiary as defined by the Employment Rights Act 1996 or the Companies Act and any company which is for the time being a holding Company as defined by the Companies Act. The Employee [*EXECUTIVE/MANAGER, ETC.*] is . . . . of . . . .
2. Date employment began, continuous employment and hours of work	The Employee [*EXECUTIVE/MANAGER, ETC.*]'s employment began on . . . . and the Employee [*EXECUTIVE/MANAGER, ETC.*]'s date of continuous employment began on . . . . The Employee [*EXECUTIVE/MANAGER, ETC.*]'s employment is subject to the probationary period and other conditions set out in the Letter of Appointment/ Offer Letter. *OR* [The Employee [*EXECUTIVE/MANAGER, ETC.*]'s employment began on . . . . and will continue for a [. . . . .] year fixed period. The employment may be terminated during the fixed period as provided for hereafter, and, subject to termination as set out hereafter, after the end of the fixed period by the giving of [. . . . .] months' notice. *Hours of work* The Employee [*EXECUTIVE/MANAGER, ETC.*]'s normal hours of work are . . . a.m. to . . .p.m. However, the nature of the Employee [*EXECUTIVE/MANAGER, ETC.*]'s position is such that he will be expected to work such hours as are necessary on business for the Employer or Group Companies in order that he can fully carry out his duties and this may entail the Employee [*EXECUTIVE/MANAGER, ETC.*] spending time travelling or away from the place of work or

2.	Date employment began, continuous employment and hours of work (cont.)	home on business. The Employee [*EXECUTIVE/ MANAGER, ETC.*] is not entitled to additional remuneration for such time save as has been agreed with the Company and in respect of additional work carried out for Group Companies this will be agreed between the Company/Group Company and Employee [*EXECUTIVE/MANAGER, ETC.*].
3.	Job title and duties	The Employee [*EXECUTIVE/MANAGER, ETC.*] will be employed as [*SENIOR MANAGER/SENIOR MARKETING MANAGER/FINANCE DIRECTOR, ETC.*] from the date his employment began. The Employer may change the Employee [*EXECUTIVE/MANAGER, ETC.*]'s job title in its absolute discretion and as it considers necessary and may appoint an Employee [*EXECUTIVE/ MANAGER, ETC.*] to act in a joint capacity if it considers it necessary.

Description
The Employee [*EXECUTIVE/MANAGER, ETC.*]'s job description [*WAS PROVIDED WITH THE LETTER OF APPOINTMENT*] [*IS APPENDED TO THIS CONTRACT*].

Duties and flexibility
During the period of his Employment:

1. The Employee [*EXECUTIVE/MANAGER, ETC.*] will well and faithfully serve the Company and the Group Companies and will do all in his powers to promote the interests of the Company and the Group Companies.

2. The Employee [*EXECUTIVE/MANAGER, ETC.*] will not accept or take up any employment during the hours that he has agreed to work for the Company or a Group Company nor will he accept, whether indirectly or directly, any form or paid or unpaid Consultative or other work [*WITHOUT THE PRIOR PERMISSION IN WRITING OF THE MANAGING DIRECTOR OF THE COMPANY, WHICH WILL NOT BE UNREASONABLY WITHHELD*].

3. The Employee [*EXECUTIVE/MANAGER, ETC.*] agrees that he will carry out such duties as may from time to time be assigned to him by the Company, or instructed by [. . . . . .] whether or not those duties fall within the job title or

3. Job title and duties (cont.)	description, provided that they are consistent with his status and position with the Company. 4. The Employee [*EXECUTIVE/MANAGER, ETC.*] agrees that he will carry out such duties for other Companies in the Group if so instructed and that his employment may be transferred to any one of the Group Companies in which case this Agreement shall continue to apply with suitable modifications. Where the Employee [*EXECUTIVE/ MANAGER, ETC.*]'s employment has been assigned to another Group Company then this Agreement shall remain in force, with necessary modifications, and the Employer shall mean that Group Company to which the Employee [*EXECUTIVE/MANAGER ETC.*] has been assigned.
4. Remuneration and other benefits	*Salary* 1. The Employee [*EXECUTIVE/MANAGER, ETC.*] will be paid the sum of £[. . . . .] per annum. 2. The salary will be calculated and accrue on a daily basis and will be paid by credit transfer on the [. . .] day of each month, provided that the Employee [*EXECUTIVE/MANAGER, ETC.*] acknowledges that the salary may be paid at a later date if, for reasons beyond the control of the Company salary was not paid on the above date and such late payment shall not be regarded as any breach of this Agreement. Salary will be paid once the Employee [*EXECUTIVE/MANAGER, ETC.*] has provided details of the bank to which it is to be transferred. 3. The salary will be reviewed by the [*MANAGING DIRECTOR/ BOARD/ REMUNERATION COMMITTEE, ETC.*] on . . . . . or by the end of the [. . .] month each year and a salary rise may be awarded in the absolute discretion of the [*MANAGING DIRECTOR/ BOARD/ REMUNERATION COMMITTEE, ETC.*]. There is no guarantee of any salary rise [*BUT THE SALARY WILL NOT BE ADJUSTED DOWNWARDS*]. *Bonus* 4. The Employer may award a bonus at the [*SET OUT WHEN*]. The bonus is based upon [*SET OUT HOW — E.G. PROFITABILITY OF THE GROUP, DIVISION,*

4. Remuneration and other benefits (cont.)	*TURNOVER BROUGHT IN BY THE EMPLOYEE [EXECUTIVE/MANAGER, ETC.]].* The bonus is paid at the absolute discretion of the Employer [*AND THE EMPLOYEE [EXECUTIVE/MANAGER, ETC.] ACKNOWLEDGES THAT HE HAS NO SET EXPECTATION THAT HE WILL BE PAID A BONUS*]. *Commission* 5. Commission is paid as follows: [*SET OUT HOW IT IS CALCULATED*] 6. Where commission is paid in advance of sales and employment terminates the Company may offset any commission that would be otherwise payable against such advance commission.
5. Share options	The Group operates a Group Share Option Scheme. If the Employee [*EXECUTIVE/MANAGER, ETC.*] is entitled to participate in the Scheme he will have been advised in his Letter of Appointment. The Options are subject to the Rules of the Scheme to which reference should be made.
6. Company car	1. The Employee [*EXECUTIVE/MANAGER, ETC.*] will be provided with a Company car, which shall be not less than [*SET OUT. . . . .*]/[*SUITABLE FOR THE EMPLOYEE [EXECUTIVE/MANAGER, ETC.]'S DUTIES AND STATUS*]. The Company will tax, insure, pay for maintenance and repairs [*PROVIDED THEY WERE NOT CAUSED BY THE EMPLOYEE'S NEGLIGENCE*]. 2. The car may be replaced when the Company (or, in appropriate circumstances Group Company) considers it appropriate. 3. The car may be used for private purposes as well as Group business. The Company will pay for petrol used for business purposes which may be claimed as part of expenses. 4. The Employee [*EXECUTIVE/MANAGER, ETC.*] warrants that he has a clean driving licence and he will bring to the attention of the Company or Group any matter that may affect his continued ability to drive the car. 5. The Employee [*EXECUTIVE/MANAGER, ETC.*] agrees that he will not do anything that may invalidate the insurance policy.

6. Company car (cont.)	6. Upon termination of this Agreement, for whatever reason, the Employee [*EXECUTIVE/ MANAGER, ETC.*] agrees that he will immediately deliver up the car or make it available for collection [and acknowledges that he will no longer be insured to drive the car from the date of termination]. *ALTERNATIVELY—* [*THE COMPANY/GROUP*] operates a car policy which the Employee [*EXECUTIVE/MANAGER, ETC.*] agrees he has read and signed — **see MANUAL PRECEDENT F10**]
7. Pension	The Employee [*EXECUTIVE/MANAGER, ETC.*] is entitled to join the Group Pension Scheme and the terms of the Scheme are incorporated into this Agreement. There is [*IS NOT*] a contracting out certificate in relation to the Pension Scheme.
8. Expenses	The Company will reimburse the Employee [*EXECUTIVE/MANAGER, ETC.*] expenses incurred in the course of his employment which were incurred in the furtherance of his duties. The Employee [*EXECUTIVE/MANAGER, ETC.*] should acquaint himself with the procedure for reclaiming expenses.
9. Holidays and other absences	*Holiday* 1. The Employee [*EXECUTIVE/MANAGER, ETC.*] is entitled to [. . . . .] days' holiday per year on full salary, in addition to the normal statutory holidays. 2. The Employee [*EXECUTIVE/MANAGER, ETC.*] must agree holiday in advance with [. . . . . . .] by giving at least twice the number of working days' notice of the number of days he intends to take on holiday and this will be subject to the Agreement of the Company. The Company may stipulate the days that the Employee [*EXECUTIVE/MANAGER, ETC.*] must take as paid holiday. 3. Holidays not taken in the calendar year which runs from [. . . . .] to [. . . . .] cannot be carried out [*SAVE WITH THE WRITTEN AGREEMENT OF . . . . .*]. 4. For the purposes of termination of employment, holidays accrue on a daily basis and the Employee [*EXECUTIVE/MANAGER, ETC.*] will be entitled to

9. Holidays and other absences (cont.)	any accrued holiday pay on the termination of his employment. *Other absences* The Company operates a maternity and paternity policy to which reference should be made. **[SEE MANUAL PRECEDENT K1]**
10. Sickness absences and benefits	*Sickness* 1. Where the Company [*EXECUTIVE/MANAGER, ETC.*] is absent due to sickness he must, as soon as is possible, inform or cause to be informed [STIPULATE WHO — *E.G.* THE MANAGING DIRECTOR] of the Company. 2. Self certificates must be provided for periods of up to 7 days and medical certificates must be provided for any longer periods. 3. The Company will continue to pay full salary whilst the Employee [*EXECUTIVE/MANAGER, ETC.*] is absent due to sickness for a period of [. . .] days. However, the Company has the right not to pay salary where: (1) The Employee [*EXECUTIVE/MANAGER, ETC.*] is absent for more than [. . . . .] days in any one period or [. . . . .] days during the calendar year. (2) The Employee [*EXECUTIVE/MANAGER, ETC.*] does not provide certificates as required. (3) The Employee [*EXECUTIVE/MANAGER, ETC.*] fails to respond to any reasonable request from the Company about his condition and prognosis. (4) The Employee [*EXECUTIVE/MANAGER, ETC.*] has repeated spells of short absence that cumulatively amount to [. . . . .] days in any six month period. 4. The Employee [*EXECUTIVE/MANAGER, ETC.*] will give credit for any statutory or other benefits he receives arising out of his absence due to sickness and which do not arise out of any private insurance taken out by the Employee [*EXECUTIVE/MANAGER, ETC.*]. 5. The Employee [*EXECUTIVE/MANAGER, ETC.*]'s employment may be terminated for sickness in the circumstances set out herein.

10. Sickness absences and benefits (cont.)	*Medical examination* The Company may require the Employee [*EXECUTIVE/MANAGER, ETC.*] to undergo a medical examination and refusal to do so may result in non payment of salary or in dismissal. **[SEE MANUAL AT J FOR FURTHER EXAMPLES OF THE ABOVE PRECEDENTS]** *Private Health Insurance* The Employee [*EXECUTIVE/MANAGER, ETC.*] [*AND HIS FAMILY WHICH SHALL CONSIST OF SPOUSE AND CHILDREN*] are entitled to membership of the Group private health insurance scheme, on the terms that may from time to time exist. If the Employee [*EXECUTIVE/MANAGER, ETC.*] chooses not to join the Scheme he is not entitled to any sums by way alternative. *Third Parties* Where the Employee [*EXECUTIVE/MANAGER, ETC.*]'s absences arise out of the actions of a third party which entitle him to claim damages the Employee [*EXECUTIVE/MANAGER, ETC.*] agrees that any sums advanced to him by way of salary will be regarded as sums that must be refunded out of any damages recovered for loss of earnings. **[SEE ALSO MANUAL PRECEDENT F 11]**
11. Place of work	The Employee [*EXECUTIVE/MANAGER, ETC.*]'s place of work will be as set out above [*OR SET OUT ADDRESS, ETC.*] or shall be the premises of any Group Company to which the Employee [*EXECUTIVE/MANAGER, ETC.*] is assigned or works from time to time. However, the Employee [*EXECUTIVE/MANAGER, ETC.*] agrees: 1. The Employee [*EXECUTIVE/MANAGER, ETC.*] may at any time be instructed to work from any Group Company premises on a temporary or permanent basis. 2. Should the Company decide to relocate, the Employee [*EXECUTIVE/MANAGER, ETC.*] may be required to move to anywhere within the United Kingdom, upon such relocation, provided that the Company will pay the reasonable costs of removal and other incidental expenses to be agreed beforehand.

11. Place of work	3. The Employee [*EXECUTIVE/MANAGER, ETC.*] will be required, as part of his duties to travel in the United Kingdom and abroad (for which he confirmed he has a valid passport) and the Company may so instruct him in the proper furtherance of his duties PROVIDED that he will not have to spend time abroad for more than [. . .] days at any one time without prior mutual agreement. The Employee [*EXECUTIVE/ MANAGER, ETC.*] can claim expenses in relation to such travel as provided for herein. **[FOR AN OVERSEAS CONTRACT SEE 5.10]** **[FOR A RESIDENTIAL REQUIREMENT SEE 5.12]**
12. Disciplinary and other procedures	The Employee [*EXECUTIVE/MANAGER, ETC.*]'s attention is drawn to the Company's Disciplinary and Grievance Procedures which are applicable to him. They do not form part of this contract. For the purposes of any disciplinary matter, the following persons are responsible: • Warnings: . . . . • Dismissal: . . . . • Appeals against warnings: . . . . • Appeals against dismissal: . . . . For the purposes of the Grievance procedure, the following individuals: • Initial informal grievance: . . . . • Formal grievance:. . . . . • Further complaint where not satisfied with outcome:. . . . . **[SEE MANUAL PARTS R AND S FOR FURTHER DETAIL]**
13. Standard of work and other duties during employment	The Employee [*EXECUTIVE/MANAGER, ETC.*] acknowledges that his title, position and the nature of his work require a high standard and breach may cause the Company or any Group Company [IRREMEDIABLE] harm. He therefore warrants that he has the requisite qualifications and abilities to perform the full functions of his job and will draw to the attention of the Company or Group any matter that may affect his ability to carry out his job. Because of the nature of his Employment, the Employee [*EXECUTIVE/MANAGER, ETC.*] recognises that, in addition to those matters set out in the

13. Standard of work and other duties during employment (cont.)	Disciplinary Policy as constituting grounds for dismissal, any negligence or act that may bring the Employer or Group into disrepute or that undermines the trust and confidence of the Company or Group may lead to summary dismissal.

The Employee [EXECUTIVE/MANAGER, ETC.] also expressly acknowledges that he will draw to the attention of the Company any act by any employee or third party that is a breach on their part or may harm the interests of the Employer or Group.

ALTERNATIVELY

The Employee [EXECUTIVE/MANAGER, ETC.] undertakes that he will disclose to the Company, forthwith upon it coming to his knowledge, any of the following information or matters:

- Any activities on the part of other employees that may be harmful to the interests of the Company or Group, including but not limited to:
  (1) any plans of employees to leave the Company or Group or to join a Competitor or to take any steps to set up or establish a business that is or may be in competition with any Group Company;
  (2) any steps taken by employees to carry out such plans.
  (3) any use of confidential information or other property or assets of the Company by employees for the furtherance of such plans.
  (4) any other matters that may adversely affect the business of the Company or Group.

[SEE MANUAL PART P ON PUBLIC INTEREST DISCLOSURE]

14. Scope of duties	*Whole Employment* The nature of the Employee [EXECUTIVE/MANAGER, ETC.]'s employment is such that the Employee [EXECUTIVE/MANAGER, ETC.] cannot be engaged in any activity that may mean he cannot give his full attention to his duties with the Company or Group or which may place him in a position of conflict. The Employee [EXECUTIVE/MANAGER, ETC.] therefore agrees that he will not accept or take up any employment during the hours that he has agreed to work for the Company or any Group Company nor

14. Scope of duties (cont.)	will he accept, whether indirectly or directly, any form or paid or unpaid Consultative or other work [*WITHOUT THE PRIOR PERMISSION IN WRITING OF THE MANAGING DIRECTOR OF THE EMPLOYER, WHICH WILL NOT BE UNREASONABLY WITHHELD*]. The Employee [*EXECUTIVE/MANAGER, ETC.*] may however, purchase shares in [*SET OUT THE EXTENT OF THE INTERESTS THAT MAY BE PERMISSIBLE*].
	Implied Duties
	The Employee [*EXECUTIVE/MANAGER, ETC.*] further acknowledges that the nature of his employment creates implied fiduciary duties and duties of fidelity to the Group and any and all covenants herein are subject to those implied duties where they be wider.
15. Covenants during employment	*Co Employees*
	The Employee [*EXECUTIVE/MANAGER, ETC.*] will not at any time during his employment solicit or seek to recruit any current employee of the Company or Group to be engaged or work for the Employee [*EXECUTIVE/MANAGER, ETC.*] or any other person, firm, company or organisation and will not make any comment, representation or statement that may facilitate, induce, persuade procure, or howsoever cause any employee to leave the employment of the Company or Group.
	ALTERNATIVELY
	The Employee [*EXECUTIVE/MÀNAGER, ETC.*] shall not at any time during his employment with the Company, whether directly or indirectly, and for his own behalf or that of any company, firm, person or other third party seek to encourage or entice any employee of the Company or any Group Company to leave the employment of the Company.
	Other activities
	The Employee [*EXECUTIVE/MANAGER, ETC.*] will not during the period that he is employed by the Company:
	1. during the Employee [*EXECUTIVE/MANAGER, ETC.*]'s working hours take any steps to seek work with any competitor;
	2. canvass solicit or otherwise make any representation or statement to any customer or

15. Covenants during employment	supplier which may cause harm or adversely affect the Group or the Company's business or entertain any offers from customers or suppliers, and in the event of the latter shall immediately inform the Company of any offers. *Secret Profits* The Employee [*EXECUTIVE/MANAGER, ETC.*] agrees that he will not take any money or other benefit from any client of the Company or any Group Company and will immediately advise the Company if any such money or other benefit is offered to the Company.
16. Intellectual property	*[SHORT FORM CLAUSE]* The Employee [*EXECUTIVE/MANAGER, ETC.*]'s duties will involve him in formulating and dealing with [*LIST E.G. MARKETING, ETC.*]. These duties will involve the production of designs, manufacturing methods, plans, processes or techniques in which any copyright or other intellectual property rights will subsist. The Employee [*EXECUTIVE/MANAGER, ETC.*] agrees that any such rights vest absolutely in the Company or relevant Group Company and will take all steps and carry out all acts that may be necessary to ensure that the intellectual property is lawfully vested in the Company or Group Company, including signing all applications and any other documents that may be necessary to apply for any patent rights or other form of application in the United Kingdom and Worldwide, and that this obligation will continue to exist when the Employee [*EXECUTIVE/MANAGER, ETC.*]'s employment has ended. *ALTERNATIVELY* Because of the nature of the employment the Employee [*EXECUTIVE/MANAGER, ETC.*] has signed an Intellectual Property Agreement [it is a condition of your employment that you sign the Company's Intellectual Property Agreement] **[SEE MANUAL Q PRECEDENT Q4 FOR AN AGREEMENT]**

17. Confidentiality	The Employee [*EXECUTIVE/MANAGER, ETC.*] agrees that he will not at any time during his Employment and after the termination of his employment without restriction in time communicate, disclose or divulge to any third person or in any way make use of the Company's Confidential Information or Trade Secrets or that of the Group [which, without prejudice to the generality of the foregoing include [*LIST*]] relating to the Company, the Group and its customers or Suppliers PROVIDED that once the Employee [*EXECUTIVE/MANAGER, ETC.*] has left the employment with the Company this restriction shall not apply where such information has been ordered to be disclosed by a court or otherwise by law and the Employee shall not be prevented from using his own skills and experience. **[FOR MORE DETAILS PROVISIONS SEE MANUAL Q PRECEDENT Q2 AND Q5]**
18. Post termination covenants: non solicitation, non dealing and non poaching	The Employee [*EXECUTIVE/MANAGER, ETC.*] agrees that for a period of [. . . . .] months from the termination of his Employment he will not: 1. Canvass, solicit or otherwise in any way seek to procure, the business or business opportunities from any customer or client of the Company or any Group Company, where the customer or client of the Company or any Group Company has been a customer or client [. . . . .] months immediately preceding the termination of employment of the Employee and with whom the Employee has had business dealings within the previous [. . . . .] months. 2. Canvass, solicit or otherwise in any way seek to procure, orders from any supplier of the Company or any Group Company where the supplier has supplied the Company or any Group Company within the previous [. . . . .] months and the Employee has had dealings with the supplier or is aware of any agreement between supplier and the Company or any Group Company . 3. Deal with any customer or client of the Company or any Group Company, where the customer or client of the Company or any Group Company has been a customer or client [. . . . .] months immediately preceding the termination of

18. Post termination covenants: non solicitation, non dealing and non poaching (cont.)	employment of the Employee [*EXECUTIVE/MANAGER, ETC.*] and with whom the Employee [*EXECUTIVE/MANAGER, ETC.*] has had business dealings within the previous [. . . . .] months.

4. Deal with any supplier of the Company or any Group Company where the supplier has supplied the Employer or any Group Company within the previous [. . . . .] months and the Employee [*EXECUTIVE/MANAGER, ETC.*] has had dealings with the supplier or is aware of any agreement between supplier and the Company or any Group Company.

5. Seek to persuade or solicit or provide work, whether directly or indirectly, or by self employment or consultancy, to any person who was an employee of the Company or any Group Company [. . . . .] years prior to the termination of the Employee [*EXECUTIVE/MANAGER, ETC.*]'s employment, or was engaged in any capacity, and who would be in a position to harm the business of the Company or any Group Company were he to accept any employment or engagement.

6. Accept, whether through himself or a third party, indirectly or indirectly and whether of his own or a third party's benefit, any orders for any products or services with which the Employee [*EXECUTIVE/MANAGER, ETC.*] was concerned whilst he was working for the Company or any Group Company and which the Company or any Group Company would have been in a position to supply.

[SEE MANUAL PRECEDENT Q5 FOR A MORE DETAILED COVENANT]

19. Post termination: working for competitors	The Employee [*EXECUTIVE/MANAGER, ETC.*] agrees that for a period of [. . . . .] months from the termination of his Employment he will not:

1. Hold any material interest in any business which is or is likely to be in competition with the Company or any Group Company.

2. Hold any material interest in any business which may require or might reasonably be considered by the Company or any Group Company to require the disclosure of Confidential information

19. Post termination covenants: non solicitation, non dealing and non poaching (cont.)	belonging to the Company or any Group Company in order to property discharge his functions in such business.
	3. Accept employment or take any engagement, whether self employed or otherwise and whether directly or indirectly, from any competitor of the Company or any Group Company which is likely to adversely affect the business of the Company or any Group Company.
	[SEE MANUAL PRECEDENT Q5 FOR A MORE DETAILED CLAUSE]
	[SEE SALESMAN AT 5.13 FOR A TERRITORIAL COVENANT]
20. Employer's property	Upon the termination of the Employee [*EXECUTIVE/MANAGER, ETC.*]'s contract for whatever reason, the Employee [*EXECUTIVE/MANAGER, ETC.*] shall immediately return to the Company all property that belongs to the Company or any Group Company, including:
	1. Any computer, printer or other such equipment, and all computer discs and other software. If the Employee [*EXECUTIVE/MANAGER, ETC.*] has a password on any computer, the detail of the password.
	2. All documents in whatever form, including any copies or summaries of the same and including the Employee [*EXECUTIVE/MANAGER, ETC.*]'s working notes.
	3. The Company car and keys.
	For the purpose of this Agreement the Employee [*EXECUTIVE/MANAGER, ETC.*] irrevocably gives the Company the right to enter any property where the Company's property is held and remove the same.
21. Severability of covenants	The Employee [*EXECUTIVE/MANAGER, ETC.*] agrees that the each of the covenants contained in this Agreement are reasonable and are necessary for the protection of the Employer's business. However, each provision of this Agreement is independent and severable and if any of them should be found by a Court of Law to be unenforceable or ineffective for whatever reason that shall not affect the validity of the separate covenants.

21. Severability of covenants (cont.)	If any covenants would become valid if any wording was deleted then the covenant shall be deemed to be applicable with such deletions and shall apply as so amended as to make the same enforceable.
	In particular, it is expressly acknowledged that if any clause is regarded as unenforceable by virtue of reference to Group Companies the same may be deleted in such manner as to make the clause enforceable.
22. Termination of contract	*Notice* Save as set out below, the Company must give the Employee [*EXECUTIVE/MANAGER, ETC.*] [. . . . .] months' notice to terminate this Agreement and the Employee [*EXECUTIVE/MANAGER, ETC.*] must give [. . . . .] months' notice.
	Payment in lieu **[FOR PAYMENT *IN LIEU* CLAUSES SEE MANUAL AT PRECEDENT V2]**
	Earlier Termination The notice period is subject to the Company's rights to dismiss the Employee [*EXECUTIVE/MANAGER, ETC.*] without notice if:
	1. He is guilty of conduct set out in the Company's Disciplinary Procedures which warrant dismissal without notice.
	2. He commits any act of negligence, neglect of duty which is serious, or does any act which causes the Company to lose trust and confidence and which justifies dismissal without notice.
	3. He is in serious or repudiatory breach of this agreement.
	4. He commits any act outside his employment which is liable to bring the Company or Group into disrepute.
	5. He is declared bankrupt or otherwise enters into any arrangement with his creditors.
	6. He is convicted of a criminal offence and in the case of a motoring offence this results in disqualification or imprisonment.
	7. He suffers from mental disorder.

| 22. Termination of contract (cont.) | 8. He is persistently absent from work for a period of [. . . . .] days in any [. . . . .] months. |
| | 9. He is guilty of any serious or repudiatory breach of this Agreement. |

| 23. Garden leave | Where notice has been given by either side to this Agreement, or the Employee [*EXECUTIVE/MANAGER, ETC.*] purports to leave the employment in breach of the notice that he is required to give: |

The Company:
1. Shall no longer be under any duty to provide work to the Employee [*EXECUTIVE/MANAGER, ETC.*] and the Employee [*EXECUTIVE/MANAGER, ETC.*] shall have not right to carry out any work or services for the Company [but the Employee [*EXECUTIVE/MANAGER, ETC.*] may be required to make himself available during normal working hours should the Company require his services].

2 May direct that the Employee [*EXECUTIVE/ MANAGER, ETC.*] cease all contact with any customers or suppliers or Employees of the Company.

3. Shall be entitled to exclude the Employee [*EXECUTIVE/MANAGER, ETC.*] from the Company's premises.

PROVIDED THAT

4. The Employer shall continue to have the right to suspend the Employee [*EXECUTIVE/MANAGER, ETC.*] in the circumstances provided for in the Disciplinary Policy.

5. During the notice period the Employee [*EXECUTIVE/MANAGER, ETC.*] will continue to receive all his contractual benefits.

6. The Company shall retain the right to transfer the Employee [*EXECUTIVE/MANAGER, ETC.*] to any Group Company.

24. Whole agreement	This Agreement forms the Whole Agreement between the parties, save that it is subject to any further terms contained in the Letter of Appointment and the Employee [*EXECUTIVE/MANAGER, ETC.*] acknowledges that he has read the Letter, this Agreement and any Company or Group Policies that are referred to in the Letter of Appointment. *[CONSIDER WHETHER EXPRESS REFERENCE SHOULD BE MADE I.E. TO EQUAL OPPORTUNITY POLICIES, ETC.]*
SIGNATURES	*[CONSIDER WHETHER THE DOCUMENT SHOULD BE SIGNED AS A DEED]*

MANAGERIAL STAFF: COMMENTARY

In the case of managerial staff the contract is likely to contain more detail than the bare statement of terms and conditions. Any precedent will by its very nature be tailor made for the particular employment. In this book I have proved two draft precedents: one where there are a number of associated companies that may have some relevance to the individual's employment (Precedent 5.8.1) and a contract where this complication does not exist (Precedent 5.8.2). However, it may be helpful to set out a checklist of items that the drafter wishes to consider in settling a contract of employment. The checklist will follow the usual format adopted in this book, which is to deal with the basics as required by the section 1 statement and to set out those other items that are likely to be of importance to a contract of this nature. Directors are considered in the Manual, **Part V**. The very scope of the Clauses in the Managerial Precedent means that many of these are commented on in the Parts of the Manual and this checklist will therefore cross reference with the Manual.

CHECKLIST FOR DRAFTING CONTRACTS OF EMPLOYMENT/ SERVICE AGREEMENTS FOR MANAGERS/SENIOR EXECUTIVES

PREAMBLE

There is likely to be a preamble that sets out the name of the parties and the formal reason for the executive entering into the Service Agreement. This is not obligatory but helps to focus the parties' attention and gives a Service Agreement a certain amount of 'gravitas'!

IDENTITY OF THE PARTIES TO THE CONTRACT	
1. The Employer	The Company may be an individual company, a Group of Companies or a Service Company. It is important that it is correctly identified as there may be considerable repercussions for the future — as in the case of a Transfer of an Undertaking for example. The identify of the Company is also likely to have a knock on effect so far as *intra* company group transfers are concerned.
2. The Employee	Identify the Employee's name and address and date of birth — the latter may have some relevance for retirement purposes, *etc*.

THE PERIOD OF EMPLOYMENT	
3. Date employment began	Identify the date when the Manager/Executive's employment began.
4. Continuous employment	It will be important to identify: 1. Whether there are any previous periods of employment that count — for example with an associated Company. 2. If the Company is part of a Group what the impact will be of intra company transfers. 3. It is often the case that the employment of a Manager will be for a fixed term. The dates should be made clear.

PROBATIONARY PERIODS AND PRE-CONDITIONS	
5. Probationary periods	It may be that there will be a probationary period — though this is less likely with senior managers. **SEE MANUAL PART H FOR COMMENTARY**

6. Continuous employment	Consider: • what qualifications are necessary as a pre-requisite for the job; • whether professional qualifications should be referred to; • whether the employment of the employee is dependent upon a medical examination; • whether a driving licence is necessary for the job; • whether the employee needs to make any warranties as to convictions (if he falls within one of the exceptions) or that he has not been subject to any regulatory action. **SEE MANUAL PART H FOR COMMENTARY**

NATURE OF THE EMPLOYMENT

7. Job title	The Manager's Job Title/Description
8. Job description	Set out where the job description is contained if it is not contained in the contract.
9. Flexibility	A flexibility clause is necessary both as to job title and job descriptions so that the Company may change both as is necessary. Any change will normally be commensurate with the employee's status. **SEE MANUAL PARTS B AND C FOR COMMENTARY**
10. Other companies	If the Company is part of a Group then a power to transfer to other companies in the Group will be needed.

REMUNERATION AND OTHER BENEFITS

11. Remuneration	The contract will provide for the rate of remuneration and will also contain provisions relating to rises. It should also state how and when the remuneration will be paid. **SEE MANUAL PART E**
12. Bonus	If a bonus is to be paid the contract should state how it will be calculated and whether it is to be discretionary. **SEE MANUAL PART F2**

13. Commission	Commission may be paid depending upon the turnover of the Company. **SEE MANUAL PART F3**
14. Share options	It is important that the provisions of any share option scheme are incorporated and the circumstances in which the share options can be/cease to be exercised is set out. **SEE MANUAL PART F7**
15. Expenses	There should be clear provision as to what expenses are claimable and the procedure for claiming expenses should be incorporated. A senior manager may be in breach of his duty of fidelity if he wrongfully claims expenses. It should be stated that wrongfully claiming expenses may be a disciplinary offence.
16. Company car	The provision of a Company car is likely to form an important part of the employee's package and provision should be made for the type of car that will be provided. Petrol and other maintenance expenses may be expressly dealt with. **SEE MANUAL PART F9**
17. Pensions	Where there is a pension scheme then it should be made clear that the terms of the scheme are incorporated. **SEE MANUAL PART F5**
HOURS OF WORK	
18. Hours of work	The contract will set out the hours of work that the employee will be expected to work as 'core' hours. However, in the case of a senior employee it is likely that the Employee will have to work such hours as are necessary to get the job done. **SEE MANUAL PART D**
19. Overtime	It may be that provision will be made for overtime in certain circumstances. **SEE MANUAL PART D2**

HOLIDAYS AND ABSENCES FROM WORK OTHER THAN SICKNESS

20. Holiday entitlement	The contract will set out the number of days holiday to which the employee is entitled and when they may be taken. Note, however, the Working Time Regulations. A statement about holiday payment should be included. **SEE MANUAL PART I**
21. Carrying over holidays	There should be a provision as to whether or not holiday may be carried over and, if so, in what circumstances. **SEE MANUAL PART I**
22. Public duties	It may be prudent to state that the employee is entitled to time off in relation to certain public duties. **SEE MANUAL PART L**
23. Maternity and paternity policies	If there are such policies then they should be referred to as being incorporated. A statement about equal opportunities is prudent. **SEE MANUAL PART K**

SICKNESS

24. Sickness absence	Where the employee is absent because he is incapacitated there will need to be provision for notifying such absences. A statement that un-authorised absence may be a disciplinary matter/lead to non payment of salary may be included. **SEE MANUAL PART J**
25. Medical insurance	Medical insurance is likely to be an important part of the employee's benefit package. The nature of the insurance and whether it is to apply to the employee's family should be stated. **SEE MANUAL PART F6**
26. Sick pay schemes	If there is a contractual sick pay scheme this should be referred to. **SEE MANUAL PART J**
27. Medical examinations	The employee will want to make provision to have the employee examined by an independent medical practitioner or the Company Doctor. **SEE MANUAL PART J**

28. Periods of absence	Given the senior nature of the employment, the employer may wish to have the right to dismiss after a certain prolonged period of absence.
29. Permanent health insurance	Senior employees may have provision for permanent health insurance in the event of permanent disability. Note that the Company should not act in such manner as to defeat the right to claim insurance. **SEE MANUAL PART J12**
30. Third parties	Where there is a claim against a third party that has given rise to absence the Company may wish to include a provision that he obtains the benefit of any damages. **SEE MANUAL PART J11**

PLACE OF WORK

31. Place of work	The contract should specify the place of work.
32. Mobility clause	Some form of mobility clause will be required if the employee is expected to move from time to time — though note that in the case of a senior employee some term is likely to be implied that the employee will move within reasonable travelling distance. An express clause will be necessary if the employer wishes to be able to instruct a more wide ranging move. **SEE MANUAL PART G**
33. Overseas employment	Where the senior employee is liable to be required to work abroad then provision will need to be made that the employer can give this instruction. Provision will need to be made, as to: • any additional remuneration; • the currency in which the employee will be paid; • relocation expenses; • the period the employee may be abroad; • whether the employee will be provided with accommodation; • other benefits that the employee and his family may receive. **See 5.10.**
34. Residential accommodation	The nature of the employee's employment may require him to occupy residential accommodation and provision must be made for the accommodation to be vacated when the employment ceases or it is no longer required to carry out the job. **See 5.12.**

VARIATION OR FLEXIBILITY CLAUSES

35. Variation clauses	It may be that variation has already been catered for in the clause relating to job functions or place of work. However, a general variation clause may assist and if there is a general handbook or manual a statement that this may be varied from time to time may be included. **SEE MANUAL PARTS B AND C**

DISCIPLINARY AND GRIEVANCE PROCEDURES AND STANDARD OF WORK

36. Disciplinary procedures	The Company's disciplinary procedure may be incorporated but this is likely to require amendment to deal with the status of the employee — *i.e.* the disciplinary panel may be at a higher level than for general employees so that the Board becomes involved at a much earlier stage. **SEE MANUAL PART R**
37. Grievance procedures	Again, where the employee has a grievance consideration may be needed at to which level the employee first makes any complaint. **SEE MANUAL PART S**
38. Standard of work	The nature of the employee's work may mean that 'one off' breaches, mistakes or acts of gross negligence make it impossible for the employee to continue in employment or destroy the trust and confidence that should exist. If this is the position it is prudent to make it clear. **SEE MANUAL PART M**

RESTRICTIONS DURING EMPLOYMENT — SEE GENERALLY MANUAL PART Q

39. Whole Employment clauses	In the case of senior employees, the Company may not be prepared to allow them to work for anyone else or have any outside interests. This should be made clear. Where limited outside interests are permitted the parameters of what is acceptable should be made clear, and when and how consent will be given to carry out these activities should be made clear. The contract should also make it clear that the employee is to use his best endeavours to forward the interests of the Company.

40. Implied duties	The employee is likely to have implied duties of fidelity or fiduciary duties, given his status. It is prudent to make it clear that any express terms are without prejudice to such implied duties.
41. Preparation during employment	Express provision may be made as to what is unacceptable during the currency of the employee's contract where the employee is actively engaged in setting up in competition.
42. Poaching	A clause against poaching employees should be included.
43. Secret profits	Whilst there will almost certainly be an implied term against making a secret profit, an express term may assist as it can set out what the employee must divulge to the Company.
44. Whistleblowing	There should be an express clause requiring the employee to notify the Company of any wrongdoing on the part of other employees.

INTELLECTUAL PROPERTY: SEE MANUAL PART Q

45. Patents and inventions	It should be considered whether the employee is likely to be involved with patents and inventions and an appropriate clause included.

CONFIDENTIALITY AND RESTRICTIVE COVENANTS: SEE MANUAL PART Q FOR FURTHER EXAMPLES OF TERMS AND CONDITIONS

46. Confidentiality	Where the employee deals with confidential matters a covenant to protect the confidential information before and after employment is necessary.
47. Non dealing/non solicitation of customers	A suitably drafted non solicitation or non dealing clause is essential.
48. Anti-poaching of employees	Since the employee is likely to be in a position of influence an anti poaching covenant in relation to employees, once the employee has left is appropriate. **SEE MANUAL PART Q**
49. Severability	A clause which permits the court to severe any parts of covenants that it considers to be unenforceable should be included. **SEE MANUAL PART Q**

50. Delivery up of material	An express clause that any documentation or other material must be delivered up at the termination the contract, identifying if possible the exact items that should be delivered up (*i.e.* computers, discs, particular documents, *etc.*) will make it easier to apply to the court if the matters are not delivered up.

TERMINATION OF THE CONTRACT — SEE MANUAL PART V

51. Notice period	The contract may be for a fixed term, but with provision that notice may be given during the fixed term. It is common for senior employees to have fixed notice periods (and in this respect see the section on Directors).
	However, where the contract is not for a fixed term it is important that a notice period be specified. (See Duggan on *Wrongful Dismissal* for a detailed consideration of the law in this area.)
52. Payment *in lieu*	A provision for payment *in lieu* of notice may be desired by the Company if it wishes to have the option of paying the employee and not requiring the notice period to be worked out. This has an interrelationship with Garden Leave and with the issue of mitigation.
	SEE MANUAL PART V for a full consideration of these issues.
53. Summary termination	There may be express areas where the Company wishes to provide for summary termination without payment in lieu in the event of certain contingencies.
54. Accrued benefits	A clause setting out what is to happen in respect of accrued benefits (*i.e.* holiday pay).

PROPER LAW AND ARBITRATION

55. Proper law	This book is based on the English jurisdiction. In the case of more senior employees some form of arbitration or mediation clause may be considered.

9. OFFICE STAFF AND THE FINANCIAL SECTOR

PRECEDENTS

In addition to the precedents contained in the Section 1 statement and in the Manual, in the financial sector, there are likely to be compliance issues and the following precedents are of relevance in dealing with those issues.

Introduction (This clause may appear in a manual introduction, letter of appointment or in the contract under duties.)	The nature of the Company's business means that it is dependant upon its reputation and its financial confidentiality and honesty to conduct its business. You are therefore under a duty to ensure that you are acquainted with and comply with all relevant legislation and the rules and regulations of the [. . . . .] Regulatory Body which covers your work. In order to assist you the Company has produced a compliance manual. This covers the rules and regulations that must be followed in carrying out your work for the Company. Failure to observe these requirements is a disciplinary offence. The Manual will be updated from time to time and you must make sure that you are acquanited with any updates. If you have any queries about any compliance matters you should immediately contact . . . .
Staff compliance	Because of the nature of your employment you must observe the highest standards of financial probity. In order that you are not placed in any position of conflict you must observe the Company's rules on dealings in stocks, shares and investments, which are there to comply with 'best practice' as well as the legislation. It is a condition of your employment that you have signed an undertaking to comply with the Company Securities (Insider Dealing) Act 1985 ('the Act') and the Company rules set out in that document. Failure to observe these rules is likely to result in dismissal. If you have any queries or concerns about any of these or your rights in relation to any transaction matters you should contact the Compliance officer or . . . .

Interests in other companies, *etc.* for compliance purposes

In order to prevent any conflict of interest arising, the Company has strict rules that must be followed:

1. You must inform........... of any outside financial interests including directorships and partnerships. You are not permitted to hold any directorships or partnerships without written permission from the Company, which will decide whether approval is appropriate after consultation with the Compliance Department. You should inform .... if you propose to enter into any directorship or partnership.

2. You must ensure that you conduct Company business in such manner that no conflict of interest arises and you must ensure that business is conducted in such manner that there is no risk of financial impropriety. In particular:

    (1) There may be a conflict of interest if a transaction or decision may result in financial gain for you or your relatives. If there is any such risk you must immediately inform .... so that a decision can be made as to the steps to be taken.

    (2) Any transactions of dealings with outside businesses must not give rise to suspicion or result in unusual financial gains or profits for those businesses.

    (3) Any forms of bonuses, bribes or other benefits that may result in gain to yourself or third parties are absolutely prohibited and you must immediately inform . . . . or the Compliance officer if you become aware of any such risks.

OFFICE STAFF AND FINANCIAL SECTOR COMMENTARY

In the case of office staff and those working in the financial sector, information technology is likely to be of some importance and a policy with regard to computers, e-mail and other technology is likely to be necessary. There will be some emphasis on flexibility in terms of job requirements and, whilst there may be set hours of work, there should be a clause requiring the individual to work the hours that are needed to get the job done. In addition to the usual matters the following, in particular, need to be considered:

Job title, description and duties

See Model Terms and Conditions/Manual: **Parts B and C and the commentaries thereto**. It is necessary for there to be a clause that is sufficiently flexible so that an employee may be transferred to other duties if so required.

Hours of work and overtime

See Model Terms and Conditions/Manual: **Parts D1 and D2 and the commentaries thereto**. The hours of work may be specified but it is more sensible to include a provision that the employee must carry out his duties and will be expected work hours to ensure that this is achieved. Additionally a power to require the employee to work extra hours may be specified and consideration should be given to whether overtime is payable or not normally payable save in exceptional circumstances (see **Part D2**).

Other benefits

See the Model Terms and Conditions/Manual: **Part F1-10 and the commentaries thereto** Consider the list of benefits at Part F, some of which may be especially relevant such as bonus or commission.

Conduct and standard at work

See the Model Terms and Conditions/Manual: **Part M and the commentaries thereto**. The nature of the job may mean that high standards of financial probity are necessary and the employee may be required to conform to the standards of a regulatory body. This may entail rules with regard to accepting entertainment or gifts from clients or offering such entertainment.

Other matters

The office environment may require a strict smoking policy (**Part M3**) as there is a risk of employers being found liable for constructive dismissal if they do not heed the objections of an employee who complains about a smoking environment. A policy relating to taking calls from work and using office equipment is also sensible (**Part M4**).

The use of information technology means that a policy on e-mail and computer use is important (**Parts M5 and M6**) especially as there is potential for abuse and there have been a number of tribunal cases that have considered these issues (**see the commentary to Part M5**).

6. Confidential information

See the Model Terms and Conditions/Manual: **Parts Q2 and 3 and the commentaries thereto**. Access to confidential information means that a policy or undertaking as to its use should be incorporated. These restrictions are also likely to be post employment where the information remains confidential (**Part Q5**).

10. OVERSEAS EMPLOYMENT

PRECEDENT 5.10

These particulars are given to you in accordance with the requirements of section 1 of the Employment Rights Act 1996 which sets out certain minimal entitlements to particulars.

Your Job Title is . . . . and your immediate supervisor is . . . . You should have been issued with a job description at the time of your employment.

1. Name and address of Employer	Your employer is . . . . of	
Name of Employee	To	
2. Date when employment began	Your employment began on . . . . [*date*].	
3. Date when continuous employment began	Your period of continuous employment began on . . . . No employment with a previous employer counts as continuous employment. [*ALTERNATIVELY: YOUR EMPLOYMENT WITH . . . . . . FROM . . . . COUNTS AS PART OF YOUR CONTINUOUS EMPLOYMENT.*]	
4. Scale or rate of remuneration	Your scale or rate of remuneration will be paid at the rate of £ . . . . a month to be paid in local currency into any bank account designated by you. The amount of each payment will be calculated by the exchange rate on the first day of the month before payment.	
5. Intervals at which remuneration is paid	You will be paid [*WEEKLY*] [*MONTHLY*] in arrears and your salary shall accrue from day to day.	
6. Terms and conditions relating to hours of work	Your normal hours of work will be in accordance with the custom in the locality: [*SET OUT*].	

7. Holiday	1. You are entitled to such statutory holidays as are customarily recognised in the country in which you will be working, being: . . . .
	2. In addition you are entitled to . . . . days' holiday a year to be taken at times agreed with [local office/head office].
	3. The holiday year runs from . . . . . to . . . .
	4. You may not carry over holiday without permission which should be obtained from . . . .
	5. You will be paid during the period that you take your holidays.
	6. If your employment terminates and you have outstanding entitlement you will be paid your basic salary representing the number of days outstanding.
8. Absence due to sickness, *etc.*	If you are going to be absent from work for any reason, [*SET OUT PRACTICE IN THE COUNTRY OF WORK WHERE THE EMPLOYEE WORKS OR THE RULES OF THE EMPLOYER IF THERE IS NO PRACTICE.*]
9. Pensions	There is no pension scheme applicable to your employment.
	[*YOU ARE ENTITLED TO JOIN THE CONTRIBUTORY PENSION SCHEME AND MAY OBTAIN DETAILS FROM . . . .*]
10. Notice	You are entitled to the following notice:
	1. Any time during the first six months' probationary period: 1 week.
	2. If your employment is confirmed: • one week's notice up to two years' service. • one week's notice for each completed year of service up to a maximum of 12 weeks.
	Your employment may be terminated summarily in the event of breach by you that warrants summary termination.
	English law is applicable to this contract and you have the statutory rights given by the Employment Rights Act 1996.
11. Job title	As set out above

12. Temporary or fixed term contracts	NOT APPLICABLE
13. Place of work	You will be required to work in . . . . for a period of . . . . months [UNTIL DATE]. Your employment shall cease at the conclusion of the aforesaid period but the Company will use its best endeavours to try to find a position for you in its business on terms that would have been applicable if you had been employed in the United Kingdom or place where the employment is available.
14. Collective agreements	There are no collective agreements affecting your employment.
15. Overseas employment	In addition to being paid as set out above you will be entitled to the following benefits: 1. You will be reimbursed for the cost of your removal expenses to and from the country in which you will work. This may be paid beforehand if a sum is agreed with . . . . 2. You and your family will be paid the cost of transport in advance and where possible tickets will be provided by your Company up to . . . . days in advance. 3. You and your family will be provided with a suitable residence that will [will not] be furnished, in which you may reside during the proper performance of your duties. The residence will be vacated when your employment ceases. [4. *UP TO £ . . . . . OF YOUR CHILDREN'S SCHOOL FEES IN THE UNITED KINGDOM WILL BE PAID.*] [5. *SET OUT ANY OTHER BENEFITS.*]
16. Disciplinary procedures	The disciplinary procedures are attached. They are not part of your contract of employment and the employer may alter them from time to time. You should especially note that you are expected to comply with the laws, morals and customs of the country where you will be working. English law is however, applicable to this Agreement.

17. If you are not satisfied with any disciplinary decision	If you are not satisfied with any disciplinary decision relating to your employment you may appeal in accordance with the terms of the disciplinary procedure.
18. Grievances	You may raise any grievance that you may have in accordance with the terms of the disciplinary procedure.
19. Further steps	Any further steps that you may take consequent upon any disciplinary procedure or grievance are set out in the procedures.
20. Contracting out	A contracting out certificate pursuant to the Pension Scheme Act is [NOT] in force.

I accept the above particulars of terms and conditions.

Or

I accept the terms and conditions as forming part of my contract of employment, subject to my Letter of Appointment and [THE STAFF MANUAL].

. . . .
SIGNED

OVERSEAS EMPLOYMENT COMMENTARY

In the case of overseas employment, section 1(4)(k) makes specific provision for particulars that should be included in the section 1 statement, which are:
- the period that the employee is to work outside the United Kingdom;
- the currency in which the employee is to be remunerated;
- any additional remuneration and benefits provided by reason of working outsider the United Kingdom;
- any terms and conditions relating to return to the United Kingdom.

Where the employee is working in the United Kingdom and the Employee wishes him to work overseas an express mobility clause will be necessary in the absence of the consent of the employee. Employment abroad may have tax implications and these will need to be considered. Prior to section 32 of the Employment Rights Act 1999 unfair dismissal and certain other rights were excluded where the employee was employed outside Great Britain.

Section 32 repealed section 196 of the ERA 1996 so that this distinction is no longer applicable.

The precedent assumes that English Law will be applicable. The following matters should be noted in relation to employment abroad:

- The scale or rate of remuneration will be expressed to be governed by the £ or by the local currency. This is likely to be of significance where there are currency fluctuations and an employee considering undertaking employment overseas will wish to bear in mind the impact of this upon his salary. Clause 4 of the Precedent provides that the remuneration is to be paid at a sterling value but in the local currency.

- Clause 7 refers to statutory holidays as being those recognised in the country in which the employee is working. However, if the contract is subject to UK law the Working Time Regulations will still give the employee the right to the statutory minimum in respect of the number of days per year to which he is entitled.

- Query whether or not the provisions relating to sickness will cover the practice in the country or be according the UK law (see Clause 8).

- Where the work that the employee is carrying out abroad ceases the employee may be entitled to a redundancy payment unless there is a provision that he may be transferred to the UK or other places of employment. Clause 13 of the Precedent recognises the position in this respect and provides that the employer will seek to find alternative employment for the employee. However, if the position is that the employee will transfer back to the UK this should be made clear so that there is no question of a redundancy situation arising.

- Clause 15 contains specific provision in relation to remuneration, provision of transport and accommodation and additional benefits that are appropriate due to the nature of the employment.

- It is important that any disciplinary procedures cover the particular customs or laws of the country in which the employee will be working as any breach will have an impact upon the ability of the employee to continue to work.

11. PART TIME WORKING

PRECEDENTS

The standard precedents can be adapted to part time workers. The thrust of the recent regulations is that part time workers must not be less favourably treated (see below). For example, in relation to salary, a statement that the worker will be paid *pro rata* may be appropriate since, the general principle will be that, other than as set out below, there should not be disparate treatment of part time workers.

PART TIME WORKING COMMENTARY

Working practices in the UK have been changing for some considerable period of time. The Government recognises this and has stated that it is "committed to improving the functioning of the UK labour market by increasing its flexibility whilst providing a framework of decent minimum standard for employees" [Government Consultation Document on Part Time Work]. To this end the Government introduced the Part Time Workers (Prevention of Less Favourable Treatment) Regulations 2000 (No 1551), which provide a number of rights for part time workers and consequent duties upon employers. A Compliance Guide and Best Practice guidance has also been introduced, which give some guidance on how employers should manage part time work. In the introduction to the Regulations the DTI have stated that the Regulations mean that part timers will be entitled to:

- the same hourly rate of pay;
- the same access to company pension schemes;
- the same entitlements to annual leave and maternity/parental leave on a pro rata basis;
- the same entitlement to contractual sick pay; and
- no less favourable treatment in access to training.

The effect of the Regulations upon drafting contracts means that, effectively, contracts for part time workers should be drafted without regard to hours of work so that there can be no discriminatory conduct on the part of the employer. Any contract of employment should be drafted in such manner that the part time worker receives the same benefits as a full time worker, but on a *pro rata* basis.

As with much of the recent employment legislation the Regulations apply to workers as opposed to employees (see 5.16). A worker is defined as:

> "...an individual who has entered into or works under or (except where a provision of these Regulations otherwise requires) where the employment has ceased, worked under-
> (a) a contract of employment; or
> (b) any other contract, whether express or implied and (if it is express) whether oral or in writing, whereby the individual undertakes to do or perform personally any work or services for another party to the contract whose status is not by virtue of the contract that of a client or customer of any profession or business undertaking carried on by the individual".

The Regulations introduce a *pro rata* principle meaning that where a comparable full time worker receives or is entitled to receive pay or any other benefit, a part time worker is to receive or be entitled to receive not less than the proportion of that pay or other benefit that the number of his weekly hours bears to the number of hours of the comparable full time employee.

A full time worker is someone who is paid wholly or partly by reference to the time he works and, having regard to the custom and practice of the employer in relation to workers employed under the same type of contract, is identifiable as a full time worker (Reg 2(1)).

A part time worker is someone who is paid wholly or partly by reference to the time he works and having regard to the custom and practice of the employer in relation to workers employed under the same type of contract, is not identifiable as a full time worker.

The Regulations set out a comparison between a full time worker and a part time worker in Regulation 2(4) where:
- both workers are employed under the same type of contract by the same employer; and are
- engaged in the same or broadly similar work having regard, where relevant, to whether they have a similar level of qualification, skills and experience; and
- the full time worker works or is based at the same establishment as the part time worker.

Full time workers may come to be treated as part time workers under Regulation 3(1) where there is a termination or variation that requires him to work less hours, or under Regulation 4 where a worker returns to work within twelve months on a different or varied contract that requires him to work less hours.

The heart of the Regulations is contained in Regulation 5, which provides that a part time worker has a right not to be treated less favourably than the employer treats a comparable full time worker as regards the terms of his contract or by being subjected to any other detriment by any act, or deliberate failure to act, of his employer. This right applies where the treatment is on the ground that the employee is a part time employee and it cannot be justified on objective grounds. The pro rata principle is to be applied unless it is inappropriate. There is, however, provision that excludes disparate treatment for overtime until the part time worker has worked the equivalent full time hours as the full time worker (Regulation 5(4).

The part time worker's remedy is to claim unfair dismissal (Regulation 7(1)) or to claim that he has been subjected to a detriment (Regulation 7(2)).

12. RESIDENTIAL STAFF

PRECEDENT 5.12
CLAUSES APPLICABLE TO RESIDENTIAL STAFF

Clause to be added in respect of accommodation at the beginning of the contract

In order to properly carry out your duties and for the better performance thereof the Company will provide you with residential premises so long as you remain in employment. You occupy these premises as a licensee and your right to occupy the premises will cease forthwith upon your employment ending for whatever reason. You must immediately vacate the premises upon such termination.

During your employment you will be permitted to quietly reside at the premises and you must keep the interior of the premises in good decorative repair. You must immediately inform the Company of any event or matter that may effect the condition of the premises.

You are not permitted to assign, sublet, share or part with possession of some or all of the premises or to have anyone live with you at the premises without the prior written consent of the Company.

If you breach the above conditions you are liable to disciplinary action which could result in your dismissal and you being required to vacate the premises forthwith. The Company agrees to pay all outgoings relating to the premises.

The Company shall have the right to enter the premises without notice at any time as it considers fit.

RESIDENTIAL STAFF COMMENTARY

If the work carried out by the employee requires him to occupy premises for the better performance of his duties it is important that the contract stipulates that occupation is commensurate with employment and is to last only so long as the individual is employed. The law of Landlord and Tenant is outside the scope of this book but the cases clearly differentiate between contracts that make it apparent the residential accommodation is related to employment and those where such a term has been omitted. Where there is no term which makes it clear that the employee is only to live in the accommodation so long as he remains employed the court will only imply a term if it is necessary. In **Hughes v Greenwich Borough Council** [1993] 3 WLR 821 the House of Lords refused to imply a term that a headmaster was occupying a house for the better performance of his duties and was not therefore secure under paragraph 2(1) of Schedule 1 to the Housing Act 1985. An order for possession was refused.

It was held in **Surrey County Council v Lamond** (Court of Appeal 16.12.1998) that where an employee was employed as a residential caretaker a term could be implied into the contract that he occupied the premises for the better performance of his duties. A property had been purchased near a school for the employee's occupation. The Court of Appeal held that the employee did not have security of tenure as he occupied the premises for "the better performance of his duties" and the premises were not secure under paragraph 2(1) of Schedule 1 to the Housing Act 1985. It was necessary to consider what duties the employee was to perform and ask whether the duties could be performed if the employee did not live at the premises. The case was distinguishable from *Hughes* since it was essential that the employee should live at the premises in order to perform his duties.

In the case of private employees, it was held in **Norris v Checksfield** [1991] ICR 632 that an employee occupied premises as a licensee, even though the occupation of the premises was not necessary for the performance of the duties and could therefore be evicted.

Under the National Minimum Wages Regulations 1999 accommodation may be taken into account in calculating salary, subject to the statutory maximum from time to time in force.

This precedent does not cover agricultural workers, which are outside the scope of the book.

13. SALESMAN

PRECEDENT 5.13

SERVICE AGREEMENT BETWEEN . . . . ('THE COMPANY') AND . . . . ('THE EMPLOYEE') WHEREBY THE EMPLOYEE IS APPOINTED AS A SALES EXECUTIVE	
1. Employer and Employee	The Employer is . . . . .of . . . . Company Registration No . . . . The Employee [*SALES EXECUTIVE*] is . . . . . . of . . . . .
2. Date employment began, continuous employment and hours of work	The Sales Executive's employment began on . . . . and the date of continuous employment began on . . . . The Sales Executive's employment is subject to the probationary period and other conditions set out in the Letter of Appointment/Offer Letter. There are no fixed hours of work. The Sales Executive will be expected to work such hours to achieve the turnover in Sales that has been agreed between the Company and the Sales Executive but is expected to work not less than [. . . . .] hours per week.
3. Job title and duties	Sales Executive *Definitions* • The Product: [*SET OUT*] • The Territory: This must be set out with clarity as it will affect any covenants. • Monthly Turnover: Sales by the Sales Executive of not less than £ . . . . per month of the Product. • Sales: A concluded agreement for the purchase of the Product. The Company is engaged in the manufacture and sale of [. . . . . . .] ('the Product') and to this end employs a number of Sales Executives to market the Product on a wholesale and retail basis.

3. Job title and duties	The Sales Executive has been engaged to actively promote the Sale of the Product within the Territory assigned to him.
	During the period of his Employment:
	1. The Sales Executive will well and faithfully serve the Company and will do all in his powers to promote the sales of the Product and to achieve the Monthly Turnover required by the Employer.
	2. The Sales Executive will not accept or take up any employment nor will he accept, whether indirectly or directly, any form of paid or unpaid Consultative or other work [without the prior permission in writing of the Managing Director of the Company, which will not be unreasonably withheld] [which may inhibit his ability to promote and sell the Product].
4. Remuneration and other benefits	*Salary* There is a base salary of £ . . . . which will be offset on a monthly basis against Commission [*OR OTHER SUCH ARRANGEMENTS*].
	Commission This is a Commission based appointment. Commission is paid on a monthly basis against Sales as follows:
	1. On the first £ . . . . sales at . . . . % of sales per month.
	2. Thereafter on sales at . . . . % per month.
	The Sales will be calculated at the end of each calendar month and payment made within 14 days thereafter subject to offset of monthly base salary.
	The Sales Executive recognises that base salary and Commission are paid before payment is received from the customer. The Company reserves the right to withhold Commission where:
	1. It reasonably believes that a customer may not pay sums due.
	2. Monthly payments received against commission generated fall to below £ . . . . per month.

5. Company car	1. The Sales Executive will be provided with a Company car, which shall be [SET OUT]. The Employer will tax, insure, pay for maintenance and repairs, [provided they were not caused by the Sales Executive's negligence].
	2. The car may be replaced when the Company considers it appropriate.
	3. The car may be used for private purposes as well as Company business. The Employer will pay for petrol used for business purposes which may be claimed as part of expenses.
	4. The Sales Executive warrants that he has a clean driving licence and he will bring to the attention of the Employer any matter that may affect his continued ability to drive the car.
	5. The Sales Executive agrees that he will not do anything that may invalidate the insurance policy.
	6. Upon termination of this Agreement, for whatever reason, the Sales Executive agrees that he will immediately deliver up the car or make it available for collection [and acknowledges that he will no longer be insured to drive the car from the date of termination].
	ALTERNATIVELY: [The Company operates a car policy which the Sales Executive agrees he has read and signed. **See MANUAL PRECEDENT F10**]
6. Pensions	There are no pension provisions relating to this position.
7. Expenses	The Company will reimburse the Sales Executive's expenses incurred in the course of his employment which were incurred in the furtherance of his duties up to the sum of £ . . . . per month. The Sales Executive should acquaint himself with the procedure for reclaiming expenses. Failure to follow the correct procedure will result in expenses claims being refused.
8. Holidays and other absences	*Holiday* 1. The Sales Executive is entitled to [. . . .] days' holiday per year on base salary and an average of commission, in addition to the normal statutory holidays.

8. Holidays and other absences (cont.)	2. The Sales Executive must agree holiday in advance with [. . . .] by giving at least twice the number of working days' notice of the number of days he intends to take on holiday and this will be subject to the agreement of the Company. The Company may stipulate the days that the Sales Executive must take as paid holiday.
	3. Holidays not taken in the calendar year which runs from [. . . .] to [. . . .] cannot be carried out [save with the written agreement of . . . .].
	4. For the purposes of termination of employment, holidays accrue on a daily basis and the Sales Executive will be entitled to any accrued holiday pay on the termination of his employment.
	Other absences The Company operates a maternity and paternity policy to which reference should be made. **[SEE MANUAL PRECEDENT K1]**
9. Sickness absences and benefits	*Sickness* 1. Where the Sales Executive is absent due to sickness he must, as soon as is possible, inform or cause to be informed [STIPULATE WHO — *E.G.* THE MANAGING DIRECTOR] of the Company.
	2. Self certificates must be provided for periods of up to 7 days and medical certificates must be provided for any longer periods.
	3. The Company will continue to pay base salary and accrued commission whilst the Sales Executive is absent due to sickness for a period of [. . . .] days. However, the Company has the right not to pay salary where: (1) The Sales Executive is absent for more than [. . . .] days in any one period or [. . . .] days during the calendar year. (2) The Sales Executive does not provide certificates as required. (3) The Sales Executive fails to respond to any reasonable request from the Company about his condition and prognosis. (4) The Sales Executive has repeated spells of short absence that cumulatively amount to [. . . .] days in any six month period.

9. Sickness absences and benefits (cont.)	4. The Sales Executive will give credit for any statutory or other benefits he receives arising out of his absence due to sickness and which do not arise out of any private insurance taken out by the Sales Executive.
	5. The Sales Executive's employment may be terminated for sickness in the circumstances set out herein.
	Medical examination The Company may require the Sales Executive to undergo a medical examination and refusal to do so may result in non payment of salary or in dismissal. **[SEE MANUAL AT J FOR FURTHER EXAMPLES OF THE ABOVE PRECEDENTS]** for loss of earnings. **[SEE ALSO MANUAL PRECEDENT F11]**
10. Place of work	The Sales Executive will work within the Territory as specifically set out in this Agreement [*OR* as delineated on the map attached]. He will not work outside this Territory. However, the Sales Executive agrees that the Company may in its absolute discretion change the Sales Executive's Territory.
11. Disciplinary and other procedures	The Sales Executive's attention is drawn to the Company's Disciplinary and Grievance Procedures which are applicable. They do not form part of this contract. **[SEE MANUAL PARTS R AND S FOR FURTHER DETAIL]**
12. Standard of work	The Sales Executive warrants that he has the requisite abilities to perform the full functions of his job and will draw to the attention of the Company any matter that may affect his ability to carry out his job. In particular loss of a driving licence for whatever reason will result in termination of the Sales Executive's employment.
13. Standard of work	*Co Employees* The Sales Executive will not at any time during his employment solicit or seek to recruit any current employees of the Employer to be engaged to work for the Sales Executive or any other person, firm,

13. Covenants during employment (cont.)	company or organisation and will not make any comment, representation or statement that may facilitate, induce, persuade procure, or howsoever cause any employee to leave the employment of the Company.

ALTERNATIVELY

The Sales Executive shall not at any time during his employment with the Company, whether directly or indirectly, and for his own behalf of any company, firm, person or other third party seek to encourage or entice any employee of the Company to leave the employment of the Company.

Other activities

The Sales Executive will not during the period that he is employed by the Company:

1. Take steps to seek work with any competitor which is likely to put him in a position of conflict;

2. Canvass solicit or otherwise make any representation or statement to any customer or supplier which may cause harm or adversely affect the Employer's business or entertain any offers from customers or suppliers. In the event of the latter, the Sales Executive shall immediately inform the Company of any offers.

Secret Profits

The Sales Executive agrees that he will not take any money or other benefit from any customer or supplier of the Company and will immediately advise the Company if any such money or other benefit is offered.

[SEE ALSO MANUAL PRECEDENT Q5]

14. Confidentiality	The Sales Executive agrees that he will not at any time during his Employment and after the termination of his employment without restriction in time communicate, disclose or divulge to any third person or in any way make use of the Company's Confidential Information or Trade Secrets [which, without prejudice to the generality of the foregoing include [LIST]] relating to the Company, its customers or Suppliers **provided** that once the Sales Executive has left the employment with the Employer this

14. Confidentiality (cont.)	restriction shall not apply where such information has been ordered to be disclosed by a Court or otherwise by law and the Employee shall not be prevented from using his own skills and experience. **[FOR MORE DETAILS PROVISIONS SEE MANUAL Q PRECEDENTS Q2 AND Q5]**
15. Post termination covenants: non solicitation, non dealing and non poaching	The Sales Executive agrees that for a period of [. . . .] months from the termination of his Employment he will not WITHIN THE TERRITORY: 1. Canvass, solicit or otherwise in any way seek to procure, the business or business opportunities from any customer or client of the Company, where the customer or client of the Company has been a customer or client [. . . .] months immediately preceding the termination of employment of the Employee and with whom the Sales Executive has had business dealings, or has canvassed, approached or sought to do business with, during the previous [. . . .] months. 2. Canvass, solicit or otherwise in any way seek to procure, orders from any supplier of the Company where the supplier has supplied the Company within the previous [. . . .] months and the Sales Executive has had dealings with the supplier or is aware of any agreement between supplier and the Company. 3. Deal with any customer or client of the Company, where the customer or client of the Company has been a customer or client within [. . . .] months immediately preceding the termination of employment of the Sales Executive and with whom the Sales Executive has had business dealings or has canvassed, approached or sought to do business with, during the previous [. . . .] months preceding termination. 4. Deal with any supplier of the Company where the supplier has supplied the Company within the previous [. . .] months and the Sales Executive has had dealings with the supplier or is aware of any agreement between supplier and the Company. 5. Seek to persuade or solicit or provide work, whether directly or indirectly, or by self employment of consultancy, to any person who

15. Post termination covenants: non solicitation, non dealing and non poaching (cont.)	was an employee of the Company [....] years prior to the termination of the Sales Executive's employment, or was engaged in any capacity, and who would be in a position to harm the business of the Company were he to accept any employment or engagement.
	6. Accept, whether through himself or a third party, indirectly or indirectly and whether of his own or a third party's benefit, any orders for any products or services with which the Sales Executive was concerned whilst he was working for the Company and which the Company would have been in a position to supply.
	and this will include the Sales Executive carrying out such activities outside the Territory which have an impact or effect within the Territory.
	[SEE MANUAL PRECEDENT Q5 FOR A MORE DETAILED COVENANT]
15a.Post termination: working for competitors	The Sales Executive agrees that for a period of [. . . .] months from the termination of his Employment he will not **in the Territory or where the activities have an effect or impact within the Territory:**
	1. Hold any material interest in any business which is or is likely to be in competition with the Company.
	2. Hold any material interest in any business which may require or might reasonably be considered by the Company to require the disclosure of Confidential information belonging to the Employer in order to properly discharge his functions in such business.
	3. Accept employment or take any engagement, whether self employed or otherwise and whether directly or indirectly, from any competitor of the Employer which is likely to adversely affect the business of the Company.
	[SEE MANUAL PRECEDENT Q5 FOR A MORE DETAILED CLAUSE]
16. Employer's property	Upon the termination of the Sales Executive's contract for whatever reason, the Sales Executive shall immediately return to the Company all property that belongs to the Company, including:

16. Employer's property (cont.)	1. Any computer, printer or other such equipment, and all computer discs and other software. If the Sales Executive has a password on any computer, the detail of the password.
	2. All documents in whatever form, including any copies or summaries of the same and including the Sales Executive's working notes.
	3. The Company car and keys.
	4. Lists of all contacts, customers including names and addresses with whom the Sales Executive has had contact, followed a business lead, entered into discussions or approached. To this end this information shall be deemed to be the property of the Company.
	For the purpose of this Agreement the Sales Executive irrevocably gives the Company the right to enter any property where the Company's property is held and remove the same.
17. Severability of covenants	The Sales Executive agrees that the each of the covenants contained in this Agreement are reasonable and are necessary for the protection of the Company's business. However, each provision of this Agreement is independent and severable and of any of them should be found by a Court of Law to be unenforceable or ineffective for whatever reason that shall not affect the validity of the separate covenants.
	If any covenants would become valid if any wording was deleted then the covenant shall be deemed to be applicable with such deletions and shall apply as so amended as to make the same enforceable.
18. Termination of contract	*Notice* Save as set out below, the Company must give the Sales Executive [. . . .] months' notice to terminate this Agreement and the Sales Executive must give [. . . .] months' notice.
	Earlier Termination The notice period is subject to the Company's rights to dismiss the Sales Executive without notice if:
	1. He is guilty of conduct set out in the Company's Disciplinary Procedures which warrant dismissal without notice.

18. Termination of contract (cont.)	2. He commits any act of negligence, neglect of duty which is serious or does any act which causes the Employer to lose trust and confidence and which justifies dismissal without notice. 3. He is in serious or repudiatory breach of this agreement. 4. He commits any act outside his employment which is liable to bring the Company into disrepute. 5. He is declared bankrupt or otherwise enters into any arrangement with his creditors. 6. He is convicted of a criminal offence and in the case of a motoring offence this results in disqualification or imprisonment. 7. He suffers from mental disorder. 8. He is persistently absent from work for a period of [. . . .] days in any [. . . .] months. 9. He is guilty of any serious or repudiatory breach of this Agreement. 10. He fails to achieve a Sales Target of £ . . . per month in any three month period. In all of the above cases the Sales Executive is liable to summary dismissal without payment for any notice period.
19. Provision of materials	The Employer will provide the Sales Executive with promotional material, *etc.* [LIST] for the better performance of his job. However, the Employer owes no duties at all to the Sales Executive in this respect and the Sales Executive is solely responsible for achieving sales.
20. Whole agreement	This Agreement forms the Whole Agreement between the parties, save that it is subject to any further terms contained in the Letter of Appointment and the Sales Executive acknowledges that he has read the Letter, this Agreement and any Company Policies that are referred to in the Letter of Appointment. *[CONSIDER WHETHER EXPRESS REFERENCE SHOULD BE MADE I.E. TO EQUAL OPPORTUNITY POLICIES, ETC.]*
SIGNATURES	*[CONSIDER WHETHER THE DOCUMENT SHOULD BE SIGNED AS A DEED]*

SALESMAN COMMENTARY

Many of the provisions contained in relation to this contract are similar to that of a contract for managerial staff. The Sales Executive is treated in many respects in a similar manner from the point of view of remuneration and benefits. However, there are some points of importance to bear in mind in drafting a contract of this nature.

- The Sales Executive's duties are related to a specific product. The Job Title and duties at Clause 3 set out the Sales Executive's responsibilities in relation to the sale of the Product. The Precedent is based upon the Sales Executive selling within a particular territory as it is envisaged that the Employer will have employees engaged in similar activities in other territories. This has a 'knock on effect' in relation to Clause 16 when one considers post termination covenants.

- The duty of the Sales Executive is to do all that he can to promote the product within the territory *i.e.* to use his best endeavours. However, if the Sales Executive does not achieve targets the Employer may wish to include a provision for summary termination (Clause 19.10). In this case it is important that it is made explicit that the Sales Executive is not to be paid for what would otherwise be the notice period.

- The contract is commission driven so that the Sales Executive receives a basic salary to be offset against commission. It should be noted, however, that where the Sales Executive has a legitimate expectation of commission this may be claimable as a deduction from wages under Part II of the ERA 1996 (**Kent Management Services Limited v Butterfield** [1992] ICR 272; IRLR 394). Where the Employee is paid advance commission there should be a provision to recoup the same or to withhold monies that may be otherwise due by way of set off. A Sales Executive may also receive a basic salary, to which is added commission. He will then be entitled to obtain his base salary in the absence of an express provision to the contrary.

- It should be noted that the Sales Executive will be entitled to holiday under the Working Time Regulations if he has the necessary continuity and is an employee.

- The contract contains some fairly stringent restrictive covenants that apply during and after employment since it must be recognised that it is the Sales Executive who has the day to day contact with clients or customers and is therefore in a good position to take away such clients having built up a relationship of goodwill with them during a period of time (see Manual **Part Q**).

14. SHOP WORKERS

PRECEDENTS

As well as the standard section 1 statement and the precedents mentioned below, which are contained in the Manual, the following precedent is necessary.

PRECEDENT 5.14
STATEMENT UNDER SECTION 42(4) OF THE ERA 1996

STATUTORY RIGHTS IN RELATION TO SUNDAY WORK

You have become employed as a shop worker and are or can be required under your contract of employment to do the Sunday work your contract provides for.

However, if you wish, you can give a notice, as described in the next paragraph to your employer and you will then have the right not to work in or about a shop on any Sunday on which the shop is open once three months have passed from the date on which you gave the notice.

Your notice must:
- be in writing,
- be signed and dated by you,
- say that you object to Sunday working.

For three months after you give the notice, your employer can still require you to do all the the Sunday work your contract provides for. After the three months has ended, you have the right to complain to an employment tribunal if, because of your refusal to work on Sundays on which the shop is open, your employer dismisses you or does something else detrimental to you, for example, failing to promote you.

Once you have the rights described, you can surrender them only by giving your employer a further notice, signed and dated by you saying that you wish to work on Sunday or that you do not object to Sunday working and then agreeing with your employer to do such work on Sundays or a particular Sunday.

SHOP WORKERS COMMENTARY

Apart from the general employment issues set out in Chapter 2 and the Manual the following specific issues are likely to be applicable to shop workers.

Sunday working

For the purposes of the provisions relating to Sunday working, section 232 of the ERA defines a shop worker as an employee who may under his contract be required to do shop work.

- Shop work means work in or about a shop on a day when the shop is open for the serving of customers. This means that if the Sunday work is utilised for purposes where the shop is not open for customers (*i.e.* shelf stacking, stock inventories) the provisions do not apply (See **Sands v Donlan** [ET case no 3226/95].)

- Shop includes any premises where any retail trade or business is carried on and retail trade or business is defined as including a barber or hairdresser, the business of hiring goods other than in the course of trade or business and retail sales by auction, but not catering or the sale in theatres and places of amusement of programmes, catalogues and similar items.

- Catering business covers the sale of meals, refreshments, or intoxicating liquor for consumption on premises where they are sold and the sale of meals or refreshments prepared to order for the immediate consumption off the premises.

- Where the premises are used mainly for other than retail or business only such part as is used wholly or mainly for retail trade or business and for the purposes of wholesale (whether considered singly or together) will be regarded as a shop.

Where the person falls within the definition of a shopworker those rights that are set out in the section on Betting Workers in relation to Sunday working will be applicable.

Deductions from salary

The second area where those in retail employment/shopworkers have specific provisions intended to give them protection is in the area of deductions from wages where there are till shortfalls. These provisions are contained in Part II of the Employment Rights Act 1996 and the full summary at the commentary to Model Conditions/Manual **F4: Deductions from salary**.

Dress and appearance

Because shop workers are likely to be in the public eye certain standards of dress and appearance are likely to be required. This may raise issues of conduct and capability where the employee does not live up to the standard that is required. It may also raise issues of discrimination where the employee alleges that differential treatment is being applied to men and women. These issues are considered at Model Terms and Conditions/Manual **M7; Dress and Appearance**.

15. TASKS: ENGAGEMENT FOR A SPECIFIC PURPOSE

PRECEDENT 5.15
AGREEMENT FOR A SPECIFIC TASK

These clauses may be inserted in the appropriate place in the statement in Chapter 2:

1. Notice	Notwithstanding 12. Your employment may be terminated by the Company giving .... days'/weeks' notice.
2. Temporary contract	You were employed for the specific task set out in your Letter of Appointment [*JOB DESCRIPTION SET OUT ABOVE*] which relates to a specific project. When the project is completed your contract will terminate as the task will have been completed. Your contract may, however, be terminated as set out in 10 or earlier if you commit any act of gross misconduct or serous breach of your contract of employment.

SPECIFIC TASK COMMENTARY

There is a clear distinction between employment for a specific task and an employee who is on an 'open ended' contract as the following cases make clear:

Holliday Concrete (Testing) Limited v Woods [1979] IRLR 310. Mr Woods was employed by the appellant company after replying to their advertisement for "a qualified concrete technician to operate the site lab near Wantage, Oxfordshire, for 15 months commencing mid-June" 1977. Following an interview, he was sent a letter confirming the company's offer of employment and stating that the contract would run for 15 to 18 months. The job finished at the end of July 1978, which was earlier than had been anticipated and Mr Woods was then dismissed on grounds of redundancy. An Industrial Tribunal found that the dismissal was unfair. In reaching its decision, the Tribunal determined that Mr Woods' contract had been for a minimum period of 15 months as stated in the job advertisement. The EAT held that Industrial Tribunal had not erred in holding that the respondent employee's dismissal on grounds of redundancy when the job on which he was working as a concrete technician came to an end was unfair. On the evidence before it, the Industrial Tribunal was entitled to conclude that it was a term of the respondent's contract of employment that he would be employed for a minimum period of 15 months and his dismissal before the end of that period was thus in breach of contract. The contract was therefore not for the specific task but was expressed to be for a minimum period.

In **Ryan v Shipboard Maintenance** [1980] ICR 88; IRLR 16, Mr Ryan was employed on a job by job basis and drew unemployment benefit between jobs. The EAT held that there was a contract to do specific work without reference to the duration of the contract which was, on each occasion, discharged by performance upon competition of each task.

In **Wiltshire County Council v NATFHE** [1980] ICR 455; IRLR 198, the employee was employed on a session and hourly paid basis, subject to there being enough students and the course not finishing early. She was not offered employment in the next session when a full time teacher was appointed. She had been bound to serve the Council for the whole of the academic session and the Court of Appeal held that she was employed on a fixed term even though her work may have ended early because there was no more work to do.

The precedent seeks to make it absolutely clear that employment will terminate on the completion of a specific task. Where the employer is dependent on funds (*i.e.* as a grant) then the clause should make it clear that the employment will come to an end upon such funding ceasing.

16. WORKERS

COMMENTARY

The scope of this book is directed at Contracts of Employment in relation to Employees. However, it must be borne in mind, in drafting such contracts, that much of the recent legislation extends statutory protection to 'Workers'. The definition of worker, which is now commonly being used, is that of someone who works under:

"(a) a contract of employment; or

(b) any other contract, whether express or implied and (if it is express) whether oral or in writing, whereby the individual undertakes to perform personally any work or services for another party to the contract whose status is not by virtue of the contract that of a client or customer of any profession of business undertaking carried on by the individual."

This definition is , for example, incorporated into:
- Regulation 21 of the Working Time Regulations.
- The National Minimum Wages Act 1998.
- The provisions incorporated into the ERA 1996 by the Public Interest Disclosure Act 1998.
- Section 230(3) of the ERA 1996 relating to deductions from wages.
- The Part Time Workers Regulations

A slightly different definition is adopted by the discrimination legislation though its impact is probably the same. Where the individual is engaged under a contract 'personally to execute any work or labour' (section 78(1) RRA 1976; section 82(1) SDA 1975; section 1(6)(a) Equal Pay Act 1970) then he will fall within the scope of the legislation. It was held in **Mirror Group Newspapers v Gunning** [1986] IRLR 27 that this definition was applicable where the dominant purpose was to execute personal work or labour (see also **Besley v Abbey Life Assurance Co Limited** [EAT 429/95]; **Parceline v Darien** [EAT 107/95]).

It must therefore be borne in mind that liability under the employment protection legislation may be applicable where the individual is not an employee and the draftsmen cannot necessarily escape liability by seeking to create a relationship of self employment.

AT A GLANCE CHECKLIST AS TO WHEN WORKERS WILL BE COVERED FOR THE PURPOSE OF EMPLOYMENT RIGHTS

THE RIGHT	
DISCRIMINATION	YES
DATA PROTECTION ACT 1988	YES
EQUAL PAY	YES
MATERNITY AND PATERNITY RIGHTS	NO
NOT TO BE REFUSED EMPLOYMENT BECAUSE OF UNION MEMBERSHIP	NO
PART TIME WORKERS REGULATIONS	YES
PROTECTION FROM VICTIMISATION ON TRADE UNION GROUNDS	YES
REDUNDANCY	NO
PUBLIC INTEREST DISCLOSURE	YES
STATUTORY MINIMUM NOTICE	NO
SIZE OF WORKFORCE FOR TRADE UNION RECOGNITION INCLUDES WORKERS	YES
STATUTORY MINIMUM WAGE	YES
RIGHT TO BE ACCOMPANIED AT A DISCIPLINARY OR GRIEVANCE HEARING	YES
TIME OFF FOR TRADE UNION ACTIVITIES	NO
UNFAIR DISMISSAL	NO
TUPE AND COLLECTIVE CONSULTATION RIGHTS	NO
WAGES FREE OF DEDUCTION IF NOT AUTHORISED	YES
WRITTEN PARTICULARS OF TERMS AND CONDITIONS OF EMPLOYMENT	NO
WORKING TIME REGULATIONS	YES
WRITTEN REASONS FOR DISMISSAL	NO

SECTION THREE

MODEL TERMS AND

CONDITIONS MANUAL

PART A: INTRODUCTION TO THE MANUAL AND THE COMPANY

Precedent A1: Introduction

1   The Company is pleased to present this Personnel Manual to you as an introduction to the work that is carried out by the Company and to set out the management structure and basis on which the company operates. You will find enclosed at the back of this Manual a diagram that sets out the management hierarchy and reporting structures from which you will be able to see where you fit into the organization.

2   Whether you are an existing member of staff or a new employee, the document is intended to provide you with information about the activities of the Company as well as details of your terms and conditions of employment. Please read it carefully and keep it safely with your other documents (such as your Letter of Appointment or the individual statement of Terms and Conditions of Employment) as it forms part of your contract of employment with the Company.

3   The Company provides generous conditions of employment, with particularly beneficial arrangements for items such as holidays, Private Health Insurance and sick pay. In return, we expect staff to be flexible in the way they work, in order to meet our objectives of providing a high level of service to members, students and others who wish to use the Company's facilities. This means that we all have to concentrate on getting the job done when it is required, balancing this where necessary with time off later. We work on a basis of trust and look to individuals to control their own time as far as possible.

4 The Company also places emphasis on employee initiative, so that we can continue to change to meet the demands of both our members and potential customers for the Company's services. We encourage staff development so that wherever possible we can respond quickly and appropriately to every opportunity or problem and we welcome suggestions from members of staff as to how their roles may be improved to further enhance the Company's services.

5 The Personnel Manual sets out the policies of the Company concerning its staff and contains important contractual information relating to your rights and duties at work. The manual supplements your Terms and Conditions of Employment and the sections that follow this introduction are incorporated into your contract. The Company has the right to vary this manual from time to time as a result of changes or developments in work or as is reasonably required in order for the Company to carry out its functions. It also may be that, from time to time, legislation requires variations to this manual. When there is a variation in the terms of this manual you shall be notified as soon as possible of the change by way of issue of new pages to the manual, which shall then be the terms governing your contract.

6 The rules and conditions in this Personnel Manual apply to all staff, and should be read in conjunction with any Statement of Terms and Conditions of Employment issued under the Employment Rights Act 1996, and with your Letter of Appointment or Conditional Offer of Employment. Your agreement to these conditions is signified by your written acceptance of employment. Should there be a conflict between this Manual and your personal Statement of Terms and Conditions or other written document issued to you, the latter will prevail.

7 The manual is intended to be a codification of good employment relations practice in accordance with the law as it is currently stated. The Company reserves the right to revise these conditions from time to time as it considers necessary and by reason of changes in legislation. In particular, statutes and related legislation are constantly changing employment obligations and there may be a need to alter this manual from time to time to ensure that it reflects the current state of the law. Any variation of your Terms and Conditions of Employment or to this manual (which is incorporated into your contract) will be notified to you in writing within one month of the alteration or within such other time period as may be required by statute (the current statutory requirement being one month). These changes will be incorporated into your contract of employment after one month of such notification.

8 You are responsible for keeping this manual up to date based upon any new pages that are issued to you from time to time. An up to date version of the manual and a document setting out your pension scheme which you may inspect upon giving notice will be maintained by the Officer of Human Resources/Personnel Manager and if you have any questions about these documents you should address them to _____.

Precedent A2: Alternative Introduction

1 This Personnel Manual sets out important terms and conditions of your employment with the Company. Your letter of appointment together with the Personnel Manual comprise your Contract of Employment ('Contract of Employment') with the Company. This Manual is however, subject to any amendments that which will be made from time to time in order to keep it up to date. The Company reserves the right to amend the terms and conditions of employment of all employees whether by amendment to this Manual and to vary them terms in respect of individual employees as necessary. Any amendments will be notified to you in writing one month before such terms and conditions are to be amended.

2 The terms and conditions of employment contained in the Handbook apply to all employees of the Company but where there is any difference between the terms and conditions specified in your Letter of Appointment and this Manual the terms and conditions contained in the letter of appointment takes precedence.

3 If you are unsure about anything mentioned in your Letter of Appointment or the Manual please contact your Line Manager or the Human Resources Department who will be pleased to answer any questions that you may have.

4 The Company reserves the right to amend its terms and conditions of employment and policies from time to time. Such amendments will be notified in writing to all employees, and this Handbook will be kept updated by the re-issue of the appropriate pages. You will be notified of minor changes of detail by way of a general notice to all employees affected by the change and any such changes take effect from the date of the notice. You will be given not less than one month's written notice of any significant changes which may be given by way of an individual notice or general notice to all employees. Such changes will be deemed to be accepted unless you notify the Company of any objection in writing before the expiry of the notice period.

COMMENTARY TO A:
INTRODUCTION TO THE MANUAL AND THE COMPANY

Part A contains two precedents for introductions to the Manual if the Parts contained hereafter are to be consolidated in a Manual. These introductions, to some extent, are an expression of general sentiments as to how the Manual is to operate and the manner in which the employer will treat its employees. They emphasise that the Manual is intended to be a codification of good working practice.

Both precedents also note that the Manual will be subject to change from time to time. It is sensible for such amendments to be produced as issue numbers (*e.g.* reflected in headers or footers) so that it is clear what is the up to date version of the Manual and for a 'Master Copy' to be available for inspection by the employee.

Whilst the fact that the Manual is subject to variation is mentioned in the precedents (see **A1.2-4**) it will be important that any flexibility/ mobility/variation clauses are brought to the attention of the employee and that the employee is quite clear about the extent to which job functions/hours/workplace and other terms and conditions may be changed, and the Model Terms and Conditions/Manual hereafter sets out a number of Precedents in this regard and the relative effectiveness of such clauses.

It is also common for some form of statement to be included at the outset of the Manual that sets out the employer's/company's objectives and aspirations. A chart setting out the structure of the organisation is also a valuable addition, especially if it shows the channels of communication and reporting channels within the business.

It is important to note that there is a distinction between a Code that lays down standards of good practice but is not meant to have contractual effect and terms and conditions that are intended to be contractually binding. In **Wandsworth London Borough Council v D'Silva** [1998] IRLR 193 the Council had a code of practice on staff sickness which included procedures for monitoring and reviewing different categories of absence. In 1995, the employers notified employees of certain changes to the code, one of which related to the level at which short-term absence would be reviewed, and the other to the period of long-term absence prompting referral to a director, which could result in redeployment or termination. These changes meant that redeployment or termination may be considered after shorter periods of absence. The staff objected to those changes. They maintained that the code formed part of their contractual terms and conditions of employment and that, accordingly, the employers were not entitled to make changes unilaterally. The Council argued that the code was not contractually binding and, in any event, could be unilaterally altered because of a provision which stated:

> "as adopted by the corporation and supplemented by its rules and other conditions as may be determined by the authority ... From time to time variations in your terms of employment may occur, and these will be separately notified to you or otherwise incorporated in the documents to which you have reference."

The Court of Appeal held that the ET had erred in holding that the code was contractually binding and could not be altered by the employers unilaterally. It stated that whether a particular provision in an employer's code of practice is contractually binding depends upon whether it should properly be regarded as conferring a right on employees or as setting out no more than good practice which managers were intended to follow. In the present case, it held, that the language of the provisions in question did not provide an appropriate foundation on which to base contractual rights. The code did no more than provide guidance for both supervisors and employees as to what was expected to happen in certain circumstances. It did not set out what was contractually required to happen. The whole procedure in its initial stages was designed to be flexible and informal in a way which was inconsistent with contractual rights being created. Therefore, the employers were entitled to amend the provisions unilaterally.

It is clear that in certain circumstances the courts will prepared to construe a manual as having contractual force. This was the position in **DAL & Ors v A S Orr** [1980] IRLR 413. The employers decided to move from a four to a three shift system due to a fall off in orders. The Employees' Handbook made provision for this eventuality. It was held that the employees were not dismissed for redundancy as there had not been a diminution in work but a requirement to work longer hours on the new shift system. The new arrangement was not in breach of contract since the Handbook provided that the employee could alter shift systems and hours. However, where there is a works rule book that sets out in detail how work is to be performed the book may not be regarded as containing the terms of the contract between employer and employee, though the instructions are to be construed and followed in a manner that is reasonable (**Secretary of State for Employment v ASLEF** [1972] 2 QB 455; ICR 7).

In some cases it has been held that conditions placed on a notice board are incorporated (**Petrie v MacFisheries Limited** [1940] 1 KB 258) though the prudent employer will expressly draw the attention of the employee to any conditions (and it should be noted that *Petrie* was before the requirements for section 1 statements).

Where the contract or manual is updated from time to time the original contract will not be destroyed and only the matters specified will be varied (**Allen v Marconi Space & Defence Systems Limited** (CA 31.1.1980).

PART B: JOB TITLE AND DESCRIPTION

Precedent B1: Terms of Engagement

1 Your employment will be with _____ Limited [your Employer] [*OR* which is a Service Company responsible for the employment of staff.]

2 New employees are reminded that employment is subject to receipt of satisfactory references and a medical report if required by the Company. New employees will have confirmed their acceptance of the 'Conditional Offer of Employment' in writing having received their Letter of Appointment. By accepting employment with the Company you have confirmed that you will be prepared to attend a medical examination if the Company does consider it to be necessary. If the Company wishes you to attend an examination it will nominate a medical practitioner and an appointment will be made that is mutually convenient. Any medical report that is obtained will be confidential to yourself and the Company. If, as a result of a medical report, the Company has any concerns they will be discussed with you by_____ before consideration is given to any further steps that may be required.

3 The date that your employment began is shown in your Letter of Appointment and Statement of Terms and Conditions of Employment. If previous service with an associated employer is to count as part of your continuous employment, then the date on which that employment began will be shown.

4 When you arrive, you should ensure that you have brought an income tax form P45 from any previous employer. This must be passed to the [DIRECTOR OF FINANCE] at

_____ together with your National Insurance number and details of your bank account. Without this information, your salary may be delayed or subject to higher tax deductions than are necessary.

5   The title of the job which you are employed to do is shown in your Statement of Terms and Conditions of Employment and your Letter of Appointment. You will have received a description of your duties and responsibilities as an Appendix to your Conditional Offer of Appointment, but this description should not be regarded as exhaustive. There will be times when you may be required to undertake additional tasks within your capabilities or be asked to transfer to an alternative job and where this is agreed on a permanent basis it will be confirmed to you in writing. However, you will not be assigned duties or required to perform services which you cannot reasonably perform, or which are inconsistent with the position or status that you hold. You will be subject to the flexibility and mobility terms contained elsewhere in this Manual.

Precedent B2: Job Title and Description Short Form

1   Your job title is stated in your Letter of Appointment or in the Written Particulars of Terms and Conditions of Employment as may subsequently have been varied or amended in writing. The Company reserves the right to ask you to undertake other duties as may from time to time be reasonably required in accordance with the status of the job to which you have been appointed.

COMMENTARY TO B:
JOB TITLE AND DESCRIPTION

The job title is likely to be contained in the Letter or Offer of Employment which may contain a brief job description (see Chapter 2). The job title or description should contain sufficient flexibility to enable the employer to alter the job functions of the employee as is considered appropriate. In smaller organisations a certain degree of flexibility is likely to be implied, as is apparent from the examples given in the cases below. The question of job title and scope of duties/status may be inextricably linked and this part should be read in conjunction with Part C. It is important to consider whether the job title is apposite. A person described as a manager may object to being required to carry out the job of a salesman. The impact of the job title may, however, vary depending on the circumstances, size and nature of the business. The job title may be of contractual significance where it was advertised as such and was instrumental in attracting the employee to the position. In some cases the job title may be inaccurate or meaningless but considered by the employee to be a reflection of his status (*e.g.* it is common to describe employees as Sales Directors when in fact they are not directors at all). Some examples where job title has been considered include:

By way of example:

- **Joseph Steinfeld & Co Limited v Reypert** [EAT 550/78] The employee was appointed as a 'Sales Manager (Sales Director Designate)' in a job where sales management experience was required. He was asked to carry out clerical duties and left after some time as he did not believe he would be given the functions of a manager in charge of a sales force. The EAT agreed with the EAT that requiring him to carry out clerical duties for a period of 8 months was a fundamental breach of contract. It stated:

> "It seems to us that the appointment of someone as a sales manager does involve work of a certain kind. It is not necessary that one should be able to define with precision the exact duties which are performed by such a person; but it is clear that a sales manager is someone who is responsible for the selling staff, who is dealing with sales statistics, marketing research and matters of that kind. He is a person who is concerned with sales and who is exercising a truly managerial role."

See also Part C which considers further the cases under job content, duties and status.

The Precedents

The two precedents contained in Part B are examples of the description of terms of engagement that one may expect to see in a Manual but are equally appropriate for an Offer of Appointment or Terms and Conditions of Employment.

Precedent B1 is the longer form, containing the following:

- a statement of the identity of the employer. This may frequently be a service company;
- a note of where to find the date of start of employment;
- a reminder about P45 and statement of method of payment of salary;
- a statement that the employer may be required to carry out other tasks and a reminder of any other flexibility/mobility clauses that may exist. This clause states that the employee may be required to transfer to an alternative job, consistent with the employee's capabilities, position or status.

Precedent B2 is a short form, setting out the job title and a statement that the employee may be required to carry out other duties, in accordance with the status of the job to which he has been appointed.

A provision that the employee must perform to the satisfaction of the employer may be a good idea since this will be measured by how the employer viewed the individual: see **Diggle v Ogston Motor Company** 84 LJKB 2165; 112 LR 1029 *but note that this may not be of any assistance in relation to an unfair dismissal claim where no procedures were followed.*

PART C: SCOPE OF DUTIES AND RESPONSIBILITIES

Precedent C1: Scope of Duties

1 You will faithfully and diligently perform such duties and job functions in accordance with your post as may be instructed and should at all times use your best endeavours to further the business of the Company. The Company reserves the right require you to carry out duties of a different nature that are additional to or instead of those specified in your Letter of Appointment provided that you are capable of performing the same and they are consistence with the status of your position.

2 You are required to work to the best of your ability and to use your best endeavours to promote, develop and expand the business of the Company and its interests generally. You will act at all times with consideration for the needs of the Company's customers and your colleagues and comply with the rules, procedures and policies of the Company.

3 If you are engaged to carry out a particular function or trade you must at all times carry out your work to the best of your ability and in a manner which is consistent with the normal standards of skill required by that particular function or trade.

4 The Company is part of a Group and you therefore agree that you will may be transferred to any Group Company and may be required to be employed by any Group or Associate company or seconded to such Company. In the event of such transfer or secondment the terms and conditions of your remuneration will be no less beneficial than they are at present.

COMMENTARY TO C:
SCOPE OF DUTIES AND RESPONSIBILITIES

The Letter of Appointment or Offer Letter is likely to set out the scope of duties and responsibilities of the employee as well as the job title. The employer will no doubt wish to build in a certain amount of flexibility so that the employee can be moved to other duties, be given other responsibilities or a change in status, or so that terms and conditions may be varied as the employer considers necessary, for example, by changing hours, work systems or policies such as sickness, disciplinary and grievance procedures to meet the needs of the business. The distinction between contractual and non contractual matters (as exemplified in the *Wandsworth* case) should be borne in mind in this respect. Furthermore, where the employer seeks to unilaterally impose change it is unlikely to be able to lawfully do so unless there is a clear power to this effect. It was said in *Wandsworth* that:

> "Although contracts of employment generally can only be varied by agreement, either party can reserve the ability to change a particular aspect of the contract unilaterally by notifying the other party as part of the contract that this is the situation. However, clear language is required to reserve to one party an unusual power of this sort. In addition, the court is unlikely to favour an interpretation which does more than enable a party to vary contractual provisions with which that party is required to comply. To apply a power of unilateral variation to the rights which an employee is given could produce an unreasonable result, which the courts in construing a contract of employment will seek to avoid."

The cases contain numerous examples where employers have sought to change the terms of employee's contracts, with varying degrees of success. Where the contract does not contain an express term the court will consider the scope of the implied term in the contract of employment. Where there is an express term its ambit will have to be construed, though it should be noted that in certain circumstances the courts may imply a term that the employer invokes the term in a reasonable manner.

Implied terms
The circumstances in which the Courts may imply terms have already been set out above. In the context of scope of job functions implied terms have particularly been considered in relation to:

1. Hours of work
This is considered in Part D.

2. Job content, duties and status

Where the employee has performed a particular function or has had a particular status over a period of time, there is likely to be an implied term, in the absence of an express power to vary, which establishes that function or status as a term of the contract. In **South Yorkshire Passenger Transport Executive v Baldwin** [EAT 518/78], Mr Baldwin, employed as a handyman, worked as a substitute charge hand for two nights a week then full time for three months when the charge hand died. Someone else was then given the job. The EAT held that the ET were correct in finding that it had become an implied term of his job, by custom and practice, that he be a relief charge hand and the whole nature of his job had been changed when this was taken away and his pay was detrimentally affected. Compare **Horrigan v Lewisham LBC** (see page 228) where the conduct of the employee after the contract had been entered into did not lead to a term being implied.

It has been seen that there may be an implied term that an employer will not behave intolerably (or breach trust and confidence) and this may occur where an employer unilaterally changes duties or status. In **Giblin v Seismographic Services (England) Limited** [EAT 305/78] the employers restructured Ms Giblin's job without consultation, which resulted in another employee being given some of her duties. When she complained it was decided to share the duties on an alternating basis but Ms Giblin resigned and claimed constructive dismissal. The EAT held that the ET had not erred in finding there was no breach of the implied term as the employer had sought to repair the situation when the found out the employee objected.

In **Walker v Josiah Wedgewood & Sons Limited** [1978] ICR 744; IRLR 105 Mr Walker had a poor relationship with his newly appointed supervisor, which resulted in an assistant being appointed without consultation, Mr Walker receiving a final warning without justification, not receiving a pay rise and the supervisor placing his secretary in Mr Walker's office and transferring him to an unfinished room. The EAT agreed that the conduct, though unreasonable, was not repudiatory. However, a series of incidents which lead to a demotion and reduction in status may be in breach of the implied term that there be no intolerable conduct on the part of the employer (**J W Carr M & Co Limited v Hammersley** (unreported); **Garner v Grange Furnishings Limited** [1977] IRLR 206) a promotion over the head of an employee may be part of the conduct, as in *Hammersley* but merely promoting another employee is unlikely to be so (**Goodchild v BL(UK)** (unreported)).

A series of incidents which in themselves do not amount to a breach of contract may lead to a breach of the implied term of mutual trust and confidence. It was said in **Woods v W M Car Services (Peterborough) Limited** [1982] IRLR 413; ICR 693 that to constitute a breach of the implied term it is not necessary that the employer intended any repudiation of the contract since the tribunal's function is to look at the employer's conduct as a whole and determine whether it is such that its effect, judged reasonably and sensibly, is such that the employee cannot be expected to put up with it. An employer who persistently attempts to vary an employee's conditions of service with a view to getting rid of the employee or varying the employee's terms of service does act in a manner calculated or likely to destroy the relationship of trust and confidence between employer and employee. Any breach is of the implied term is a fundamental breach amounting to a repudiation since it necessarily goes to the root of the contract. (In this case, as a matter of fact there was no breach.)

It is not a loss of status to insist that an employee is supervised where the employer is concerned about his work. The only loss is one of self esteem (**Mensah v London Borough of Islington** [EAT 156/79]). However, a reduction in status does not have to be permanent in order to amount to a repudiatory breach (**McNeill v Charles Crimin (Electrical Contractors) Limited** [1984] IRLR 179).

3. Mobility and relocation
This is considered in Part G.

Express Terms
It has already been noted that express terms will be strictly construed. However, where the express term is absolutely clear there will be no justification for construing it on a more restrictive basis than the term warrants. In **Nelson v British Broadcasting Corporation** [1977] ICR 469, Mr Nelson was employed pursuant to a contract which included a term that stated:

> "During the subsistence of this Agreement the employee shall perform such duties and exercise such powers and authorities as may from time to time be assigned to or vested in him .... and the employee shall at all times obey and conform to the reasonable orders and directions and restrictions given by the Board of Governors or the Director-General for the time being of the Corporation or such other person as aforesaid which shall include the right to direct the employee to serve wherever he may be required..."

Mr Nelson was dismissed when the Caribbean service closed down and he refused alternative employment. The Court of Appeal held that he had not been redundant (as the BBC had contended) as the express term made it clear that he was not employed solely for the Caribbean service. Roskill LJ stated that it is a basic principle of contract law that if a contract makes provision in almost unrestricted language it is impossible to imply a restriction as the tribunal had sought to do in this case.

The courts have, however, construed express clauses in a restrictive way, whilst playing lip service to what was said the *Nelson* case.

1. Hours of work
This is considered in Part D.

2. Job content, duties and status
The issues of job content, duties and status have been considered in the following cases (in chronological order):
- **Goode & Cooper Ltd v Thompson** [1974] IRLR 111. Mr Thompson was the general manger of a garage and taxicab business. When it was taken over another manager was appointed and he was told that he would be in charge of the garage workshop and no longer be able to sign cheques or have responsibility for buying in stores. It was held that there "...was a change of status, and a change of such a nature as to show that there was a repudiation of the contract and an intention only to employ him in some very much lower, though undefined, capacity."
- **Managers (Holborn) Ltd v Hohne** [1977] IRLR 230. It was held that Mrs Hohne was effectively downgraded in status as manageress, when she was moved to another office at which there was already a manageress as "she was in effect down-graded in status because in the Regent Street hive there was only room for one Queen Bee, and that was Mrs Falconer."
- **Coleman v S & W Baldwin** [1977] IRLR 342. Mr Coleman was promoted to acting manager with responsibility for buying groceries. When the firm was taken over he was removed from this position and his buying duties were taken away, leaving him with only humdrum duties. It was held that the employer had unilaterally changed the whole nature of the job, which they could not do unilaterally and by way of ultimatum, so that there was a constructive dismissal.
- **Gronow v GKN (South Wales) Limited** [EAT 461/78]. Mr Gronow was employed as a stock control clerk, grade 3, at a time when a job evaluation scheme was introduced and it was a term that

he could be reassessed and re-graded. He was upgraded to grade 5 on the basis that he would take a job as divisional planner but this did not happen. After 4 years he was regraded to grade 3. The EAT held that there was no provision in the scheme to reduce to a lower grade in accordance with the scheme. It is clear from this case that if the employer wishes to have the power to downgrade there must be an express provision to this effect.

- **Glitz v Watford Electric Co Limited** [1979] IRLR 89. Miss Glitz was employed in 1974 as a "Copy typist/general clerical duties clerk". In 1977 she was asked to operate a duplicating machine but refused to do so after it gave her headaches. It was held that the operation of the machine fell within the ambit of typist/clerk and she was contractually bound to operate the machine. It was said that "in the context of the case, with a small clerical staff in a small office, the ambit of general clerical duties is wide enough to include the operation of a duplicator."

- **Peter Carnie & Son v Paton** [1979] IRLR 260. Mr Paton was employed to carry out "general garage duties/stores" duties. He engaged in handyman duties, care hire and spent 25% of his time on reception. Although he liked the latter, it was taken away from him as his employers were not satisfied with him. The EAT held that he had been engaged to carry out a variety of jobs of an unskilled nature and that "it is unreasonable, if not absurd, to suggest that an employee who is engaged on general duties can insist on doing only those duties which he likes most". The employer was not bound to keep him on reception duties and the duties could be altered from time to time to meet the needs of the business.

- **Joseph Steinfeld v Reypert** (See Part B).

- **Ford v Milthorn Toleman Limited** [1980] IRLR 30. Mr Ford was appointed as a sales manager and was responsible for "sales, administration, estimating and quoting, keeping an order book, invoicing, monitoring the production development and prices of competitors." He was responsible to the MD and was paid a commission. When he gave notice a number of his functions were taken away and his commission was removed. It was held that the removal of some of his functions amounted to a demotion. Stephenson LJ indicated that loss of job satisfaction may amount to a repudiatory breach of contract.

- **Pedersen v London Borough of Camden** [1981] IRLR 173. The employer advertised for a "bar steward/catering assistant", stressing the primary function as being bar steward. Over a period of four years Mr Pedersen's duties changed to primarily that of a catering assistant. The Court of Appeal held that the ET were correct in construing the letter of appointment by reference to the surrounding circumstances including the job advert and that if the function of bar steward was substantially reduced there was a change of conditions of work which could be a breach of contract.

- **Cresswell v Board of Inland Revenue** [1984] IRLR 190; ICR 508. The introduction of computers was held not to change the nature of clerical work. The employers were employed to do clerical work and "it was recognisably the same job but done in a different way." This case shows that technological advances will not necessarily change the nature of the work.

The employer is not entitled to change the job content and demote merely because the employee has given notice (**Milthorn Toleman Limited v Ford** [1978] IRLR 306; see the Chapter on SOSR in Duggan, *Unfair Dismissal, Law Practice and Guidance*).

3. Mobility and relocation
This is considered in Part G.

4. Remuneration
This is considered in Part E.

Limits of flexibility clauses
1. Construction
Where there is a flexibility clause it will be for the tribunal/court to construe its meaning. The courts will not seek to expand upon it as the following cases make clear:

- **SmithKline Beecham PLC v Johnston** [EAT 559/96]. The employees were employed on a 40 hour week under a three shift system. The contract provided that the shifts could be changed to 12 hour shifts. The terms were changed so that employees worked under this system for 42 hours. After a re-organisation the hours were again changed to 40. The EAT held that there was no power to vary the hours in this way so as to reduce the employees' basic salary.
- **National Semiconductor (UK) Limited v Church & Ors** [EAT 252/97]. Four employees were engaged to work a total of 25 hours at weekends. The contract provided that "Although you are employed in the shift/position quoted, production requirements may change from time to time and it is a condition of employment that you should be able, with due notice, to change to other shifts/positions." The employers sought to change the conditions so that the employees worked 42 hours during the week on a shift

system. It was held that they had been constructively dismissed. The new shift patterns necessitated longer hours. The contract provided that the employees' work could be relocated in terms of time, not in terms of an extension of hours. The EAT stated that "in order for there to be an express term in a contract which entitles the employer to increase the working hours it must be thus, *i.e.* express". The EAT also recognised that if an employer seeks to unilaterally change the conditions of employment, even within the band of an express term, so as to achieve a result which precludes the employee in practical terms from complying with the change he may act unreasonably and create a constructive dismissal. (See *Akhtar* below.) It is thus necessary that the flexibility clause contemplates the variation that is proposed.

2. Reasonable behaviour and implied terms

Where there is an express mobility clause, there may nevertheless be implied terms that the clause is operated reasonably as in **United Bank Limited v Akhtar** [1989] IRLR 507. An alternative way in which a term may be implied is that the employer does not operate the express clause in such a way as to destroy mutual trust and confidence between the parties. In **French v Barclays Bank PLC** [1998] IRLR 646 Mr French was employed under a contract that contained a mobility clause entitling the employer to transfer the employee to any of the offices throughout the country. There were also terms for financial assistance, including an interest free bridging loan, which was stated to be at the bank's discretion and not part of the contract of employment. Mr French was provided with a bridging loan on relocation but this was withdrawn when house prices fell and he could not sell the house he had moved from. He was forced to sell it to the bank for less than the loan and repay the balance which he did by taking out a further loan. The Court of Appeal held that the employers were in breach of the obligation of mutual trust and confidence that, having ordered the employee to relocate and given an interest free loan, they then sought to change the terms of the loan to the employee's detriment. The employer was in breach of the obligation in that, once they had exercised their discretion to grant a bridging loan, they were under an obligation to maintain that position. The employer was therefore in breach but was not entitled to damages for distress (on this point see Duggan, *Wrongful Dismissal, Law Practice and Precedents*).

Employee's liability

It should be noted that, where the employee fails to achieve a standard of reasonable care he may be liable to indemnify his employer for his negligence. In **Semtex Limited v Gladstone** [1954] 1 WLR 945 it was held that the employee was liable to indemnify the employer in respect of negligent driving.

Precedent C.1 ties in and overlaps with the precedents in **B**. It requires a certain standard of competence and application to the job as well as stipulating for flexibility.

- The clause makes it clear that the Employee is expected to well and diligently perform his duties and to achieve a certain standard where he is engaged in a certain function or trade. The following propositions are applicable here:

  (1) Where the employee professes to have a particular skill he is taken to have guaranteed a reasonable level of competence. In **Harmer v Cornelious** [1858] 5 CB (NS) 236 two workers were engaged as "first rate panorama and scene painters". They were not competent and were dismissed after two days. The Court stated that:

    > "When a skilled labourer...is employed, there is on his part an implied warranty that he is of skill reasonably competent to the task he undertakes....An express premise or express representation in the particular case is not necessary."

  (2) It is a question of fact whether the standard has been achieved. This must be looked at on an objective basis. The test is that of a reasonably competent man and not angels. (**Jupiter General Insurance Co Limited v Schroff** [1937] 3 All ER 67).

  (3) However, where the employer is expressed to be the judge of the standard the test is whether the employer honestly believed that the employee was not up to the position and it is a subjective test. In **Diggle v Ogston Motor Company** 84 LJKB 2165; 112 LR 1029 the employee was engaged for one year with a provision that if he performed his duties "to the satisfaction of the directors" his contract could be extended for a further six years. The directors were not so satisfied. It was held, in the King's Bench Division, that it was not necessary for the employer to show reasonable cause for the dissatisfaction. It was for the claimant to prove that "the directors were in fact satisfied with his services or dishonestly professed to be dissatisfied or were at least capriciously dissatisfied."

- The clause re-iterates that the employee may be expected to carry out duties of a different nature within the scope of his capability and status (see also Part B).

- Where the employer is part of a Group or is the service company for a Group, it is important that it is made clear to the employee that he may be transferred to another Company within the Group in a situation where the Transfer of Undertakings (Protection of Employment) Regulations 1981 apply to the Company from which an employer is transferred prior to a transfer taking place.

PART D: HOURS OF WORK

D1: Normal Hours of Work

PRECEDENT D1.1 NORMAL HOURS OF WORK

1   Your normal working hours are as set out in your Statement of Terms and Conditions of Employment or as modified and confirmed in writing by mutual agreement. The Company may make reasonable changes in your working hours having regard to its core 'open for business' hours and the needs of the Company. You will be given reasonable notice of any changes and you are expected to be flexible.

2   The Company aims to provide a high level of personal service to its clients and you may therefore be required to work additional hours in order to ensure that the needs of the business are met.

3   Your starting and finishing times allow for an unpaid meal break during each working day. You must always take this break, which is a statutory requirement. If you exceed the allotted time, you are expected to extend your working day either on that day or, by mutual agreement with your _____, on some subsequent day. If you need to be away from the office for personal reasons which you do not wish to be counted against your holiday entitlement you are required to make up for lost time and must first seek the agreement of _____.

4   The Company reserves the right to vary your hours of work as necessary to meet its business requirements.

PRECEDENT D1.2 NORMAL WORKING HOURS

Your normal hours of work are _____ to _____ Monday to Friday. You are expected to work _____ per week. You are entitled to take a lunch break of 45 minutes to be taken between _____ and _____ or at a time to be agreed with your manager. The Company reserves the right to vary your hours of work as necessary to meet its business requirements.

PRECEDENT D1.3 NORMAL WORKING HOURS

1   Your normal hours of work are as follows

Monday   . . . . to . . . .
Tuesday   . . . . to . . . .
Wednesday   . . . . to . . . .
Thursday   . . . . to . . . .
Friday   . . . . to . . . .

2   You are entitled to take a lunch break of 45 minutes to be taken between _____ and _____ or at a time to be agreed with your manager.

3   The Company reserves the right to vary your hours of work as necessary to meet its business requirements.

D2: Overtime

PRECEDENT D2.1 OVERTIME

It is expected that you will be able to finish your work within your normal hours. However, you may be required to work overtime if it is necessary for the proper performance of your duties. Your Letter of Appointment or Statement of Terms and Conditions will set out your entitlement to overtime payments if applicable. You will not be required to work for more than 48 hours per week as an average over a period of 17 weeks.

PRECEDENT D2.2: OVERTIME

It is not the Company's normal policy to pay overtime to office staff. You are expected to manage your time and complete your work within the normal working day. If you work in an office and it is necessary to work overtime you must first obtain the agreement of your Head of Department in relation to the hours of overtime. If you need to work overtime you will be entitled to time off *in lieu* with the prior consent of your Head of Department. If overtime is a contractual requirement you will be paid for any overtime you are required to undertake. You will not be required to work for more than 48 hours per week as an average over a period of 17 weeks.

PRECEDENT D2.3: OVERTIME

You shall be available, when required by the Company, to work outside your normal working hours. This includes Saturdays, Sundays and public holidays. Overtime may be required at short notice although the Company will try to give you as much notice as possible. If you are entitled to be paid for overtime it will be specified in your Letter of Appointment. You will not be required to work for more than 48 hours per week as an average over a period of 17 weeks.

PRECEDENT D2.4: OVERTIME

Overtime where applicable is calculated on annual basic salary and will be paid at the following rates:

Monday to Friday:	time and a half
Saturday:	double time
Sunday:	double time
Statutory public holidays:	treble time or, at the discretion of your Manager, double time together with one day's holiday *in lieu* of the statutory public holiday worked to be taken at such time as is agreed with your Manager.

You will not be required to work for more than 48 hours per week as an average over a period of 17 weeks.

Precedent D3: Flexitime

1   The Company's standard hours of work are _____am until
_____ pm with a one hour lunch break to be taken between
_____ and _____ unless your manager agrees that such
breaks may be taken a different time.

2   The Company operates a flexitime system where it is
possible for employees to carry out their duties and to start
and leave work on flexitime. It recognises the benefit of
flexitime in co-ordinating your time and whilst the
essential needs of the office are of paramount importance,
if working conditions permit the operation of the system
your Manager may permit you to operate on this basis. The
flexitime system will comply with the requirements of the
Working Time Regulations 1998.

3   Your Manager may approve flexitime or set your schedule
at standard hours of operation. If you wish to work flexitime you must obtain prior approval from your Manager.

4   Flexitime operation will operate within the following
restrictions:

1.   The Company's premises are open to employees
(except for certain statutory holidays which will be
announced in advance) between the hours of
_____. You must attend work on Monday to
Friday subject to the rules set out below.
2.   The hours when you must be present at work are
between _____ and _____ ('the core hours') and you
must work a minimum of _____ per day.
3.   You are free to arrive and depart at any time provided
that you attend within the core hours and provided
that:
      (1) you comply with the departmental requirements
      as laid down by your Manager,
      (2) you must take a break of at least _____ during
      the day in order that the provisions of the
      Working Time Regulations are complied with and
      you will in any event not be paid for this period.
4.   At the end of each month no more than _____ hours
may be carried forward into the next calendar month

and any hours in excess of this will not be carried over nor will remuneration be paid for these hours unless you have been prevented by working requirements from taking off those hours.

5. The operation of flexitime may be suspended at any time by your Manager as the operational needs of the business so require.

Precedent D4: Time Keeping

1 All employees are required to record time actually worked and salaried workers will be expected to complete appropriate time sheets.

2 Hourly paid workers will be required to use the time clock which is located at _____. It will be the responsibility of your Manager to approve your time and he will forward the time sheet or card to Payroll. You are required to clock in when arriving for work and to clock out on leaving work for any reason. You must not clock in or clock out for any other person, or request or permit any other person to clock in or out for you and it will be a disciplinary offence to do so.

3 An employee found tampering or interfering with the time clocks or the time system will be liable to summary dismissal for gross misconduct.

Precedent D5: Shiftworkers

1 The Company operates on a _____ hours _____ days a week basis due to the nature of its business. If you have been appointed to work as a shift worker the hours that you will be required to work will have been set out in your Letter of Appointment. You will be given reasonable notice of any requirement to the shifts you are required to work and of the times you will be required to take a break from work during your shift.

2   The rates of pay for shiftwork will have been set out in your Letter of Appointment and will vary as follows depending on the hours that you work:
[RATES OF PAY FOR DAYS AND SHIFTS TO BE WORKED]

3   Managers are responsible for drawing up shift rosters to conform with operational requirements.

4   Requests to change shifts must be submitted at least _____ hours in advance whether by your Employer or if you wish to alter your shift. Changes to shifts among employees will be restricted to _____ shifts per month and may be allowed in order to extend holidays where the employee has ____ days holiday outstanding.

5   Where your hours of work involve night shift work you will be required to undergo an annual medical examination to ensure that you are fit for such work.

D6:   Factory Workers

PRECEDENT D6.1: SHIFTWORK

The Company needs operates on a 24-hour/seven day a week basis in order to fully utilise its production process and comply with orders from its customers. You have agreed to work a shift system in order that the business can continue to operate. You will be advised of the shifts that you are required to carry out on a weekly basis and will be given ____ hours notice should these be varied.

PRECEDENT D6.2: CLOCKING IN PROCEDURES

You have been provided with a clocking in number and card and are required to clock in when arriving for work and to clock out on leaving the work premises for whatever reason. You must personally clock in and out. You are not allowed to clock in or out for any other person and it will be regarded as a dismissable offence to clock in for any other person, tamper with clock cards or to in any way interfere with the clocks.

PRECEDENT D6.3: FACTORY CLOSURE TIMES

It is the Company's practice to close down the factory for a period of _____ each year in order to carry out maintenance work. You will be required to take part of your annual holiday during this period but the Company reserves the right to require you to work during this period if a skeleton staff is needed. You will be notified of these requirements at least _____ weeks in advance.

PRECEDENT D6.4: LAY OFF

From time to time it is necessary to close down the factory or to reduce manpower due to the fact that there is a diminution in the requirements of the business for work of the kind which you carry out due to a shortfall in orders. In that event the Company is entitled to lay you off for a period of _____ days during which you may be paid _____ [will not be paid].

D7: Retail Employment

PRECEDENT D7.1 HOURS OF WORK

1   The hours of work that you will normally be required to carry out are _____ and will normally be during the following hours:

Monday   .... to....
Tuesday   .... to....
Wednesday   .... to....
Thursday   .... to....
Friday   .... to....
Saturday   .... to....
Sunday   .... to....

2   You are entitled to take a lunch break of _____ which should be taken at a time agreed with your Manager, and to other breaks as follows:
[SET OUT]

3 Your hours may be varied in order to meet particular requirements and you may be required to work overtime in excess of your normal hours upon being given reasonable notice. If you work overtime then you will be paid at the rate of _____.

PRECEDENT D7.2 SUNDAY WORKING

It is a condition of your employment that you will work on Sundays. You are entitled to give written notice stating that you object working on Sundays and this notice must be signed and dated by you. It will become effective three months after you have given notice and after that date you will not be required to work on Sundays unless you decide to withdraw the notice.

D8: Working Time

PRECEDENT D8.1 EXCLUSION OF THE 48 HOUR WEEK UNDER THE WORKING TIME REGULATIONS 1998

You have agreed that the limit of an average working time of 48 hours including overtime for each seven day period as set out in Regulation 4 of the Working Time Regulations shall not apply to your employment and you have signed a document to this effect. You may however, give three months written notice to the Company to terminate this Agreement.

PRECEDENT D8.2: EXISTENCE OF A WORKFORCE AGREEMENT

There is a workforce agreement in effect whereby the Company and the employees have agreed to opt out of the Regulations in the terms set out hereafter. This agreement came into force on _____ and will remain in force for a period of five years unless it is terminated by either party giving not less than three months notice in writing. The terms of the agreement are as follows:

1) The maximum weekly working time of 48 hours shall not apply [but shall be _____].

2) The reference period of 17 weeks shall be consecutive periods which commenced on _____.

3) The provisions relating to daily rest periods, weekly rest periods and rest breaks shall not apply. Equivalent rest periods shall be permitted to be taken wherever possible.

PRECEDENT D8.3: A PRECEDENT WORKFORCE AGREEMENT

1   This Workforce Agreement is dated .... and is made between .... [the Employer] and the workers listed in Schedule 1 to this Agreement.

OR

2   [This agreement is made between .... the Employer and the Worker's representatives. All definitions contained in this Agreement may be found in Regulation 2 of the Working Time Regulations 1998 (SI 1998 No. 833) as amended.]

3   This Agreement applies to [the whole of the workforce of the Employer] [*OR SPECIFY GROUP*] and it is agreed that it will remain in force for a period of [not more than five years after date it is signed] when it will automatically cease to have effect, or until terminated by either party at any time by giving not less than [three months] written notice to the other.

4   Pursuant to the terms of the Regulations the Employees hereby agree with the Employer to opt out of the Regulations to such extent as is set out hereafter.

5   REGULATION 4: WORKING HOURS
The maximum weekly working time (including overtime) of 48 hours for each seven day period shall not apply to the Employees.
[The maximum working week (including overtime) shall be _____ for each seven day period.

6   REGULATION 4(3): REFERENCE PERIOD
The reference period of 17 weeks shall be successive periods as permitted under Regulation 4(3), the first to commence on_____.

7 REGULATION 6: LENGTH OF NIGHT WORK
The normal hours of work in any 24 hour period may exceed 8 hours for night workers.

8 REGULATION 10-DAILY REST PERIOD
Adult workers shall not be entitled to 11 hours' consecutive rest in each 24 hour period but will be entitled to a compensatory rest period where appropriate.

9 REGULATION 10: WEEKLY REST PERIOD
Adult workers will not be entitled to a rest period of 24 hours in each seven day period but shall be given a compensatory rest period where appropriate.

10 REGULATION 12: REST BREAKS
Adult workers shall not automatically be entitled to a rest break where they work more than six hours but will be given a compensatory rest period as appropriate.

11 SIGNED BY THE EMPLOYER:

SIGNED by the Elected Representative(s) of the Employees:
or
SIGNED by the majority of the Employees where less than 20 employees.

COMMENTARY TO D:
HOURS OF WORK

It is necessary to consider hours of work within the context of the Working Time Regulations since they will govern what is permissible (subject to opting out *etc*) in the normal working environment. Consideration will then be given to the precedents.

NORMAL HOURS

Implied terms

The employee's hours of work are an essential term of the contract of employment. Where the working hours are not specified it will be necessary for the court to imply a term as to normal working hours.

- **Dean v Eastbourne Fisherman's & Boatmen's Protection Society** [1977] IRLR 143; ICR 556. The employee worked as a part time barman, working such hours as were required, being over 21 hours for 86 weeks and less for 18 weeks. The EAT considered the hours that were worked and held that there was a contractual obligation to work the hours required which were normally more than 21 a week.
- **Scott v Victor Blagden (Barking) Limited** [EAT 367/82]. As a matter of practice, a maintenance fitter had worked weekends over the years to carry out major maintenance work. He was dismissed when he refused to work on a Sunday. The EAT held that it had become an implied term, by custom and practice, to work on weekends and to be paid double time.

THE WORKING TIME REGULATIONS 1998

The Working Time Regulations came into effect on 1st October 1998. They have subsequently been amended as set out below. This commentary will summarise the effect of the Regulations.

DEFINITIONS

Regulation 2 of the WTR sets out a number of definitions that are important in understanding the scheme of the Regulations:

1. Working time means:
   - Any period during which the worker is working, at his employer's disposal and carrying out his activity or duties. These three elements must be satisfied in order for the worker to be regarded as working during 'working time'. The DTI have published Guidance Notes which are of some assistance in considering what may be regarded as working time. The following points arise:
     — Where the worker is on call but is free to pursue his or her own activities during this time then he is unlikely to be regarded as working unless called out. This will also be the position where the worker is required to be at the place of work 'on call' but is

sleeping. The particular circumstances of the case will govern whether someone is regarded as working; for example, shop assistants are likely to be regarded as working even when they are idle because there are no customers in the shop — **SIMAP V Conselleria de Sanidad y Consumo de la Generalitat Valencia** C303/98.

— The Guidance Notes state that time spent travelling to and from work are unlikely to be working time as the worker is probably not working or carrying out his duties. However, the worker may work on the train or have to travel for the purpose of the job and this may be working time.

— Working lunch breaks may be working time.

— The Guidance Notes state that if a worker takes work home this will only count as working time if previously agreed by the employer. Difficulties may arise where the worker simply takes work home without express agreement but to the knowledge of the employer and it is prudent for some form of agreement to have been reached so that the position is clear.

— A further grey area is that where the worker has to read reports or literature to keep up to date. It is not clear whether this will amount to working time. It is to be noted that training is catered for.

• Any period during which he is receiving training. Training is defined as work experience provided pursuant to a training course or programme, training for employment or both other than the immediate provider being an educational institution or a person whose main business is the provision of training.

• Any additional period which is to be treated as working time under a relevant agreement. The parties may agree to extend the definition of working time by a relevant agreement but they cannot reduce it.

2. The Regulations apply to workers (see 5.16).

3. 'Day' is a period of 24 hours starting at midnight and the calendar year runs from 1st January

4. 'Night time' is a period of not less than 7 hours which includes the period between midnight and 5 am as determined by a relevant agreement, or in default the period between 11pm and 6am, and night work means work during night time.

5. A 'nightworker' is a person who as a normal course (*i.e.* the majority of days) works at least three hours of his normal working time during night

time, or works such proportion of his annual working time as may be specified in a collective or workforce agreement.

6. A relevant agreement (RA) is:
   - a workforce agreement (WA)
   - a provision in a collective agreement (CA)
   - any other agreement in writing that is legally enforceable.

   It is to be noted that there are four means by which the Regulations may be modified; the above three and, in the case of the 48 hour week, a non contractually binding agreement (NCBA).

7. An 'adult worker' is a person who has reached the age of 18. A 'young worker' is someone who has attained the age of 15 but not 18 and is over compulsory school age.

8. A 'workforce agreement', is an agreement between the employer and workers which satisfied the conditions set out in Schedule 1 being:
   - it is in writing;
   - it has effect for a specified period of not more than 5 years;
   - it applies to all relevant members, or particular group of members of the workforce;
   - it is signed by the representatives of the workforce or group or, if there are 20 or less employees, a majority;
   - before the agreement was made available for signature the employer provided all the workers to whom it was intended to apply on the date on which it came into effect with copies of the text of the agreement and such guidance as those workers might reasonably require in order to understand it fully.

The Scope of the Regulations

It is necessary to consider:

1. The 48 Hour week
2. Night work
3. Monotonous Work
4. Daily Rest Periods
5. Weekly Rest periods
6. Rest Breaks
7. Annual Leave — The requirements relating to annual leave are considered under holidays.
   Exceptions

1. Maximum Weekly Working Time: the 48 hour week

Regulation 4 of the WTR imposes a contractual duty and may therefore be enforced in the ordinary civil courts (**Barber v RJB (Mining (UK) Limited** [1999] IRLR 308). By Regulation 4(1):

- the maximum working time shall not exceed an average of 48 hours for each seven days in any reference period.
- the reference period is 17 weeks in the course of employment unless:
  — a relevant agreement provides for the 17 weeks to be successive;
  — the worker has worked for less than 17 weeks in which case it is the period elapsed. This provision will protect temporary workers;
  — or (under Regulation 23(b)) for objective or technical reasons or reasons concerning the organisation of work, a collective or workforce agreement has substituted a different period being a period not more than 52 weeks.
- In arriving at the 17 weeks, account is not taken of periods of annual leave, sick leave, maternity leave or periods where the worker has agreed the 48 hour limit shall not apply.

Since the 48 hour week is taken as an average over 17 weeks the fact that the employee is required to work in excess for some weeks will not necessarily infringe the Regulations if, averaged out, the excess is not 48 hours (see **King v Scottish & Newcastle (Retail) North Limited** (Newcastle upon Tyne ET *IDS Brief* 641). Regulation 4(2) places on the employer a duty to take all reasonable steps, in keeping with the need for health and safety, to ensure that the limit is complied with.

By Regulation 5 where the worker has agreed in writing that the limit shall not apply the 48 hour week may be excluded. This may be for a definite period or indefinitely and can be terminable by the worker giving not less than 7 or more than 3 months' notice. A Collective or Workforce Agreement cannot disapply the 48 hour week; it must be by consent of the worker in writing, whether or not legally enforceable. Workers may not be subjected to any detriment if they refuse to consent to the 48 hour week being disapplied (section 45A ERA 1996).

2. Night work and Nightworkers

By Regulation 6 a nightworker's normal hours in any reference period shall not exceed an average of 8 hours for each 24 hours. The reference period is again 17 weeks or such period, if less, that the worker has worked. However:

- there is no provision to extend this up to 52 weeks;
- rest periods are deducted in arriving at the calculation;

- An employer shall take all reasonable steps to ensure that the limit is complied with in accordance with the need to protect the health and safety or workers but where the worker has been identified as involving special hazards or heavy physical or mental strain the employer shall ensure that the limit is complied with (6(7)).

The definition of night work may be modified by a Collective or Workforce Agreement. There remains a question mark over the extent to which a worker on call may be regarded as working.

The employer shall ensure that a worker has an opportunity for a free health assessment before night work is carried out (Regulation 7) and a young worker should have a free health assessment as to his health and capacities. The Guidance notes that, as a minimum, this should consist of a screening questionnaire before beginning night work. Where a worker is suffering from health problems and it is possible to transfer him to non nightwork that is suitable, the employer shall transfer the worker (7(6)). It should be noted that there will in any event be duties under the DDA 1995 in respect of reasonable adjustments.

3. Work Patterns - Monotonous Work
By Regulation 8 where the pattern of work:

> "Is such as to put the health and safety of a worker employed by him at risk, in particular because the work is monotonous, or the work rate is predetermined, the employer shall ensure that the worker is given adequate rest breaks."

There is no definition of adequate rest breaks but this duty is likely to overlap with duties under the health and safety legislation in any event.

4. Daily Rest Periods
An adult worker is entitled to a rest period of not less than 11 consecutive hours in each 24 hour period during which he works for his employer. A young worker is entitled to 12 hours though this may be interrupted in the case of activities involving periods of work that are split up over the day or of short duration (Reg 10). This entitlement does not apply to shift workers where they change shift and cannot take a daily rest period between the end of one shift and the start of another (Reg 22(1)). There is then an obligation to provide a compensatory rest period (24(a)) though in exceptional cases if this is not possible the employer should provide protection as is appropriate to safeguard health and safety (24(b)).

5. Weekly Rest Periods

An adult worker is entitled to not less than 24 hours in each seven day period, which may be two periods of not less than 24 hours in each 14 day period or one period of not less than 48 hours. A young worker is entitled to not less than 48 hours during each 14 days period but this may be reduced to not less than 36 hours if justified by technical or organisational reasons in the case of activities that involve periods of work split up over the day or of short duration (Reg 11). In the case of shift workers the entitlement does not apply where the worker changes shift (22(1)(b)). There is then an obligation to provide a compensatory rest period (24(a)) though in exceptional cases if this is not possible the employer should provide protection as is appropriate to safeguard health and safety (24(b)).

6. Rest Breaks

Where an adult worker's daily working time is more than 6 hours he is entitled to a rest break which, subject to any collective or workforce agreement, shall be not less than 20 minutes, and a young worker is entitled to 30 minutes where the working time is four and a half hours (Reg 12). Payment does not have to be made unless this is agreed. In the case of young workers who work for more than one employer the number of hours must be aggregated (11(8)).

7. Annual Leave

Regulations 13 to 16 cover annual leave and this is dealt with under Part I.

Exceptions

Regulations 18 to 27 contain a large number of exceptions and exclusions. The table at the end of this section provides a ready means of identifying the modification or exclusions. There are five broad categories:

1. The excluded sectors under Regulation 18

- air, rail, road, sea, inland waterway and lake transport.
  Where workers involved in the transport industry are non mobile (*i.e.* clerical staff) it is is not clear whether they will be included within this exclusion. The DTI Guidance refers to the nature of the work that is actually being undertaken. However, in **Bowden v Tuffnells Parcels Express Limited** (Ashford ET *IDS Brief* number 641) a part time clerical worker who worked for a parcel delivery company was held to fall within the scope of the exclusion. The EAT have now referred this case to the ECJ for clarification. It is intended by the Commission to remove this blanket exception in any event.
- sea fishing
- other works at sea

- the activities of doctors in training
- where characteristics peculiar to certain specified services such as the armed forces or police or to certain specific activities in the civil protection services inevitably conflict with the Working Time Regulations.

2. Domestic Servants

Domestic servants in private household are excluded from those areas identified in the chart below. Domestic servants will cover employees working at domestic establishments who sleep on the premises (See **Re Junior Carlton Club** [1992] 1 KB 166; **Re Wilkinson** [1992] 1 KB 584).

3. Unmeasured working time

An important exception relates to 'unmeasured working time'. To cover the situation:

> "(2) Where, part of the working time of a worker is measured or predetermined or cannot be determined by the worker himself but the specific characteristics of the activity are such that, without being required to do so by the employer, the worker may also do work the duration of which is not measured or predetermined or can be determined by the worker himself, regulations 4(1) and (2) and 6(1),(2) and (7) shall apply only to so much of his work as is measured or predetermined or cannot be determined by the worker himself."

This amendment was made by the Working Time Regulations 1999 in order to cover the situation where the employee did in fact have certain pre-determined hours but also had a measure of choice as to the time during which he carried out his work.

4. Special cases

Regulation 21 contains a list of special cases which are excluded from the Regulations set out in the chart. The special cases cover:

- where the worker's activities are such that his place of work and place of residence are distant from one another or his different places of work are distant from one another.
- where the worker is engaged in security or surveillance requiring a permanent residence in order to protect property or persons.
- where the worker's activities involve the need for continuity of service or production, as may be the case in services relating to reception, treatment or care by hospitals or similar establishments or prisons; work at docks or airports, press, radio, television, postal and telecommunications services and civil protection services; gas, water and electricity services; industries where work cannot be interrupted

on technical grounds; research and development activities and agriculture.

- where there is a foreseeable surge in activity as in the case of agriculture, tourism and postal services.
- where the worker's activities are affected by an occurrence due to unusual and unforeseeable circumstances beyond the control of the employer or exceptional events, the consequences of which could not have been avoided despite the exercise of all due care by the employer or an accident or the imminent risk of an accident.

5. Agreements to modify or exclude
These are set out in the table below.

6. Others
The exceptions relating to shift workers have been noted.

An at a glance chart as to the applicability of the Working Time Regulations follows.

AT A GLANCE GUIDE TO THE WORKING TIME REGULATIONS 1998

An agreement may be reached to add to what is the definition of working time, but not to exclude (Regulation 2)	
Effect of Regulation	Working time defined in Reg. 2 as any period when working, at employer's disposal and carrying out his activity or duties, or receiving relevant training may be added to.
Automatic Exclusion	N/A
Reference Period	N/A
Exclusions & Modifications	May add to definition by RA (2)
Compensatory Rests	N/A

AT A GLANCE GUIDE TO THE WORKING TIME REGULATIONS 1998 (cont.)

48 hours working week (Regulations 4 and 5)	
Effect of Regulation	Working time in the reference period shall not exceed 48 hours subject to automatic exclusions and agreement to exclude (4(1)).
	Employer is to take all reasonable steps in keeping with the need to protect the health and safety of workers to ensure that (1) is complied with (4(2)).
Automatic Exclusion	1. Excluded Sectors (18) 2. Domestic Servants (19) 3. Unmeasuredworking time (20)
Reference Period	1. Average worked in 17 weeks (4(3)b). 2. If worked less than 17 weeks then average of period worked (4(4)). 3. Where Reg 21 special cases the period is 26 weeks (4(5)).
Exclusions & Modifications	1. Employee may agree to work in excess by NCWA (5(1)). 2. Employee may give 7 days notice to terminate agreement to work in excess. By NCBA the notice period may be extended to 3 months 5(2)) 3. May agree 17 weeks to be successive rather than rolling by RA (4(3)(a)) 4. Reference period may be extended to 52 weeks under Reg 23 by CA or WA.
Compensatory Rests	N/A

AT A GLANCE GUIDE TO THE WORKING TIME REGULATIONS 1998 (cont.)

Night Workers: average hours not to exceed 8 in any 24 hour period: Regulation 6	
Effect of Regulation	Normal hours of work in any reference period that is applicable shall not exceed average of 8 in any 24 hours (6(1)). Employer is to take all reasonable steps in keeping with the need to protect the health and safety of workers to ensure that the limit in (1) is complied with (6(2)).
Automatic Exclusion	1. Excluded Sectors (18) 2. Domestic Servants (19) 3. Unmeasured Working time (20) 4. Special cases (21)
Reference Period	1. 17 weeks (6(3)(b)). 2. If worked less than 17 weeks then average of period worked (6(4)).
Exclusions & Modifications	1. 17 week period may be successive by RA (6(3)(a)). 2. Definition of night time may be defined by RA. 3. CA, WA may modify or exclude or define number of hours to be a night worker (r 23).
Compensatory Rests	N/A

AT A GLANCE GUIDE TO THE WORKING TIME REGULATIONS 1998 (cont.)

Night work where there are special hazards or heavy physical or mental strain	
Effect of Regulation	An employer shall ensure that no nightworker whose work involves special hazards or heavy physical or mental strain works for more than 8 hours in any 24 hour period during which he performs nightwork (6(7)).
Automatic Exclusion	1. Excluded Sectors 2. Domestic Servants 3. Unmeasured Working time 4. Special cases
Reference Period	No reference period
Exclusions & Modifications	As above + definition of hazards or heavy physical or mental strain may be defined in CA, WA (6(8)).
Compensatory Rests	N/A

Night work where there is a right to a health assessment before transfer to night work	
Effect of Regulation	A worker cannot be assigned to nightwork unless the worker has had an opportunity of a free health assessment or one has already been undertaken and there is no reason to believe it is no longer valid and the employer ensures there are free health assessments at regular intervals (7(1)).
Automatic Exclusion	1. Excluded Sectors except for young workers (7(2)). 2. Domestic Servants (includes young workers).
Reference Period	No reference period
Exclusions & Modifications	Cannot exclude or modify this provision.
Compensatory Rests	N/A

AT A GLANCE GUIDE TO THE WORKING TIME REGULATIONS 1998 (cont.)

Night work where there is a duty to transfer to suitable day work for health reasons	
Effect of Regulation	Where a registered medical practitioner has advised that a nightworker is suffering health problems connected with night work and it is possible to transfer to suitable work so the worker will cease to be a nightworker he will transferred accordingly (7(6)).
Automatic Exclusion	1. Excluded Sectors 2. Domestic Servants
Reference Period	No reference period
Exclusions & Modifications	N/A
Compensatory Rests	N/A

Night work: duty to provide for adequate breaks	
Effect of Regulation	Where the work pattern is such as to put the health and safety of the employee at risk, in particular because the work rate is monotonous or the work rate is predetermined the employer shall ensure that the worker is given adequate rest breaks (8).
Automatic Exclusion	1. Excluded Sectors 2. Domestic Servants
Reference Period	No reference period
Exclusions & Modifications	There is no power to exclude or modify this provision.
Compensatory Rests	N/A

AT A GLANCE GUIDE TO THE WORKING TIME REGULATIONS 1998 (cont.)

Daily rest periods of 11 hours in each 24 hour period: Regulation 10(1)	
Effect of Regulation	Adult worker is entitled to a rest period of 11 consecutive hours in each 24 hour period during which he works (10(1)).
Automatic Exclusion	1. Excluded Sectors (for young workers see below). 2. Unmeasured working time (not young workers). 3. Special cases (not young workers). 4. Adult shift workers, changing shifts where he cannot take a daily rest period between the end of one shift and the start of another (r. 22(1)(a)) 5. Minimum period may be interrupted in the case of activities split up over the day or of short duration (10(3)).
Reference Period	No reference period
Exclusions & Modifications	CA,WA may modify or exclude except for young workers (23).
Compensatory Rests	Where a CA or WA excludes or modifies and the worker works through what would be a rest period the employer: 1. shall wherever possible allow him to take an equivalent period of compensatory rest; 2. in exceptional cases where it is not possible, for objective reasons, to grant such a period of rest, afford such protection as may be appropriate to safeguard the worker's health and safety (24).

AT A GLANCE GUIDE TO THE WORKING TIME REGULATIONS 1998 (cont.)

Daily rest period for young workers: Regulation 10(2)	
Effect of Regulation	A young worker is entitled to a rest period of 12 consecutive hours in each period of 24 hours (10(2)).
Automatic Exclusion	Minimum period may be interrupted in the case of activities split up over the day or of short duration (10(3) 22(1)(c)).
Reference Period	No reference period
Exclusions & Modifications	10(2) will not apply where: 1. no adult worker is available; 2. work is occasioned by an occurrence due to unusual and unforseen circumstances beyond the employer's control or exceptional events, the consequences of which cold not have been avoided with the exercise of all due care by the employer and is of a temporary nature and must be performed immediately (27).
Compensatory Rests	Where the young employer is required to work during a period which would otherwise be a rest period, his employer shall allow him to take an equivalent period of compensatory rest within the following three weeks (27(2).

AT A GLANCE GUIDE TO THE WORKING TIME REGULATIONS 1998 (cont.)

Weekly rest period of 24 hours in each 7 day period: Regulation 11	
Effect of Regulation	An adult worker is entitled to not less than 24 hours in each 7 day period (11(1)). This does not include reg 10(1) rest periods unless justified by objective or technical reasons or reasons relating to the organisation of work (11(7)).
Automatic Exclusion	1. Excluded Sectors (except young workers) 2. Unmeasured working time 3. Special cases (except young workers) 4. Adult shift workers changing shift and not a weekly rest period between the end of one shift and the start of another (22(1)(b). 5. Adult workers whose work is split up over the day (22(1)(c).
Reference Period	No reference period
Exclusions & Modifications	1. Employer can determine 2 periods of 24 hours in each 14 day period or 1 period of 48 hours in each 14 day period (11(2)). 2. RA may determine when each period of 7 or 14 days is to begin (11(4)(5)(6)). 3. CA, WA may modify or exclude (23).
Compensatory Rests	N/A

AT A GLANCE GUIDE TO THE WORKING TIME REGULATIONS 1998 (cont.)

Weekly rest period for young workers: Regulation 11(3)	
Effect of Regulation	A young worker is entitled to a rest period of not less than 48 hours in each 7 day rest period (11(3)).
Automatic Exclusion	N/A
Reference Period	No reference period
Exclusions & Modifications	The minimum period may be interrupted in the case of activities involving short periods of work that are split up over the day or are of short duration or where it is justified by technical or organisational reasons but not to less than 36 consecutive hours (11(8)).
Compensatory Rests	Where the young worker is required to work during a period which would otherwise be a rest period, his employer shall allow him to take an equivalent period of compensatory rest within the following three weeks (27(2)). He shall be allowed such a period of compensatory rest (25(3)).

AT A GLANCE GUIDE TO THE WORKING TIME REGULATIONS 1998 (cont.)

Rest breaks of 20 minutes in each 6 hour period: Regulation 12	
Effect of Regulation	Where an adult worker's working time is more than 6 hours he is entitled to a rest break of 20 minutes, away from a workstation if he as one (12(1),(3)) — subject to 12(2).
Automatic Exclusion	1. Excluded Sectors (except young workers) 2. Unmeasured working time (except young workers) 3. Special cases (except young workers)
Reference Period	N/A
Exclusions & Modifications	The details of a rest break, duration and terms on which granted may be contained in a CA, WA.(12(2) CA,WA may exclude or modify (23).
Compensatory Rests	Where a CA or WA excludes or modifies and the worker works through what would be a rest break the employer: 1. shall wherever possible allow him to take an equivalent period of compensatory rest; 2. in exceptional cases where it is not possible, for objective reasons, to grant such a period of rest, afford such protection as may be appropriate to safeguard the worker's health and safety (24).

AT A GLANCE GUIDE TO THE WORKING TIME REGULATIONS 1998 (cont.)

Rest Breaks of 30 minutes in each 6 hour period for young workers: Regulation 12(4)	
Effect of Regulation	Where a young worker's daily working time is more than four and a half hours he shall be entitled to a rest break of 30 minutes which shall be consecutive possible and he shall be entitled to spend it is away from his workstation (12(4)).
Automatic Exclusion	None
Reference Period	No reference period
Exclusions & Modifications	1. Where a young worker is employed by more than one employer his daily working time shall be determined by aggregating the number of hours worked for each employer (12(5)). 2. 12(4) will not apply where: (1) no adult worker is available; (2) work is occasioned by an occurrence due to unusual and unforseen circumstances beyond the employer's control or exceptional events, the consequences of which cold not have been avoided with the exercise of all due care by the employer and is or a temporary nature and must be performed immediately (27)
Compensatory Rests	N/A

OTHER ISSUES

Varying Hours of Work

We have seen that, in the absence of an express term, a unilateral variation of terms is likely to be a repudiatory breach of contract. This is the position where it is sought to change working hours.

- **Risk Management Services (Chiltern) Limited v Shrimpton** [EAT 803/77]. The employee applied for a day job as a security guard. After certain problems at work the company decided to put him on night work, as he would be supervised. The EAT held that the ET was entitled to find that this amounted to a constructive dismissal on the basis that the contract was for a day job only.
- **Brechin Bros v Kenneavy & Strang** [EAT 373 & 374/82]. The employees were given written statements which provided that their hours of work were as set out on a notice board and that any variation would be similarly exhibited. The EAT held that this provision did not have any meaning and that any power to vary a 20 hour week within the framework of 48 hours must be "unequivocally contained in the contract of employment". This was not done so that there was a fundamental breach of contract when the cmployer sought to change the hours.

COMMENTARY ON THE PRECEDENTS

D1: Normal hours

Precedents D 1.1 to D1.3 contain standard provisions relating to hours of work, with a reservation in each case that the employer has the ability to vary the hours of work to meet its business requirements. These precedents assume that the employee is not expected to work more than a 48 hour week. Regard should be had to **D8.1** if this is to be the position. Without the power to vary the hours of work, there is likely to be a breach of contract should hours be altered without consent.

D2: Overtime

Overtime may be obligatory so that the employee has a contractual right to payment. In certain cases some degree of flexibility may be required and the provisions of the Working Time Regulations may need to be considered in so far as they relate to unmeasured time. Where overtime is part of the employee's normal working hours this will have an impact upon calculations for the purposes of holiday under the Working Time Regulations or for the purposes of a redundancy payment.

Examples of cases involving express and implied terms:

Express terms

- In **Pearson & Workman v William Jones Limited** [1967] ITR 471 the appellants were paid a redundancy payment based upon a 40 hour week. They had a clause incorporated into their contracts which provided that

  > "The Federation and Trades Unions agree that systematic overtime is deprecated as a method of production, and that when overtime is necessary the following provisions shall apply, namely: No union workman shall be required to work more than 30 hours overtime in any four weeks after full shop hours have been worked...It is agreed that employers have the right to decide when overtime is necessary, the work people or their representatives being entitled to bring forward...any cases of overtime they desire discussed...".

  The Divisional Court held that the overtime was permissive and not compulsory so that the employees were entitled to redundancy based upon a 40 hour week.

- **Martin v Solus Schall** [1979] IRLR 7. Mr Martin's contract stated that "you will be expected to work such overtime as is necessary to ensure continuity of service." He was dismissed when he refused to work overtime. The EAT held that the document he had signed implies that he had accepted the need to work such overtime as was necessary to ensure continuity of service so that this was a contractual obligation.

Implied terms

- **Darlington Forge Limited v Sutton** [1968] ITR 196. The Respondent was a furnace man whose statement provided that he work 40 hours per week, though he worked more to cover for other staff. The Divisional Court held that he was only entitled to a redundancy payment based on 40 hours as there was no term in his contract that he work such overtime as was necessary.

- **Horrigan v Lewisham Council** [1978] ICR 15. Where the employee was employed as a driver on a contract that stipulated 40 hours a week, but regularly worked overtime for which he was paid and there was an agreement that he would not be pressed if he had a specific reason for not wishing to work late on a particular day, there was no implied term, to give business efficacy to the contract, that he must work sufficient overtime to complete his rounds. This was so even though he had worked overtime in the past.

- **Lake v Essex County Council** [1979] ICR 577; IRLR 241 (See WTR Reg 20). Ms Lake was a part time teacher, on duty for 19 hours 25 minutes, of which there were three hours forty minutes when she was not teaching. She was to undertake marking and preparation during these sessions but would spend several hours a week preparing classes at home. At the time she could only succeed in an unfair dismissal claim if she had 21 hours a week service. The Court of Appeal held that the extra hours she worked were voluntary and were so unpredictable that they could not be regarded as contractual. "If she chose to do more, it is was a voluntary act on her part outside her contractual obligations."
- **Ali v Christian Salvesen Food Services Limited** [1997] ICR 25; IRLR 17. Mr Ali and four others had an annualised hours agreement incorporated into their contracts through a collective agreement, whereby they were paid for a 40 hour week and, at the end of the pay year, would be paid overtime if they had worked for more than 1,824 hours in the year. They were made redundant after six months before the 1,824 threshold was reached. The Court of Appeal held that there was no scope to imply a term that the employees would be paid overtime where the employee had not worked more than the annual hours figure but had worked more than the weekly hours. The collective agreement had not provided for this contingency and to deal with every eventuality would have required an immense degree of elaboration.

Precedents D 2.1 to D2.4 are different examples of overtime precedents. The first three precedents make it clear that overtime will not normally be paid as the employee will be expected to manage his job within his normal working hours. These precedents are for more senior staff where some degree of flexibility can expected. The fourth precedent is more suitable for those on set hours such as factory workers who will expected to be paid for any extra hours that they put in.

D3: Flexitime
D3 contains a suggested precedent for flexitime. It may be that the employer will wish to make it clear that flexitime is not a contractual right in order that the system may be abolished if the employer finds that is is being abused by employees or is not conducive to the best interests of the business.

D4: Timekeeping

D.4 contains a precedent for timekeeping/clocking in procedures that one would expect to find in the factory environment and other work environments where set hours are of importance. Note the importance of specifying that it is gross misconduct to tamper with clocks or to clock in for any other person. In **Dalton v Burton's Gold Medal Biscuits Limited** [1974] IRLR 45, the dismissal of an employee after twenty years' service was fair where he falsified a fellow worker's clock card. He was fully aware of the fact that such conduct would warrant dismissal.

D5/6: Shiftworkers/Factory workers

Precedents D5 and D6 contain a set of precedents for shiftworkers and/or factory workers.

D5 deals with the requirements to carry out shiftworking. Note the requirements of the Working Time Regulations in this respect.

D6.1 contains an alternative shiftworking precedent.

An alternative clocking in procedure to D4 is contained at **D6.2.**

It is common for factories to have a closure period during the year and **D6.3** sets out the entitlement of the employer to require the employee to take holiday during this period.

D6.4 contains important terms relating to the right to lay off and the importance of having an express term is shown by the cases set out below.

Express Terms
There may be an express term giving a right to lay off as with **Precedent D6.4.** Where there is such a right two issues may arise:

1. **The right to a guaranteed payment**
    By section 28 of the ERA 1996 there is a right to a guaranteed payment where there is a diminution in the requirements of the employer's business for work of the kind that the employee is required to do or any other occurrence affecting the normal working of the employer's business in relation to work of the kind that the employee is employed to do. Where the worker can turn down work then he is not entitled to a guarantee payment (**Mailway (Southern) Limited v Willsher** [1978] ICR 511). There are also exclusions in respect of trade disputes or where there has been an offer of suitable alternative work (s.29 ERA 1996). The guarantee payment cannot exceed five days in any three months and any

contractual payments both go to offset the guarantee payment and are counted in calculating the number of workless days in any three months (**Cartright v G Clancy Limited** [1983] ICR 552).

2. **Redundancy by reason of lay off or short time working**

In cases where the employee is considered to be laid off because he receives no pay of any kind or there is no work for him to do during that week (section 147 ERA 1996) or where the employee is on short time because he receives less that half a week's pay (section 147(2) ERA 1996):

— A redundancy payment may be claimed where he gives notice in writing of his intention to claim and the claim is submitted within four weeks of a continuous period of lay off or short work of four weeks' duration or the end of the period of six weeks' lay off or short time out of thirteen weeks (where not more than three weeks were consecutive) (section 148 ERA 1996).

— Where notice of intention has been given, he will not be entitled to a redundancy payment if it was reasonably to be expected that he would, not later than four weeks after service, enter into a period of employment of not less than thirteen weeks during which he would not be laid off or kept on short time (section 152(1) ERA 1996). However, the employer cannot take advantage of this provision unless he has, within seven days after service of the notice of intention, served a counter notice that he will contest liability to make payment (section 152(1)(b)) and a tribunal may then be asked to determine whether he is entitled to a payment (section 149 ERA 1996).

The contract must then be terminated by the employee giving the contractual period of notice or one week's notice:

- Where no counternotice has been served within seven days after the notice of intention to claim, then three weeks after the end of those seven days;
- Where a counternotice has been served in seven days after the notice of intention to claim, then three weeks after the end of those seven days;
- Where a counternotice has been served in seven days but then withdrawn, three weeks after service of the notice of withdrawal;
- Where a counternotice has been served and not withdrawn and the matter is referred to a tribunal, three weeks after the tribunal has notified to the employee its decision on the reference (section 140,141,156,157 ERA 1996 in particular).

It should be noted that there are various exclusions from the right to claim (see section 141, 156).

Implied Terms

Where there is no express term, there may still be a right to lay off by reason of custom and practice, as the following cases illustrate.

- **Devonald v Rosser & Sons** [1906] 2 KB 728. The employer alleged that they were entitled to lay off Mr Devonald when there were no profitable orders so that the works were closed. The Court of Appeal held that, in order for such a term to be implied, it must be certain and notorious which was not the case here.

- **Browning v Crumlin Valley Collieries Limited** [1926] 1 KB 522. Men were temporarily laid off whilst the mine where they worked was made safe. Greer J held that it is it is was an implied term to give business efficacy to the contract that where the mine had to be closed, through no fault of the employers, the risks would be shared so that the employers would lose production and the employees lost their wages.

- **Jones v Harry Sherman Limited** [1969] ITR 63. In order for there to be an implied term giving a right to lay off the custom must be reasonable, certain and notorious so that, where the employee knew nothing of it and it was unclear how it would operate there was no such implied term.

- **Puttick v John Wright & Sons Limited** [1972] ICR 457. Mr Puttick worked on a job by job basis for 23 years. Between jobs he would do no work or may carry out odd jobs on the employer's premises. He was not dismissed between jobs and, after a long period of not working, he applied for a redundancy payment. The NIRC held that there had been an implied term "empowering the employer to suspend, in the sense of to lay off temporarily, the employee."

- **Waine v Oliver (Plant Hire) Limited** [1977] IRLR 434. Mr Waine had been absent for six months and when he was reported back was told that there was no work for him on the Monday and to report on Wednesday. The EAT held that a right to lay off could not be implied from this one incident and that it is was necessary to look at the custom of the trade in order to ascertain whether there was a right to lay off in the particular industry.

- **Neads v CAV Limited** [1983] IRLR 360. Setters were laid off in a department C19 because work was running low. At the time there was a dispute with an other department about machines that were being used and they had been told not to report to work unless they would work normally. A collective agreement, which was incorporated into the contracts provided that "The guarantee of employment for hourly rated manual workers ... is subject to the following conditions ... In the event of a disruption of production in a federated establishment as a result of an industrial dispute in that or any other federated establishment the operation of the period of guarantee shall be automatically suspended." Pain J held that the agreement did not apply as there was work available. There was no general right to lay off without pay. (See also **Johnson v Cross** [1977] ICR 872 on which Pain J relied.)

- **Window Centre Limited v Lees & F Lees** [EAT 742/85]. a working rule agreement provided that if work was temporarily stopped the employee was entitled to a guaranteed minimum weekly pay *in lieu* for the first week of lay off and the employer could thereafter require him to register as unemployed. The ET and EAT held that this did not give an indefinite right of lay off and that a period of four months and one of nine months were unreasonable and could not be said to be for a temporary period.

D7: Retail employment

D7 is a standard clause relating to retail employment. Note that certain procedures must be followed in relation to Sunday working, in the context of Betting Workers/Shopworkers (see Chapter 5.2 and 5.14.).

D8: Working Time

There are a number of ways in which the various requirements of the WTR may be excluded, as set out in the commentary above. The three precedents **D8.1. to 8.3** contain:

- exclusion of the 48 hour week;
- confirmation that there is a Workforce Agreement;
- a draft Workforce Agreement.

The law relating to these areas is considered earlier in this Chapter.

PART E: BASIC SALARY

Precedent E1: Salaries

1 The rate of your starting salary and the method and frequency of payment are contained in your Statement of Terms and Conditions of Employment. (Subsequent changes will be advised in writing.)

2 Salaries are subject to annual review on _____ January each year.

3 Salaries are paid monthly in arrears by credit transfer to a bank account so that the money will be available in your bank or building society accounts on the ... day of each month or on the nearest working day beforehand.

4 At or before the time when your salary is paid you will be given a written itemised statement which will detail:

(a) the gross amount of salary;

(b) the amount of any variable or fixed deductions from that gross amount and the purposes for which they are made;

(c) the net amount of salary payable;

(d) where different parts of the net amount are paid different ways, the amount and method of payment of each part payment.

5 Deductions from salary are made for:

(a) National Insurance, State Pension and Income Tax where applicable, and any other deductions which are or become legally required;

(b) any Additional Voluntary Contributions to the appropriate Pension Scheme from your date of entry;

(c) any other contributions or subscriptions, such as to a Private Medical Insurance scheme, or repayments of loans such as season ticket advances, for which you have been given written authority. Requests for special deductions relating to your individual situation will be considered but the Company reserves the right to refuse such a facility.

6 A day's pay will be calculated as annual pay divided by 260. For calculating hourly rates for overtime purposes, an hour's pay is annual pay divided by 52, divided again by the number of hours worked per week.

Precedent E2: Salaries

1 Your rate of pay is as set out in your Letter of Appointment or your Written Particulars of Terms and Conditions of Employment which may be amended from time to time.

2 Your salary is paid by credit transfer monthly in arrears on _____ in twelve equal monthly amounts. If your employment terminates part way through a month your salary will be calculated on a daily basis.

3 You will receive a monthly itemised salary slip setting out your gross salary, statutory and other deductions and the net sum paid.

Precedent E3: Collective Agreements for Salaries

There is currently a collective agreement in force between the Company and _____ which covers all matters relating to pay which is negotiated from time to time with the union. Your employment is subject to this collective agreement and you are therefore bound by any agreement that is reached between the union and the Company regardless of whether you are a member of the union. You will be notified of any variations in your pay within one month of the same having been agreed with the union.

Precedent E4: Salary Reviews

Salaries are reviewed annually on ____ and any rise is awarded at the absolute discretion of the Company. Whilst the Company always endeavours to reward performance and effort it must be borne in mind that other factors have to be taken into account, including the profitability of the Company, team work and the competitiveness of the industry at the time. Salary increases will normally be announced _____ and will be notified to you in writing. [Your salary increase will remain confidential to you and the Company.]

Precedent E5: Salary Reviews

The Company has a policy of reviewing salaries based upon the contribution that the employee has made to the Company. The Company will normally consider the following matters in deciding whether there should be a salary increase for any one individual:

1) The self motivation of the employee and the contribution that has been made to the Company;
2) The current market rates and benefits in the industry. The Company prides itself on offering competitive market rates.
3) The profitability and turnover of the Company.
4) The responsibilities of the employee, including whether the employee has taken on increased responsibilities or duties.

Salaries will only be adjusted upwards.

COMMENTARY TO E:
BASIC SALARY

Agreed remuneration

The remuneration agreed between employer and employee is subject to the National Minimum Wages Act 1998.

Where no remuneration has been agreed then the court will imply a term that it be a reasonable remuneration for the services (**Way v Latilla** [1937] 3 All ER 759) and a similar approach will be taken where it is agreed a bonus will be paid but the method of assessment has not been agreed (**Powell v Braun** [1954] 1 WLR 401).

Late payment of wages may be a fundamental breach of contract but this is not necessarily so where the employee knows that salary is on the way and of the reason for late payment (**Adams v Charles Zub Associates** [1978] IRLR 551).

Varying salary and other benefits: Express Terms

In the absence of any express power in the contract, or the agreement of the employee, any unilateral change in the employee's remuneration will be in breach of contract and can be resisted by the employee. Note that it is likely to be an unlawful deduction under Part II of the Employment Rights Act 1996 to make any deduction without the express consent of the employee (See Part F4). Where the employer commits a repudiatory breach of contract by reducing the salary the employee may refuse to accept this and stand by his rights under the contract or to resign and claim constructive dismissal.

- **Managers (Holborn) Limited v Hohne** [1977] IRLR 230. The employer repudiated the contract of employment by reducing the employee's status and salary so that she was entitled to claim constructive dismissal and to a redundancy payment.
- **Miller v Hamworthy Engineering Limited** [1986] ICR 846; IRLR 461. The Court of Appeal held that the employers were not entitled to place employees on a three day week, with consequent reduction in salary without consent. It is stated that "...the defendants must show some agreed variation of the contractual terms binding upon the plaintiff".
- **Rigby v Feredo Limited** [1988] ICR 29; IRLR 516. The employer cut the wages of its employees as part of a strategy of survival. Employees of CSEU refused to accept this and continued to work as normal. The House of Lords held that, on the facts, there had been no notice of termination and the employees were entitled to work on under protest and sue on the original terms of the contract. The

claims were for the sums due under the continuing contract that had never been terminated. Lord Oliver pointed out that the employer could have chosen to terminate on notice or dismiss out of hand and face the consequences but it chose neither of these options. It continued to employ the employees week by week under contracts which entitled them to a certain level of wages.

- **Burdett-Coutts & Ors v Hertfordshire County Council** [1984] IRLR 91. The Council sent a letter which purported to reduce the salary of its school dinner ladies. The letter stated that "This letter is the formal notice of these changes in your contract of service...". The claimant brought a claim for arrears of wages and a declaration that the Council were not entitled to unilaterally vary the contracts of employment. Kenneth Jone J held that the claimants were entitled to stand and sue on the contract. The letter was not a notice of termination and offer of re-engagement but an attempt to unilaterally vary the terms which was not effective.

The Precedents

The five precedents for salaries contained at Part E are relatively straightforward. **Precedents E1** and **E2** cover the timing and means of payment and confirm that an itemised pay statement will be sent whilst **E3** deals with the position where the salary amount is governed by a collective agreement. **E4** and **E5** cover salary reviews. The following points should be noted:

- Where the employer awards pay rises to its staff there may be an implied term that the employer will not treat an employee in a manner which is arbitrary, capricious or inequitable. In **F C Gardner Limited v Beresford** [1978] IRLR 63, the employee had not been given a pay rise for two years whereas other staff had received one. She resigned and claimed constructive dismissal. The EAT held that there was such an implied term, stating:

  "if there was evidence to support the finding, that the employers were deliberately singling her out for special treatment inferior to that given to everybody else and they were doing it is arbitrarily, capriciously or inequitably, if they did victimise in that sense, one could see it is might well lead the tribunal to say that she had a good claim..."

  See also **Deniet & Son Limited v Eagle** [EAT 409/79] where the implied duty of trust and confidence was breached by the employer when the employee was not given a pay rise after a quarrel with a director and other employees were awarded a rise.

PART F: REMUNERATION AND BENEFITS OTHER THAN SALARY

Precedent F1: Overtime

You will be entitled to be paid overtime for the hours you work in addition to your normal working hours. Overtime will be paid on an hourly basis at the rate of time and a half. For bank holidays and Sundays it will be paid at the rate of double time at the discretion of the Company. The Company reserves the right to vary overtime rates.

F2: Bonus

PRECEDENT F2.1: BONUS

The Company may award an annual bonus and if you are entitled to such bonus it will have been specified in your Letter of Appointment. The bonus payment is entirely discretionary and the fact that you may have been paid a bonus in previous years does not mean that you are entitled or can have an expectation that you will get a bonus in any particular year. Bonuses are intended to reward exceptional effort which has increased the profitability of the Company. The size and nature of the bonus is at the absolute discretion of the Company.

PRECEDENT F2.2: BONUS

The Company has a discretionary bonus scheme which applies to management and which depends on the Company's turnover as set out the rules of the scheme. If you are entitled to participate in the scheme this will have been set out in your Letter of Appointment. The payment of bonus depends upon the Company attaining certain targets. However, it must be emphasised that the scheme is entirely discretionary and you are not entitled as a matter of contract or expectation to payment under such scheme.

Precedent F3: Commission

In addition to your basic salary you are entitled to commission on orders as set out in your Letter of Appointment. Commission is only payable on monies received in respect of any order and will be paid in the monthly salary payment following clearance of an order through the Company's bank accounts.

F4: Deductions from Salary

PRECEDENT F4.1: DEDUCTIONS FROM SALARY

The Company will be entitled:
1) At any time to deduct by way of reimbursement from your salary any overpayment of wages or expenses that have been paid to you for whatever reason.
2) Upon the termination of your employment to make any such deduction, including deduction in respect of holiday, loans or other advances that have been made to you and which represent an overpayment at the date of the termination of your employment.

PRECEDENT F4.2: DEDUCTIONS FROM PAY IN RETAIL EMPLOYMENT

The Company will be entitled at any time during employment or upon termination of employment to deduct from your wages any cash shortages or stock deficiencies for which you were responsible and any such deduction will be made in accordance with the provisions relating to retail employment contained in Part II of the Employment Rights Act 1996.

F5: Pensions

PRECEDENT F5.1: COMPANY PENSION SCHEME

1 You are entitled to join the Company's Pension Scheme
and will be subject to the rules of that scheme as are in
force from time to time. The Pension scheme may be
amended or withdrawn by the Company at any time.

2 A contracting out certificate under the Pensions Schemes
Act 1993 is [not] in force in respect of your employment.

3 The rules of the scheme provide that you may be a member
if:
1) you are a permanent employee of the Company;
2) you are aged between _____ and _____ years old;
3) you have completed at least _____ years service with
the Company.

4 Copies of the scheme are available for inspection at
_____.

5 You are entitled to make additional voluntary
contributions to the Scheme to increase your pension.
Advice about this may be obtained from _____.

PRECEDENT F5.2: EMPLOYER CONTRIBUTIONS TO PERSONAL PENSION SCHEME

If you have your own personal pension plan the Company
is prepared to contribute to it at rates which may be
obtained from _____. [The Company will pay _____ per
annum to a personal pension scheme approved by the
Inland Revenue. There is no pension scheme arising from
your employment with the Company.]

PRECEDENT F5.3: GROUP PERSONAL PENSION SCHEME

There is a group pension scheme and you are entitled, if
you so wish, to join the scheme. Contributions to the
scheme will be deducted from your salary and you must
inform _____ of the sum that you wish to be deducted from
your salary and paid into the scheme. The Company will

also pay a percentage into the scheme. These sums are subject to maximums permitted by the Inland Revenue and details may be obtained from _____.

F6: Medical Insurance

PRECEDENT F6.1: PRIVATE MEDICAL HEALTH INSURANCE

Private Medical Health Insurance is available for all employees other than employees who are on probation or are temporary. The scheme may be extended to family members for an additional contribution. Full details of the scheme may be obtained from _____.

Precedent F7: Share Schemes

PRECEDENT F7.1: APPROVED EMPLOYEE SHARE SCHEMES

There is an employee share scheme for which you will be eligible if this was stated in your Letter of Appointment. The membership of the scheme is in accordance with the Trust Deeds and Rules of the scheme for the time being in force.

Precedent F8: Loans

PRECEDENT F8.1: EDUCATIONAL LOANS

F8.1.1   The Company may, at its discretion, give an interest free loan to assist you in a course of study for approved professional qualifications that relate to your job and you may obtain information about what courses are approved from _____.

F8.1.2   However, you should note that the Company will only grant such loan on the basis that you expressly agree that any sums advanced will be repaid if you fail to complete the course without sufficient justification or you leave the

Company's employment either during the course or within ____ months of completing the course. The Company may also recover any sums advanced if you have been dismissed for gross misconduct.

PRECEDENT F8.2: SEASON TICKET LOANS

The Company will be prepared, at its discretion, to grant you an interest free season ticket loan for an annual season ticket on the following conditions:
1) The loan will be repayable by deductions from your salary on a monthly basis;
2) The loan will be repaid before the season ticket expires or is given up;
3) You will repay the balance of the loan in full if you leave the company's employment;
4) You will sign a document consenting to deductions being made before any loan is advanced to you.

F9: Cars

PRECEDENT F9.1: CAR/CAR ALLOWANCE

1 Your letter of Appointment set out the basis on which the Company will provide you with vehicle of a make and model determined by reference to the Company's Car Policy in effect from time to time for both business and private use.

2 If your Letter of Appointment so provided the Company will pay for all expenses of the vehicle save for private petrol and any additional costs that you incur in using the vehicle for private purposes.

3 The Company will replace the vehicle as provided for in its Car Policy and you agree that you will run the vehicle in accordance with the car policy.

4 Only employees who are aged over 21 (for insurance reasons) and who have a valid licence may drive any Company vehicle. Failure to comply with this requirement could lead to police prosecution as the driver will be uninsured and it will lead to disciplinary action by the Company for misconduct.

5   Employees using Company vehicles must not carry any unauthorised passengers.

PRECEDENT F9.2: PROVISION OF A VEHICLE

1   If you are provided with a vehicle by the Company it will be subject to you complying with the conditions set out hereafter.

2   **Care of vehicle:** You are responsible for ensuring that the vehicle is properly looked after at all times. You may only retain the vehicle if you have a full driving licence. You have the vehicle at the discretion of the Company and it may change its procedures at any time. Vehicles are insured on a third party basis and the Company may seek to recoup any losses in the event of negligence.

3   **Nature of vehicle:** You will be entitled to a vehicle in accordance with the terms of your Letter of Appointment and the vehicle may be replaced after ____ miles or at the discretion of the Company. You have no right to a replacement.

4   **Car documents:** The Company will retain all documents relating to the registration of the vehicle. You are responsible for ensuring that the car has an MOT certificate and a valid licence disc.

5   **Personal Use:** Your spouse may use the vehicle provided that he/she has a valid licence. Other members of staff may use it provided that they have a licence and are covered by the Company's insurance scheme.

6   **Upkeep:** You are responsible for ensuring that the car is properly maintained and serviced and that the car is in roadworthy condition. The Company will bear the cost of repairs and service provided that they are not caused by your negligence or default.

7   **Motoring offences:** You are responsible for the payment of any fines incurred as a result of a motoring offence, including parking fines. You must notify the Company of any serious offence that may result in the loss of your licence or cause the Company any loss.

8   **Tax:** You agree to bear any tax liability in respect of the use of the vehicle.

9   **Termination of employment:** Should your employment terminate for whatever reason, you agree that you will immediately return your vehicle and deliver up the keys to _____.

10 **Alternative allowance:** You may be entitled to an allowance as an alternative to the provision of a Company vehicle and should contact _____ for details of the same.

Precedent F10: Luncheon Vouchers

Luncheon vouchers are provided by the Company if this was set out in your Letter of Appointment. They are issued at the rate of _____ per day. Vouchers are a taxable benefit and must be declared on your tax return. Vouchers are provided at the Company's discretion and may be withdrawn at any time.

Precedent F11: Permanent Health Insurance

The Company operates a permanent health insurance scheme of which you are eligible to be a member. The Scheme is in the absolute discretion of the Company and may be discontinued at any time. You should also note that it is the decision of the insurer as to whether you qualify for permanent health benefits under the Scheme and the Company has no responsibility or liability for decisions made by the insurer. You are referred to the rules of the Scheme which sets out eligibility.

COMMENTARY TO F:
REMUNERATION AND BENEFITS OTHER THAN SALARY

There are a wide range of benefits that may be available to employees other than salary, whether by way of cash payments or benefits in kind, with different tax consequences and consequences should there be a dismissal (See Duggan on *Wrongful Dismissal, Law Practice and Precedents*). Fringe benefits are often an important part of the employee's remuneration package so that withdrawal of the same may amount to a fundamental breach of contract or found a claim for constructive dismissal. In **McColl v Gael Motors (Dumbarton) Limited** [EAT 63/80] the employee was given the use of a company car to travel to and from work and the company did not object to her using it at weekends. She also received a petrol allowance. When insurance terms were re-negotiated she was no longer able to use the car at weekends. She alleged constructive dismissal. The EAT stated that the withdrawal of a fringe benefit could be of sufficient materiality to amount to a dismissal. In this case, however, the essential element was transport to and from work which was not affected in any way by the proposed variation.

Each of the benefits set out in the Precedents above will be reviewed briefly.

F1: Overtime
A precedent is contained at **F1**. Further precedents can be found at **D2**.

F2: Bonus
Bonus is likely to be expressed to be discretionary and based upon the profitability or turnover of the Company or upon the effort of the individual employee. Although expressed to be discretionary caution should be exercised in this respect as the payment of bonus may become a 'legitimate expectation'. The two precedents in **F2** state that the payment of bonus is entirely discretionary. However, in **Kent Management Services Limited v Butterfield** [1972] ICR 272; IRLR 394, it was held that a commission scheme that was expressed to be non contractual nevertheless gave rise to a claim for deduction from wages as there was a legitimate expectation that the employee would be paid. (See also **Clark v Nomura International PLC** [2000] IRLR 766 — which formulates how discretion should in any event be exercised as a matter of contract law.)

Where the terms of a bonus scheme are contained in a collective agreement they will remain in force if incorporated into the contract, even if the collective agreement is terminated (**Robertson v British Gas Corporation** [1983] ICR 351).

Implied Terms

In the absence of express terms the implied terms may still have a part to play as the following cases show:

- **Frischers Limited v Taylor** [EAT 386/79]. Where a week's wages had been paid as a Christmas bonus for several years this consistent conduct made it is an implied term that the bonus would be paid as part of the employee's remuneration.

- **Noble Enterprises v Lieberum** [EAT 67/98] *IDS Brief* 623 BP provided money to participating companies, which provided labour for BP explorations, to be paid to employees as an incentive bonus scheme. The companies decided what proportion of the monies should be paid to its employees. When Mr Lieberum resigned on 21st January 1997 he was not paid a bonus. The employer argued that it was discretionary and was, in any event, not payable if the employee was not employed on 30th January of each year. The EAT held that the scheme was contractual in that, once BP had paid monies to the company, the scheme became contractually operative, the consideration from the employee being that a certain standard was achieved. Moreover, there was no evidence that the requirement of being employed at a certain date had ever been drawn to the attention of the employee.

- In **Pendragon PLC v Jackson** [EAT 108/97] *IDS Brief* 622 it was held that the fact that the employers had inserted a term into a share incentive scheme stating that it was non contractual was an indication that the employer did not intend the scheme to create legal relations so that there was no legally binding obligation to pay out under the scheme.

- It may be a breach of an implied term to provide work to refuse to allow an employee to work a shift where there is a duty so that the employee can earn a shift premium or overtime (**Langston v AUEW & Anor (No 2)** [1974] ICR 510; IRLR 182).

F3: Commission

For many employees commission may be an important part of remuneration and, in some case, the only remuneration (see **5.15** for a Salesman's contract). Again in the absence of express terms implied terms are likely to play an important part.

Implied terms

Where the employee earns part of his remuneration by way of commission there may be an implied term on the part of the employer that the employee be provided with work so that a suspension on basic salary can be a repudiatory breach of contract. In **Re Rubel Bronze & Metal Co Limited**

and Vos [1918] 1 KB 315 the employee was suspended during an investigation into allegations of inefficiency on his part. McCardie J held that where an employee is paid by way of commission he must be given an opportunity to earn it.

Where an employee receives advance commission and the employment terminates, or the monies upon which the commission was paid is not forthcoming for some reason, then there will be an implied term that the employee will account for the excess (**Bronester Limited v Priddle** [1961] 1 WLR 1294). The employee will be liable for any secret profits that he has earned during employment, even if they would not have been earned by the employer (**Boston Deep Sea Fishing & Ice Co Limited v Ansell** [1988] 39 ChD 339).

As stated in **F3** it is should be made clear that commission will only be payable in respect of payments actually received rather than orders placed. This will have the effect that sums are likely to remain due after the employee has left the employment of the employer and some consideration may be given as to whether there should be a provision whereby any sums received may be set off against any monies that may be owed by the employee.

F4: Deductions from Salary

Part II of the Employment Rights Act 1996 (previously the Wages Act 1986), sections 13 to 27 sets out rights not to suffer unauthorised deductions from wages and there are specific provisions relating to retail employment. **Precedent F4** sets out two clauses which permit the employer to deduct certain sums from wages. However, these clauses must be incorporated into the contract if they are to be effective (See **5.14** Shop workers). The provisions of the ERA 1996 will be here summarised.

1. Right not to suffer unauthorised deductions

By section 13 of the ERA an employer may not make a deduction from wages of a worker employed by him unless:

- the deduction is required or authorised to be made by virtue of a statutory provision or a relevant provision of the worker's contract (which means a provision on a contract comprised in one or more written terms given before the deduction or the existence and effect of which has been previously notified in writing); or
- the worker has previously signified in writing his agreement or consent to the making of the deduction.

If there is a variation of the contract then a deduction will not be authorised until the variation takes effect (13(5)) nor will an agreement or consent authorise making the deduction on account of the conduct of any worker before the agreement or consent takes effect (13(6)).

Where the total amount of wages payable is less than the amount properly payable on that occasion the amount of the deficiency is treated as deduction (13(2)) but this does not apply to an error of computation (13(4)).

2. Wages and excepted deductions

By section 14, section 13 does not apply to a deduction where:
- it relates to the reimbursement of an overpayment of wages;
- it relates to an overpayment in respect of expenses incurred by the worker in carrying out his employment;
- it relates to a deduction in consequence of any disciplinary proceedings if the proceedings were held by reason of a statutory provision;
- it relates to a deduction by reason of a statutory requirement to pay amounts over to a local authority;
- it relates to arrangements which have been established in accordance with the contract, the inclusion of which the worker has signified his agreement or consent in writing or with the prior agreement or consent of the worker in writing;
- it is made where the worker has taken part in a strike or other industrial action;
- it is made with proper agreement or consent where there is an order of a court that money be paid to the employer.

3. Payments to the employer and excepted payments

As with deductions, there is protection for workers in relation to payments that may otherwise have to be made. By section 15:
- an employer may not receive a payment from a worker unless the payment is required or authorised to be made by virtue of a statutory provision or a relevant provision of a worker's contract; or
- the worker has previously signified in writing his agreement or consent to the making of the payment.

The section contains the same restrictions in relation to variations or modifications as section 13.

Payments are, by section 16, excepted where:
- it relates to the reimbursement of an overpayment of wages;
- it relates to an overpayment in respect of expenses incurred by the worker in carrying out his employment;

- it relates to a deduction in consequence of any disciplinary proceedings if the proceedings were held by reason of a statutory provision;
- it is made where the worker has taken part in a strike or other industrial action;
- it is made where there is an order of a court that money be paid to the employer.

Retail Employment: Restrictions on Deductions

There are special protections for retail workers in sections 17 to 22 of the ERA. "Retail transactions" mean the sale or supply of goods, or the supply of services, including financial services, and "retail employment" means employment involving:

- the carrying out by the worker of retail transactions directly with members of the public or with fellow workers or other individuals in their personal capacities;
- the collection by the worker of amounts payable in connection with retail transactions carried out by other persons directly with members of the public or fellow workers or other individuals in their personal capacities.

The protection applies to deductions or payments due to cash shortages which cover deficits arising in relation to amounts received in connection with retail transactions and to stock deficiencies arising in the course of such transactions, whether or not a deduction of payment is made on account of dishonesty or any other event in respect of which the worker had any contractual liability.

By section 18(1) where the employer of a worker employed in retail employment in accordance with the powers under section 13 makes on account of one or more cash shortages or stock deficiencies a deduction or deductions from wages payable to the worker on a pay day, the amount shall not exceed one tenth of the wages payable on that pay day. Any deduction must be made in any event within 12 months of when the shortage or deficiency was established or ought reasonably to have been established (18(3)). Where the wages are determined by reference to shortages or deficiencies this will be treated as a deduction so that sections 13 and 18 apply.

There are similar protections for payment contained in section 20. By section 20 the worker should have first been notified in writing of the total amount and required to pay by means of a demand, not earlier than the first pay day following the date when the worker was notified and not later than 12 months after discovery of the shortage. By section 21 the amount to be paid shall not exceed one tenth.

Where the worker receives a final instalment of wages there are no restrictions on the amount of any deduction or payments (section 22). This means that, provided section 13 applies, the one tenth rule is not applicable to a final payment on termination.

Enforcement
A worker may apply to the tribunal where there has been an unauthorised deduction from wages (see section 23 ERA 1996).

Precedents
The two precedents at **F4** contain provisions relating to deductions from salary in relation to retail and non retail employment.

F5: Pensions
It is likely that the rules of any pension scheme will be in a separate document and the Manual or contract will merely state what entitlement the employee has and refer to the Rules of the Scheme. The precedents at **F5** adopt this approach. The employee cannot be required to join a personal or occupational pension scheme and any term to this effect is void (section 160 Pension Schemes Act 1993). It should be noted that, since the rules of the scheme are likely to change from time to time, there may be a duty on the part of the employer to tell the employee of his rights and any matters that may affect the value of his pension (see **Scally v Southern Health and Social Services Board** [1992] 1 AC and page 54 above). However, it was held by the Court of Appeal in **Outram v Academy Plastics** (CA 10.4.2000) that there was no duty owed in tort to the employee by the employer. Moreover, in **University of Nottingham v Eyett** [1999] IRLR 87, the High Court held that there was no implied contractual duty on the part of an employer to advise the employee that if he waited one month before retiring he would be entitled to an enhanced pension. The scope of the implied term still remains unclear and the prudent employer will make it clear that it accepts no contractual liability in relation to advice.

F6: Medical Insurance
This clause relates to the provision of health insurance to cover medical bills for hospital, operations, etc. and is likely to be regarded by a senior employee as an important part of the package. Consideration should be given as to whether this benefit is to cover members of the employee's family as well as the employee. It may be that the employer will also wish to have a right to

withdraw such insurance if it becomes too expensive and a clause giving the employer such a general discretion may be advisable.

F7: Share Schemes

This benefit will usually be subject to the rules of the particular scheme and the employee will need to refer to the express rules of the scheme in order ascertain when options may be exercised. Issues have arisen in the cases as to when a scheme may automatically lapse and as to the effect of termination of employment before an option is exercised. These matters will, of course, depend upon the wording of the scheme.

- In **Thompson v ASDA MFI Group PLC** [1988] IRLR 340, Mr Thompson, who was employed by a wholly owned subsidiary, Wades Limited, was given an option to subscribe for shares. The option certificate provided that the option would lapse in the event of "the option holder ceasing to be in the employment of the company or a participating subsidiary." ASDA sold all its shares in Wades Limited and wrote to Mr Thompson stating that the shares lapsed when Wades ceased to be a member of the Group. Scott J held that the shares options lapsed when the shares in Wades were sold and it is was not possible to imply any term to the effect that ASDA would not do anything to cause the option to lapse or sell off the participating subsidiaries. There was no breach of duty on the part of ASDA so that it is could not be argued that they could not take advantage of their own acts.

- **Micklefield v SAC Technology Limited** [1990] IRLR 218. Mr Micklefield had the benefit of a share option scheme of the parent company. He was entitled to six months' notice of termination of employment. The share scheme provided that the option was not exercisable until three years after grant and that if an option holder ceased to be an executive for whatever reason he would not be entitled and would be deemed to have waived any entitlement by way of compensation for loss of any rights under the scheme. On 19th February 1985 he was granted an option. On 3rd February 1988 he wrote stating that he wished to exercise the option on 19th February 1988. His contract was terminated forthwith on 12th February and he was paid *in lieu*. It is was held that he was not entitled to exercise the option as his contract had terminated before the option became exercisable. Liability was clearly excluded and the clause did not fall within section 3 of the Unfair Contract Terms Act 1977 as it is fell within the exclusion of "any contract so far as it is relates to the creation or transfer of securities or of any right or interest in securities". (Cf. **Chapman v Aberdeen Construction Group PLC** [1991] IRLR 505 for the position in Scotland).

However, where an employee is dismissed in breach of contract the employer may not be able to rely on a clause that provides that the option would lapse in the event of the employee being dismissed following disciplinary action. In **Levett v Biotrace International PLC** [1999] IRLR 375 the Court of Appeal held that an employer was not entitled to rely on its own breach in these circumstances.

F8: Loans

Where the employee is provided with training paid for by the employer or the employer pays for the employee to go on a course, there may be a term in the contract that the employee will refund part of the costs of the training if he leaves before a certain period of time. In **Neil v Strathclyde Regional Council** [1984] IRLR 14 the employee was given paid leave to go on a training course as a social worker. She signed a contract that stated she would stay in employment for two years and would repay "an amount proportionate to the unexpired service period" covering her salary and the cost of training. She resigned after fifteen months and a liquidated sum was claimed. It is was held that she was liable to repay the proportionate amount.

F9: Cars

Express Terms

The employee may be contractually entitled to a car or a car allowance. Once he has become contractually entitled it is will be a breach of contract to take away the benefit unless there is an express power to do so.

- **Knox v Down District Council** [1981] IRLR 452. The National Joint Council conditions of service provided that
  "any officer whose employing authority so resolves that it is essential in the interests of the efficient conduct of the business of the Authority that the officer shall be permitted to use his private car for the carrying out of his official duties shall be eligible for financial assistance in accordance with this scheme".
  It was further provided that the authority may on receipt of an application, subject to the terms of the scheme, authorise the grant of a loan not exceeding the purchase price. The Council turned down an application because of lack of financial resources. The Northern Ireland Court of Appeal held that there was an implied term that, once the conditions had been complied with, the applicant would receive a loan under the scheme.

- In **Keir & Williams v County Council of Hereford and Worcester** [1985] IRLR 505 the Council paid an 'essential user allowance' to certain employees under terms agreed by the National Joint Council, depending upon authorisation by the Council. The NJC Conditions defined essential users as "those whose duties are of such a nature that it is essential for them to have a motor car at their disposal when required" and casual users as "those for whom it is merely desirable that a car will be available when required". An essential user received a greater allowance than a casual user. Keir and Williams were told that their essential user allowance was to cease and that they could use a pool car and therefore would receive a casual user allowance. The Court of Appeal held that once an employee had been given authority to use his car for Council business he was entitled to an essential user allowance. The Council could not take away the essential user allowance in the case of someone who needed to use his car simply because a pool car was available.

- It is was held in **Ropaigealach v THF Hotels Limited** [EAT 180/80] that the withdrawal of free transport which only cost the employer £1 per week was not so fundamental as to amount to a breach of contract on the part of the employer. On the other hand where employees were provided with free transport in a company car over several years, at a loss in excess of £14 per week and that entailed two hours walking, such provision had become a term by custom and practice so that the employer could not withdraw the same (**Power Lines Pipes & Cables Limited v Penrice** (EAT 29.1.1987)).

F10:   LUNCHEON VOUCHERS

This is a common perk for office workers and a sample precedent is at **F10**.

F11:   HEALTH INSURANCE SCHEMES

Any express terms may be affected by implied terms as the following cases illustrate.

Implied terms

- **Aspen v Webbs Poultry & Meat Group Holdings Limited** [1996] IRLR 521. Mr Aspen was entitled to the benefit of income replacement insurance which applied from 26 weeks after incapacity and continued until death, retirement or "the date on which the group member ceases to be an eligible employee". His contract provided that the Company could dismiss him if he was absent for

183 days in any twelve months due to illness of accident. He was absent on sickness certificates and was given three months' notice of dismissal as the employer thought he was malingering. Sedley J held that there was an implied term that he would not be deprived of his entitlement under the scheme whilst incapacitated for work save for summary dismissal in response to a repudiatory breach of contract on his part. This term could be implied notwithstanding the contract provided for termination after a period of absence. The contract had been entered into during the currency of the employment and was not intended to replace the scheme nor was it is drafted with the scheme in mind.

Where an insurance policy is terminated without notice to the employee and the contract permits this, any sickness benefits will not thereby automatically terminate unless and until the employee is informed that the contract has been varied (**Bainbridge v Circuit Foil UK Limited** [1997] ICR 541; IRLR 305).

It was held in **Briscoe v Lubrizol Limited and Anor** (CA 15.10.1999) that once a claim has been rejected by the insurer the only remedy lay in suing the employer for breach of contract as the insurer did not owe any duty of care to the employee.

PART G: PLACE OF WORK AND MOBILITY

G1: Place of Work and Mobility

PRECEDENT G1.1: Your normal workplace is _____.

However, you accept that you will work at any other establishment of the Company within the United Kingdom whether on a temporary or permanent basis as your contract with the Company shall so require for the needs of the business. You also agree that you will make visits to clients or other establishments of the Company throughout the United Kingdom and abroad as may be required.

PRECEDENT G1.2: You agree that you are employed to work from the Head Office of the Company and that you are prepared to work from the Head Office wherever it may be located. You also agree that you will be mobile and prepared to work from any establishment of the Company to which you may, on reasonable notice, be instructed to move.

PRECEDENT G1.3: The Company operates [on the following territories] [on a worldwide] basis. You agree that, subject to having been given [days][reasonable] notice, you will transfer to any of the Company's locations within the area where the Company carries out its activities.

PRECEDENT G1.4: You agree to carry out work for the Company within a radius of [   ] miles from the Company's premises at _____.

COMMENTARY ON G:
PLACE OF WORK AND MOBILITY

Implied Terms

In the absence of any express terms there is considerable scope for the implication of a term. However, such a term will be applied in such way as does not breach the implied duty of trust and confidence (see Chapter 4).

Scope of implication

It is clearly preferable that the employer stipulates the place of work and makes it clear that the employee can be moved as required where a degree of mobility is required. In the absence of an express term there must be an implied term as to the place of work since this is one of the essential terms of the contract of employment.

- **O'Brien v Associated Fire Alarms Limited** [1968] 1 WLR 1916; [1969] 1 All ER 93. The Appellants were employed as electricians, installing fire and burglar alarms. The Respondents operated nationwide but divided the business into regions and the Appellants were employed in the Northwest region, based at Liverpool. During their employment they had only visited customers in the Liverpool area. They were asked to visit a customer in Barrow, 120 miles away and were dismissed when they refused. The Court of Appeal held that the tribunal had erred in finding that there was an implied term that they would work anywhere in the Northwest area. The proper term to imply was that they would work within reasonable or daily travelling distance from their homes. The case illustrates the importance of an express term if the employer wishes to have the power to instruct its employees to be mobile.

- **Stevenson v Tee-Side Bridge & Engineering Limited** [1971] 1 All ER 296. Mr Stevenson was employed as a steel erector. He said at interview that he would be prepared to work away from home, worked at sites in different parts of the country and was paid travel and subsistence. When he refused to transfer from a site near his home because the overtime would not be as good he was dismissed. The Divisional Court held that he could be contractually required to work anywhere in the country. Parker CJ held, taking into account the aforesaid factors, that there was every reason to imply such a term to give business efficacy to the contract. The position may be different where the course of conduct shows that the employee worked within daily commuting distance, as in **Mumford v Boulton & Paul (Steel Construction) Limited** [1970] ITR 222.

- **Express Lift Co v Bowles** [1976] IRLR 99; [1977] ICR 474. Where there was an implied term that the employee would work anywhere in the UK a further term could not be implied that it would be subject to exceptions in certain circumstances, as in the present case where Mr Bowles refused to transfer because his wife was ill. However, it may be that there is an implied term that the employer would not operate an implied condition in an unreasonable fashion as in BBC v Beckett [1983] IRLR 43 (and see **Prestwick Circuits Limited v McAndrew** below).

- **Burnett v F A Hughes & Co Limited** [EAT 109/77]. The EAT held that a term could be implied into the contract of a salesman that his territory be changed as management must have an overriding power to make such alterations to the areas and functions of their sales representatives as they may reasonably require.

- **Little v Charterhouse Magna Assurance** [1979] IRLR 19. Mr Little was a senior employee (effectively the Managing Director) on a five year fixed term with no stated place of work. He was entitled to mileage and accommodation expenses. The Head Office moved from Uxbridge to Bletchley. The EAT held that he was contractually required to move to whatever location the company had as its head office.

- **Prestwick Circuits Limited v McAndrew** [1980] IRLR 191. Mr McAndrew was ordered to attend at another factory the following day, which was fifteen miles away even though there was no mobility clause in his contract. It was held that the Industrial Tribunal had not erred in holding that the respondents' conduct in requiring the appellant to change his place of work at short notice amounted to a fundamental breach of an implied contractual term that he would not be transferred to another location except on reasonable notice and, therefore, was conduct justifying the appellant in resigning and claiming that he had been constructively dismissed.

- **Jones v Associated Tunnelling Co Limited** [1981] IRLR 477. Mr Jones worked from 1964 at colliery sites that were within reach of his home. In 1973 he was given a statement of terms that provided his employers could move him as they decided and in 1976 he was given a statement that provided he could be moved between sites. He did not object at the time but in 1980 he considered that he had been constructively dismissed when he was ordered to move. The EAT held that where there was no express term then a term must be implied. The employer had some power to transfer Mr Jones and, based upon the nature of the employer's business, whether the employee had been moved, what the employee had been told when he started work and provision as to expenses, in this case a term was implied that Mr Jones work at any place within reasonable daily reach of his home. Mr Jones had not acquiesced in a variation of his contract when he received the statements of terms and conditions.

- **Courtaulds Northern Spinning Limited v (1) Sibson (2) TGWU** [1988] IRLR 451; ICR 305. Mr Sibson who was employed as a lorry driver, was required to move site after he resigned from the TGWU and they threatened action if he remained at the depot where there was a closed shop. The Court of Appeal held that he could be required to move to a site within daily reach of his home, the depot being the starting and finishing place for his job, so that the employer was entitled to require him to move one mile to another depot. There was no need or justification to import into the implied term a requirement that the request be reasonable. (Cf **Prestwick Circuits v McAndrew**).

- **Aparau v Iceland Frozen Foods PLC** [1996] IRLR 119. In the absence of a mobility clause, the EAT held that it is was not possible to unilaterally transfer a checkout supervisor to a different store. There was no need to imply such a term given the nature of the work or to give the contract business efficacy. It was also held that the employee had not accepted a unilaterally imposed mobility clause merely by continuing to work.

An employee may rely upon the implied term of trust and confidence in relation to a proposed relocation. However, this must amount to a repudiatory breach of contract. In **Brown v Merchant Ferries Limited** [1998] IRLR 682 it was held that the fact that a proposed location left an employee felling unsettled and concerned about his future did not, viewed objectively, amount to a breach of contract as there was no evidence that his position was insecure.

Express mobility terms

The issue of place of work and mobility is likely to be an important one as employers are likely to want to have a large degree of flexibility in being able to move its workforce around as it considers appropriate. It is therefore likely to want to have mobility clauses drafted in the widest possible terms. There has been a considerable amount of case law on the issue of mobility clauses, both in the context of whether or not an employee is entitled to a redundancy payment on the basis that the workplace has closed down, or whether there has been unfair dismissal.

- **Parry v Holst & Company Limited** [1968] ITR 317. Mr Parry worked in the construction industry and his contract provided that "an operative may be transferred at any time during the period of his employment from one job to another". He finished one job in South Wales and was asked to transfer to Chard, in Somerset. He was dismissed when he was refused and it is was held that he was not entitled to a redundancy payment. Parker CJ stated that the clause, which was on its face unlimited, permitted the transfer that had been proposed, though he considered it is necessary to decide whether it is would permit transfer in the whole of the United Kingdom.

- **Scott v Formica Limited** [1975] IRLR 104. A clause which entitled the employer to transfer the employee to different jobs or departments did not enable the employer to transfer to a job where there was a reduction in salary.

- **Wilson-Undy v Instrument & Control Limited** [1976] ICR 508. Mr Wilson-Undy was employed in a labour force which transferred from site to site in the UK. At the time of his appointment he stated that he could only accept the job, which was in daily travelling distance, on the basis that when it ended he would not be transferred due to family commitments. When the employer sought to transfer him he claimed a redundancy payment. The EAT held that it was the common intention of the parties that he would only be employed within daily travelling distance.

Where the employer purports to vary the contract to include a mobility clause but this does not have any immediate effect, an employee will not be taken to have affirmed the variation merely because he has continued to work for the employee. In a case where the employee worked on for a year after the employer purported to introduce a clause which did not have immediate effect the EAT held that no consent to variation could be implied (**Aparau v Iceland Frozen Foods PLC** [1996] IRLR 119).

A temporary transfer may not be a repudiatory breach if it is for a short or specific time but where an employee is transferred until work picked up, with uncertainty as to how salary will be affected, this may amount to a breach on the part of the employer (**Millbrook Furnishings Industries v McIntosh** [1981] IRLR 309).

The precedents contain examples of different scope ranging from limited miles to worldwide mobility and should be tailored to the employment.

PART H: PRECONDITIONS OF EMPLOYMENT OR CONTINUED EMPLOYMENT

Precedent H1: References

1 Your employment with the Company is subject to the receipt of satisfactory references. If any reference is not satisfactory the Company shall be entitled to terminate your employment with immediate effect.

2 The Company may, at its absolute discretion, provide a reference upon request from a prospective employer. It will not provide a general reference but only provide references upon request. The Company will also provide references in respect of any mortgage, financial or other applications upon receipt of a written request from both the employee and the person seeking the reference.

3 The Company does not accept any liability for any references that it may give.

Precedent H2: Probationary Period and Confirmation of Employment

1 There is a minimum probationary period of ____ months for all new employees. This may have been varied by your Letter of Appointment. Moreover, the Company may, at its absolute discretion, extend the period of your probation if it considers this to be an appropriate course to adopt. You will be informed of the reasons for this.

2   Your performance will be continuously reviewed during your probationary period. If at any time during the period your performance is not considered to be satisfactory you will be advised and if there is no improvement you may be given notice.

3   At the end of the probationary period if your performance was satisfactory your continued employment may be confirmed. Your probationary period will count towards your continuous employment.

4   You will have been advised in your Letter of Appointment of what benefits you are entitled to receive during your probationary period.

Precedent H3: Car Driving and Driving Licence

You must have a full driving licence as a condition of your employment. Loss of a licence will result in immediate dismissal unless you demonstrate that you can make satisfactory alternative arrangements. The use of public transport will not be regarded as a satisfactory alternative.

Precedent H4: Qualifications

If your employment is subject to you having certain qualifications, which will have been notified to you in your Letter of Appointment, and you have not yet achieved the qualification because you are awaiting exam results or for some other reason, the employer reserves the right to terminate your employment forthwith, without notice or any compensation, should you fail to achieve the qualification by the notified date.

COMMENTARY ON H:
PRE-CONDITIONS OF EMPLOYMENT OR CONTINUED EMPLOYMENT

H1: References

Where an employer provides a reference in respect of an ex-employee it will be under a duty to take reasonable care in preparing the reference and if a negligent reference is provided that results in the employee suffering loss then the employer may be liable in damages (**Spring v Guardian Assurance PLC** [1994] ICR 596; IRLR 460; **Lawton v BOC Transhield Limited** [1987] ICR 7; IRLR 404) (Cf **Kapfunde v Abbey National PLC** [1999] IRLR 246 in relation to medical reports provided by a doctor). In **Bartholomew v London Borough of Hackney** [1999] IRLR 246 it was held that an employer did not act negligently when it stated in a reference that the employee had left the employment whilst being investigated for gross misconduct. The employer was under a duty not to mislead the prospective employer and the reference had not been drafted in a way that was unfair to the employee.

The precedent makes it clear that no liability is accepted in relation to the reference. However, this is unlikely to be effective if the employee knows that he has provided a reference that is not correct.

H2: Probationary Periods

It should be noted that an employee who is advised that he will be given a certain position or be promoted after a probationary period may bring a constructive dismissal if such is not forthcoming (**D H Russell (London) Limited v Magee** [EAT 201/78]).(Any precedent relating to probationary periods should make it clear that the employer is entitled to give notice at any time during the probationary period and is not bound to wait until the end before it terminates the contract.)

H3: Driving Licences

The nature of the employment may mean that a driving licence is essential. In **Roberts v Toyota (GB) Limited** [EAT 614/80] the employee was employed as an area sales manager. He was provided with a vehicle and it was ascertained at his interview that he had a valid driving licence. He was dismissed after nine years following a conviction for drunk driving and loss of licence for one year. He claimed unfair dismissal. It is was held that there was an implied term that he have a valid licence. The EAT stated:

> "The written contract of employment is fairly comprehensive and includes a provision to the effect that a company car would be provided for use on the company's behalf and for private purposes.

> It does not specifically state that the employee must be in possession of a driving licence but the provision with regard to the supply of a company car would be meaningless without it."

There was also evidence that the area managers had been told they would lose their job if they lost their licence. Notwithstanding this case, it is prudent to contain a provision that a licence is a condition of employment where this is intended to be the position, particularly where the driving is not as extensive as in the *Roberts* case. Other cases in which it has been held to be fair to dismiss on the loss of a licence include **Appleyard v Smith (Hull) Limited** [1972] IRLR 19 and **Fearn v Tayford Motor Co Limited** [1975] IRLR 336.

The precedent makes it clear that a licence is essential to the job. It should also be made clear that other alternatives are not acceptable. In *Roberts* the offer to employ a chauffeur was rejected and this was regarded as acceptable by the Tribunal where it had been made clear that a driving licence was required.

H4: Qualifications

Employers should ensure that they have made it clear any employment or continued employment turns upon obtaining qualifications within a certain time. In **Stubbes v Trower Still & Keeling (a firm)** [1987] IRLR 321 the employer had given articles but failed to state that continued employment turned upon passing the solicitor's exams. The Court of Appeal held that there was no necessary implication that the continued employment turned upon passing the exams. The employer had the means of securing their position through the medium of an express term. The precedent makes it clear that continued employment is subject to the possession of the required qualifications.

PART I: ABSENCES FROM WORK DUE TO HOLIDAY

Precedent I1: Annual Holidays

1 Your holiday entitlement is set out in your Letter of Appointment.

2 Your holiday entitlement is based on your length of service with the Company as follows:
[SET OUT YEARS OF SERVICE AND HOLIDAY ENTITLEMENT]

3 Holiday entitlement is calculated on the basis of a calendar year which will run from 1st January to 31st December. If you commenced work part way through the year you are entitled to holiday calculated on a *pro rata* basis.

4 You will be paid your basic salary whilst on holiday.

5 It is important to the Company that it is aware of when holiday entitlement is to be taken. Accordingly the following rules apply in respect of obtaining authorisation for holidays:
1) You must obtain prior written permission *[FROM . . . .]* before you book any holiday.
2) The Company has a holiday booking form which must be used for this purpose.
3) The maximum holiday that may be taken is two weeks, unless special permission is obtained for a longer period.
4) It will be expected that two weeks of your holiday will be taken in the Summer and any proposal to take

holiday at other times must be notified at least the same number of days in advance as the length of holiday that it is proposed to take.

5) You may not take holiday for at least 13 weeks from joining the Company and your Letter of Appointment will set out your entitlement if you are subject to a probationary period.

6) If you had already booked a holiday before joining the Company then the Company may, at its absolute discretion, authorise you to take the holiday.

7) Holiday entitlement will not be carried over from year to year without express written permission.

8) You may be required to take any accrued holiday entitlement during your period of notice where you have given notice or the Company has given notice to terminate your employment.

9) Holiday entitlement accrues at the rate of ____ days per month so that, in the event of termination of your employment, outstanding holiday will be calculated on an accrued basis. If you have taken in excess of your entitlement then, upon termination, the Company will be entitled to reimbursement for any overpayment.

10) If you resign or are dismissed you will be paid for your accrued entitlement up to the date of termination of your employment.

11) You will be paid for all Bank and public holidays.

Precedent 12: Public Holidays

You are entitled to the statutory public holidays each year which are:

New Years Day
Spring Bank Holiday
Good Friday
Later Summer Bank Holiday
Easter Monday
Christmas Day
May Day
Boxing Day

Precedent I3: Shutdown Periods in Relation to Factory Workers

The Company shuts down its factory premises during
_____. You will be required to take _____ days of
your holiday entitlement during this period.

COMMENTARY TO I:
ABSENCES FROM WORK DUE TO HOLIDAY

Contracts of employment should now be drafted with one eye on the
Working Time Regulations 1998 since this lays down certain minimum
requirements for paid holiday leave. However, these requirements can be
modified or excluded by a Relevant Agreement. This exclusionary power is of
great importance to the employer who does not wish to have to comply with
the requirements of the WTR (see also Part D to this Manual) and may be
contained in:

- A Workforce Agreement
- A provision in a collective Agreement
- Any other Agreement in writing that is legally enforceable.

The Working Time Regulations 1998 and holidays

Regulations 13 to 16 of the WTR give specific rights in relation to leave
entitlement in each leave year (which runs from January 1st on an annual
basis). The Regulations have caused some difficulty in practice because of the
manner in which they have been drafted to give entitlement to four weeks'
leave after working for a set period of time, and also entitlement to payment
for that period. This causes difficulties where employee has hitherto been
calculating entitlement on an accrued basis, month by month, or where
employees have not been paid whilst on leave but their earnings have been
'topped up' during the year to take holiday into account. It will be seen that
tribunals are having difficulty with the interpretation of the Regulations.

Entitlement

In any leave year after 23rd November 1999 a worker is entitled to four
weeks' leave (Reg 13(2)(c)). The leave year begins:

- on such date as may be provided for in a relevant agreement during
the calendar year;

- if there is no provision in a relevant agreement, where employment began the date on which the employment began and the anniversary of that date;
- the entitlement does not arise until the worker has been continuously employed for 13 weeks which means that his relations with his employer must have been governed by a contract during the whole or part of each of those weeks.

It was held by the Southampton ET in **Wellicome v Kelly Services (UK) Limited** (*IDS Brief* 641) that an worker is entitled to take the full holiday when the period to continuous service was satisfied so that a clause providing that holiday accrued at 0.29 days per week was void insofar as it is purported to exclude or limit the operation of the Regulations.

Notices to take leave

By Regulation 15(1) the worker may take the four weeks' leave by giving notice to his employer. The scheme is as follows:
- the worker may give notice relating to all or part of the leave to which he is entitled in a leave year and shall specify the days on which leave is to be taken;
- the notice must be given twice as many days in advance of the earliest date specified as the number of days or part days to which the notice relates.

The employer may require the worker:
- to take leave to which the worker is entitled, notice for which shall be given twice as many days as the earliest day specified in the notice as being the date on which leave must be taken.
- not to take leave in which case the notice must be given as many days in advance of the earliest date to which the notice relates. This means that if the worker gives 10 days' notice to take five days' holiday the employer may give notice five days before that he may not take the leave.

The Notice Provisions may be excluded or varied by a relevant agreement (15(5)).

Payment

A worker is entitled to be paid for any period of annual leave at the rate of a week's pay for each week of leave. There has been considerable difficulty in cases where workers have been paid at an 'enhanced' rate to cover holidays so that they do not receive holiday pay whilst they are actually on leave. The employment tribunal cases were reviewed in *IDS Brief* 649. In **Chapman v**

Eurostaff Personnel Limited (London (Stratford ET)) it was held that the entitlement was to paid leave and this could not be dealt with by paying an enhancement, which had been in place at the time the Regulations came into force, whilst in **Ackerman v Stratton** (Manchester ET) it was held that the practice of making a supplementary payment included in a rate was not acceptable as the worker would not earn the rate whilst on leave and the practice therefore effectively prevented the entitlement to any minimum paid leave. However, in **Davies v M J Wyatt (Decorators) Limited** (Manchester ET) the ET considered it acceptable for the hourly rate to be reduced as the employees would otherwise have been, effectively, paid twice. There will remain considerable confusion in this area until the matter is reviewed by the Higher Courts.

Termination
Where the worker's employment is terminated during the leave year and the proportion of leave to which he is entitled differs from the proportion which has expired he is entitled to a payment *in lieu* in respect of the leave not taken. If the worker has already taken in excess of his entitlement then a Relevant Agreement may provide that any payments be paid back. Where the employee is entitled to contractual holiday pay over and above the entitlements set out under the Working Time Regulations the case of **Morley v Heritage PLC** [1993] IRLR 400 will remain of relevance in deciding whether an employee is entitled to holiday pay that has been accrued on termination. The Court of Appeal held that there is no implied term that an employee will be entitled to accrued holiday pay and whether such a term exists depends on the nature of the contract and the status of the employee. In the particular case there was no need to imply such a term to give business efficacy to the contract.

The Directive
The Court of Appeal have held that the European Working Time Directive (93/104) is unconditional and not sufficiently precise to have direct effect so that it cannot be directly enforced against a State employer (**Gibson v East Riding of Yorkshire Council** [CA 21.6.2000]).

WORKING TIME REGULATIONS AND HOLIDAYS SUMMARISED

Entitlement to Leave: Regulation 13

Entitlement	4 weeks in any leave year beginning after 23.11.99 (13(2)) or where R governs start of leave year and employment commences after, then it is proportioned (11(5)).
	May take in instalments in the leave year in which due but may not replace by payment *in lieu* (13(9).
Qualification	1. Leave year begins on date provided in relevant agreement; or
	2. Date on which employment began. 13 weeks' continuous employment is needed (13(7)).
Notice by Employee	Worker may take leave by giving notice, relating to all or part of leave, which shall:
	1. specify the days on which leave is to be taken;
	2. be given at least twice as many days in advance of the earliest date specified in the notice.
Notice by Employer	The employer may require the worker to take leave, by giving notice, which shall
	1. specify the days on which leave is to be taken.
	2. be given at least twice as many days in advance of the earliest date specified in the notice.
	The employer may require the worker not to take leave by giving notice as many days in advance of the earliest date that leave is intended to be taken as the number of days to which the worker's notice related.

Payment and compensation relating to entitlement to leave — Regulations 16 and 14

Entitled to be paid in respect of any period of annual leave at the rate of a week's pay and ss 221-224 of the ERA apply. May be entitled to contractual sum.

Where employment is terminated during the leave year then payment will be for the proportion of leave that has not been taken. A relevant agreement may provide that the worker will pay back the employer where he had taken leave in excess of the proportion of the leave year to which he is entitled.

Variations of Holiday Times

In some cases holidays may be traditionally taken at specific times and there is, in any event, an entitlement to statutory holiday unless there is an express provision to the contrary. An attempted unilateral variation is likely to be in breach of contract.

- **Tucker v British Leyland Motor Corporation** [1978] IRLR 493. British Leyland sought to move the August bank holiday and New Year's Day bank holiday to the week between Xmas and the New Year, which they agreed would be with the consent of all the unions. The TGWU did not consent and members alleged that they were entitled to be paid for 30th and 31st December. It was held that the claimants were entitled to take the stand they did unless their contracts of employment obliged them to accept transfer of statutory holidays without their consent. Since there was no express term or regular usage to this effect the claimants succeeded. The judge stated that the employer "may insert in a contract of employment a term on the following lines":

  "You may be required to work on public holidays. If you are required to work on any public holiday you will be given another day's holiday on a day to be determined by the management."

- **Evans v Gwent County Council** [Ch Division 5.7.1982]. The Council designated half term as being from 26th May to 3rd June, during which nine days' paid holiday would be given. The claimant wished to take holiday from 24th May to 8th June and applied for unpaid leave from 24th/25th May and 4th/8th June. He was only permitted to take holiday on the basis that all the holiday was to be unpaid. Foster J held that the claimant was entitled to be paid for the half term as the claimant had not accepted this unilateral variation.

The Precedents

I1   Contains a precedent agreement that takes into account the Regulations.

I2   Is a precedent that may apply where the provisions of the Working Time Regulations have been excluded.

I3   Is a standard provision relating to public holidays.

I4   Relates to factory shutdowns and is dealt in Chapter 5 at 5.5.

PART J: ABSENCES FROM WORK DUE TO SICKNESS AND THE PROVISION OF SICK PAY

Precedent J1: Sickness or Injury Absence

1 If for any reason you are unexpectedly unable to attend work for sickness reasons, you must inform your Manager as early as possible on the first day of absence. Whilst absent due to sickness you are to keep your Manager informed of the place where you are living and can be contacted.

2 If you are absent between one and _____ days (inclusive of Saturday, Sunday and Bank Holidays) you should complete a Company Self-Certification Form on your return to work. This form will be available from _____.

3 If you are absent for more than _____ days you must obtain a medical certificate from your doctor.

4 If you are absent again with a gap of 14 days or less between sicknesses, the two periods of illness may be linked. Therefore, even if you fall sick again on Saturday or Sunday, you should complete a Company self-certification form on your return.

5 After receiving 28 weeks of Statutory Sick Pay in any tax year, you will be transferred to State Sickness benefit, which will be paid by the DSS following its standard procedure.

6 The Company reserves the right to require any employee, who is absent due to sickness, to be examined by a medical practitioner appointed by the Company. If the Company wishes you to attend an examination it will nominate a medical practitioner and an appointment will be made that is convenient to you.

7   The efficient running of the Company depends upon employees regularly attending work. Long term or persistent short term absence jeopardises the ability of the Company to carry out its functions. In such circumstances your future employment with the Company may become an issue or the Company may have to consider altering your job functions or conditions or adjusting your working environment to accommodate your needs. In these circumstances the Company will first require you to be examined by a doctor appointed by the Company. They will nominate a medical practitioner and an appointment will be made that is convenient to you.

8   Upon receipt of a medical report as provided for in clause 7, the Company may arrange an interview between yourself and the _____ to consider your future employment with the Company, which may lead to:

(1) Your employment being terminated on notice;
(2) The terms and conditions of your employment being altered.

9   If your Manager, with the concurrence of _____, considers that you are persistently absent from work such that you are not properly performing your job functions or other employees have to cover for you the procedure set out in clauses 7 and 8 may be implemented.

Precedent J2: Sick Pay

During periods of authorised absence due to your own sickness, it is the Company's policy to supplement Statutory Sick Pay (SSP) and DSS State Sickness Benefits with additional benefits sufficient to maintain your income at approximately the same level as your normal salary. Details of your entitlement to sick pay if applicable will have been set out in your Letter of Appointment.

Precedent J3: Sickness Absence & Unauthorised Absence

It is a contractual requirement that you are available during your normal working hours or such other hours as have been agreed. You must attempt to attend work but if you are delayed your must inform your Manager by telephone as soon as possible and explain the reason for absence of delay. Failure to attend without justification may result in your pay being reduced and could also result in disciplinary action. When your absence is due to sickness you must:

1) Ensure that your manager has been notified on the first day of your absence and that your manager is told of the reason for absence. It is not acceptable to simply leave a message.

2) Complete a self certification form on your return.

3) Where the absence is for _____ days or more (including weekends) you must submit a doctor's certificate to _____ and further certificates must cover the total period of absence, at least once every seven days. You must keep the Company informed of your likely return date.

4) If you fall ill whilst you are on holiday this will not count as sick leave unless you have obtained a doctor's certificate and the Company agree, in their absolute discretion, to treat it as sick leave.

Precedent J4: Long-term/Persistent Sickness Absence & Medical Reports

1   The efficiency of the Company depends upon its employees attending work on a regular basis as agreed in their terms and conditions of employment. Long term or persistent absence can create difficulties for the Company.

2   Long term absence is defined as _____ days at any one time during the calendar year.

3   Persistent absence is defined as _____ days of absence which may be separate or at one time during the calendar year.

4 In such cases the Company may consider it appropriate to terminate your employment. Before doing so it will make full investigation. The Company reserves the right to have a medical examination from a medical practitioner which it will nominate at the Company's expense.

5 In any event you are required at any time during the course of their employment at the request of the Company to a medical examination by a registered medical practitioner nominated by the Company for the purpose of considering whether you are fit to carry out your duties.

Precedent J5: Return to Work

You should not return to work until you have been certified as fit to return to work in cases where a premature return to work may affect your physical or mental well being or create a risk to health and safety. In certain circumstances the Company may wish you, in the exercise of its discretion to attend a medical examination, at the Company's expense, before it allows you to return to work.

Precedent J6: Suspension on Medical Grounds

The Company has the right to suspend you from work on medical grounds under section 64 of the ERA 1996. It will endeavour to find you suitable alternative work but if no such alternative work is available you will be paid during the period of suspension in accordance with the provisions of sections 64 and 65 of the ERA for a period of up to 26 weeks. If you are absent due to sickness you will be paid under the Company's sick pay scheme.

Precedent J7: No Payments while Absent due to Sickness

You are not entitled to sick pay but if you are unable to perform your duties through illness or injury the Company may pay you in its absolute discretion.

Precedent J8: Payments while absent due to sickness

You may be paid sickness pay from your first day of absence if you comply with the rules as to notification of sickness and the Statutory Sick Pay Scheme. The Company may withhold any pay if you fail to adhere to the rules as to notification and such absence may be treated as unauthorised.

Precedent J9: Payments while absent due to sickness dependent upon length of service

1 You will be entitled to receive payment for periods of absence during any consecutive 12 month period through illness as follows:
1) Full salary for absences up to _____;
2) Half salary for absences between _____ and _____.

2 These payments are made entirely at the Company's discretion and may be withheld if it is considered that you should not be entitled to payment for any reason, including abuse of the sick pay entitlement.

3 The Company reserves the right to terminate your employment at any time during your absence from work even though at the time of giving notice you remain entitled to sick pay under the sick pay scheme.

4 Absence due to sickness has a significant cost implication for the Company's business. A high level of periodic absence for minor ill health causes will be of concern to the Company.

5 The Company maintains a permanent health insurance scheme to cover long term absence. The said scheme provides benefits for employees when the absence is longer than 26 weeks. Details of its scheme can be obtained from [the Human Resources Department.]

Precedent J10: Statutory Sick Pay

You will be paid statutory sick pay in accordance with the Statutory Sick Pay scheme that is in force from time to time. The relevant forms are available from _____.

Precedent J11: Claims in Relation to Accidents Occurring Outside Work

Should you be absent from work due to the negligence or other actionable conduct of a third party all payments made to you during absence because of such injuries by the Company shall be regarded as loans and you agree that if you recover compensation for loss of earnings such sums will be repaid to the Company from the compensation that you have recovered.

Precedent J12: Permanent Health or Disability Insurance

See F12 for a Precedent.

COMMENTARY ON J:
ABSENCES FROM WORK DUE TO SICKNESS, AND THE PROVISION OF SICK PAY

A number of issues are likely to arise in relation to questions of sickness and the Precedents in Part J are intended to cover all of these eventualities. In particular:

- A proper sickness or injury absence scheme is essential and this is set out in full at precedent **F1**
- For the employee, the question of payment during absence due to sickness is likely to be of paramount importance and there are a number of possibilities. The Company may maintain the employee's income (**J2**; **J8**; **J9**) dependent upon a number of factors or limit payment to statutory sick pay (**J1**).
- Unauthorised absence should be catered for (**J3**).

- Long term or persistent sickness raises its own issues and, in this case, the ability to carry out a medical examination should be included (**J4**).
- The employer may wish to stipulate that the employee cannot return to work until he is fit (**J5**) and, in some cases, statute may require medical suspension (**J5**).
- Permanent Health or Disability insurance may be a consideration.

J1: Sickness or Injury Absence

In the case of absences due to sickness or illness there should be a clear scheme so that the employee knows what steps it should take in order to notify the employer of absence due to sickness and the likely impact of sickness. The procedure should provide for the possibility of examination by a nominated medical practitioner. Where it is apparent that the employee can no longer carry out the job the employer will wish to be in a position to terminate the contract after carrying out a proper procedure, which will involve warnings about the likely consequences of absence and a proper review of the employee's record (see **Lynoch v Cereal Packaging Limited** [1988] ICR 670 and see Duggan, *Unfair Dismissal, Law and Practice*, at pages 139-144 for a full consideration of this topic).

As part of any sickness procedure it would be prudent for the employer to obtain a medical report and failure to do so may make any dismissal unfair (see **Parsons & Co Limited v Kidney** [EAT 788/87] and Duggan on *Unfair Dismissal* at page 134).

The procedure should contain a right to request a medical report as there may be a constructive dismissal if a report is demanded without any express right (see **Bliss v South East Thames Regional Health Authority** [1987] ICR 700; [1983] IRLR 308).

Where a report is sought from the employee's own GP or consultant then the procedures of the Access to Medical Reports Act 1988 will apply.

J2: Sick Pay

Where there is no express term as to the payment of sick pay there is no presumption in common law that sick pay will be payable (**Mears v Safecar Security Limited** [1992] IRLR 183; ICR 626). The tribunal is to approach the matter with an open mind and decide, on the facts and circumstances, what term would have been implied. Sick pay was never asked for in this case, no certificates were ever sent in and other employees were never paid sick pay. The Court refused to imply any term. This case reflects earlier authorities such as **Petrie v MacFisheries** [1939] 4 All ER 258 where the

Court of Appeal stated that there was no general principle that employees were entitled to sick pay, and **Hancock v BSA Tools Limited** [1939] 4 All ER 538 where a term could not be implied when employees were only paid for work done. In **O'Grady v M Saper Limited** [1940] 2 KB 469 the employee had been absent for periods of weeks on several occasions without asking for sick pay. It was only when he read a reported case in the newspapers that he asked for sick pay. The Court of Appeal held that the evidence was clear that he was not entitled to sick pay.

In a case where sick pay is payable but the period for which it will be paid has not been expressed the court will imply a reasonable period during which it should be paid, which is applicable to the particular industry in which the employee is engaged (**Howman and Son v Blyth** [1983] ICR 416).

There may also be an implied term that the employer will not dismiss an employee whilst he is incapacitiated, save for repudiatory conduct or some other terminating event specified in the contract (**Aspen v Webbs Poultry & Meat Group (Holdings) Limited** [1996] IRLR 521 — see Part **J12**). In **Hill v General Accident Fire & Life Assurance Corporation PLC** [1998] IRLR 641, Mr Hill was entitled to full salary for the first 104 weeks with the possibility of permanent accident insurance thereafter. He was absent from work from March 1994 and was dismissed for redundancy in November 1995. He alleged that the employer was in breach of the implied term of good faith and mutual trust as his dismissal frustrated his entitlement to long term sickness benefit. There was a genuine redundancy situation. The Court of Session held that the employer was not in breach of contract even if the practical effect of the dismissal brought an end to any entitlement. Insofar as *Aspen* laid down any principle that such a dismissal was in breach of the implied term of trust and confidence, this could not be accepted. The Court stated that:

> "...the employer cannot, solely with a view to relieving himself of the obligation to make such payment, by dismissal bring that sick employee's contract to an end. To do so would be, without reasonable and proper cause, to subvert the employee's entitlement to payment while sick. The same unwarranted subversion may occur if a sick employee were to be dismissed for a specious or arbitrary reason or for no cause at all."

Express Terms
Precedent **F2** expressly provides for the payment of sick pay during absence at the same level of normal salary. Other alternatives are set out at **F7, 8, 9** and **10**).

J3: Unauthorised Absence

Where the employee does not comply with established procedures as to sickness absence or fails to advise the employer of the reason for absence then there should be provision that this will result in non payment of salary and may amount to a disciplinary offence. However this will not negate the employer's duty to carry out an investigation into the reason for absence if disciplinary measures are being considered (as to this, see the detailed consideration in Duggan, *Unfair Dismissal, Law Practice and Guidance*).

J4: Long-term/Persistent Sickness Absence and Medical Reports

Long term and persistent sickness absence raise specific issues if the employer considers that the business cannot continue to tolerate such absence on the part of the employee. It may be that long term absence has caused the contract to become frustrated (see **Marshall v Harland and Woolf Limited** [1972] ICR 101 for a consideration of the circumstances when this may be the case; and see Duggan, *Unfair Dismissal* at page 64-66). The employer is likely to want to investigate the reasons for long term or persistent sickness and, indeed, will be under a duty to carry out an investigation into the reasons for illness and inform itself of the true medical position (see **Spencer v Paragon Wallpapers Limited** [1976] IRLR 373 and Duggan, *Unfair Dismissal* at pages 131-137). In the case of persistent short term illness the employer will wish to have a definition of what is regarded as persistent short term illness that is not acceptable (see **International Sports Company Limited v Thomson** [1980] IRLR 340 and Duggan, *Unfair Dismissal* at pages 137-8). In either case there should be a full investigation and provision for medical examination.

J5: Return to Work

The prudent employer will ensure that the employee is not permitted to return to work until it is certain that he is fit to return. There is a danger that if the employee returns before he is fit he may bring claims in respect of any injuries he sustains or, alternatively, may be a danger to his co-workers. Precedent **J5** is therefore intended to ensure that there are appropriate safeguards agains an employee's return until the employer is satisfied that he is fit.

J6: Suspension on Medical Grounds

By section 64 of the ERA 1996 an employee who is suspended from work on medical grounds is entitled to be paid remuneration whilst he is suspended for a period of 26 weeks. The employee is regarded as being so suspended if he is suspended:

- in consequence of a requirement imposed by or under a provision of an enactment or an instrument made under an enactment;
- in consequence of a recommendation in a provision of a Code of Practice issued or approved under section 16 of the Health and Safety at Work *etc.* Act 1974;

and

- the provision is specified in the Control of Lead at Work Regulations 1980, Regulation 24 of the Ionising Radiations Regulations 1999 or Regulation 11 of the Control of Substances Hazardous to Health Regulations 1988. At present these are the only enactments that will give rise to a claim in respect of suspension.

He will be regarded as suspended if he continues to be employed but is not provided with work or does not perform the work that he normally performed before the suspension.

There are exclusions from the right to claim in section 65 ERA 1996, namely:

- less than one month's employment;
- where the contract is for a fixed term of less than three months, unless three months has already elapsed;
- where the employee is incapable of being able to work by reason of disease or bodily or mental impairment;
- where suitable alternative employment has been offered or the employee does not comply with reasonable requirements imposed with a view to ensuring his services are available.

The employee will be entitled to a week's pay in respect of each week of suspension, as calculated in accordance with sections 220 to 229 of the ERA 1996. Any contractual payment will go towards discharging this liability.

J11: Claims in relation to Accidents occurring Outside Work

Where the employee is unable to attend work due to an accident or other claim which gives him a right to claim damages against a third party and the employer has paid remuneration for a period where the employee is incapacitated as a result of the accident or other claim, then, in such circumstances, the employer will wish to include a provision whereby any payment will be regarded as a loan to be repaid if, and when, any claim for damages is satisfied (see **Dennis v London Passenger Transport Board** [1948] 1 All ER 779). The requirement to repay the debt should entitle the employee to recover damages, though some form of adjustment is likely to be necessary in terms of PAYE once the outcome of any claim is known.

J12: Permanent Health Insurance

Issues relating to permanent health insurance have already been considered at Manual Part **F11**. It is an important facet of permanent health insurance that, once granted, the employer should not act in a manner that effectively removes the benefit from the employee. Where there is a contractual disability benefit for the short or long term, it may be an express or an implied term that the employer will not do anything that will defeat the employee's entitlement under the scheme, including terminating the employee's employment.

Express terms
- In **Adin v Sedco Forex International Resources Limited** [1997] IRLR 280, Mr Adin was entitled to long and short term disability benefits set out in the Group's employee guide. The short term scheme provided full pay for six months and 60% for six months, whilst the long term benefit covered the employee till death if disability continued. Where employment was terminated after total disability employees would continue to receive the long term benefits. Mr Adin was dismissed after receiving short term benefits for three months and it was asserted that he was not entitled to long term benefit as he had not received short term benefit for 12 months. His contract provided that he could be dismissed without cause at any time and would only be paid to that date. The Court of Session held that the express terms of the contract provided that the employer could not defeat his entitlement to short and long term benefits as the stated purpose was to provide income protection when the employee could not work. The disability plans would not give this protection if they could be taken away at the employer's discretion by dismissing without cause. The right to benefit was established by the combination of the contract terms and the unfitness of the employee and, once established, remained due.

Implied Terms
- See **Aspden v Webbs Poultry and Meat Group (Holdings) Limited** [1996] IRLR 521 referred to at the commentary to **F11**.

The scope of Insurance schemes
Where there is an insurance scheme between employer and employee any restrictions in the term of the scheme should be drawn to the attention of the employee. In **Villella v MFI Furniture Centres Limited** [1999] IRLR 468 it is was held that a former employee was entitled to receive payments

under a Permanent Health Insurance scheme even though the insurance policy stated that it is would cease on the termination of employment. The restriction had never been drawn to the attention of the employee so that it was not incorporated into the employment contract. The restriction was merely contained in the policy between the employer and the insurer.

Where the terms of a permanent health plan are underwritten by an insurance scheme, no duty of care is owed by the insurer to the employee so that the only redress is by suing the employer for breach of contract. In **Briscoe v Lubrizol Limited & Anor** [Court of Appeal 15.10.1999 *IDS Brief* 655] it was alleged, *inter alia*, that the insurer was negligent in ascertaining the employee's entitlement under the health plan. The plan was in a common form and provided that:

- it had to be shown to the insurer's satisfaction that the employee had been totally unable to perform his occupation and had not engaged in any other gainful occupation or employment;
- the employer was under a duty to provide all particulars and information necessary to decide whether the employee fell within the definition.

When a claim was rejected the employee argued that the insurer was negligent in failing to take proper steps to commission the necessary medical evidence. The claim was struck out on the ground that there was no duty of care owed by the insurer. However, the Contracts (Rights of Third Parties) Act 1999 came into force in May 2000 and this may give an employee the right to claim against the insurer in such circumstances.

PART K: ABSENCES FROM WORK DUE TO MATERNITY OR PATERNITY LEAVE

Precedent K1: Maternity and Parental Leave Policy

Under Part I of Schedule 4 to the Employment Relations Act 1999 certain rights are incorporated into the Employment Rights Act 1996 which substitutes new sections 71 to 76 to that Act and sets new rights out in relation to maternity leave and in relation to parental leave. The Company will at all times comply with the legislation that is in force from time to time. The Company values the work of their female staff and will make such arrangements as it can to ensure that employees are able to combine their family commitments with gainful employment. The enclosed policies are intended to meet the requirements of the legislation whilst providing for the smoothest possible transition for maternity leave and return to work.

MATERNITY LEAVE

1   You will be entitled to the following maternity leave under the provisions of the legislation:

1.   You will be entitled to maternity leave, known as ordinary maternity leave, for a period of 18 weeks, which cannot begin more than 11 weeks before the expected date of your confinement.
2.   You will be entitled to additional maternity leave if you have completed one year's continuous service by the 11th week before the expected week of childbirth. This will commence at the beginning of the end of

ordinary maternity leave and will end 29 weeks after the date of childbirth.

2 Notification provisions

1. In order to qualify for ordinary maternity leave you must inform the Company at least 21 days before you intend to start your ordinary maternity leave period. The Company may require the notice to be given in writing and the provision of a certificate from your doctor or midwife confirming the expected week of childbirth.

2. You do not need to notify the Company if you are entitled to additional maternity leave. It will begin automatically after your ordinary maternity leave finishes if you are entitled to such leave.

3. It is the Company's practice to confirm whether or not you intend to take additional maternity leave and you will be asked in writing to confirm this no later than 21 days before your ordinary maternity leave expires. If you do not respond within 21 days you could lose certain rights under the employment legislation.

3 Right to return to work

1. You will be entitled to return to work in the same employment at the end of your ordinary maternity leave unless your job has been made redundant.

2. Where you have opted to take additional maternity leave you will be entitled to return to the same job if it remains practicable for you to return to the same job and your post has not been made redundant. If it is not reasonably practicable for you to return to the same job the Company will seek to provide you with another job that it suitable and appropriate.

3. You will be permitted to return early from your ordinary maternity leave period upon giving 21 days notice to the Company. The Company may reduce this period at its discretion.

4 Payment

You will be entitled to Statutory Maternity Pay during the period of your ordinary leave but will not be entitled to any payment during the period of your additional leave.

PARENTAL LEAVE

5   Employees of both sexes are entitled to parental leave under the legislation. The Company will comply fully with the provisions of the legislation and you are entitled to parental leave as set out in the following paragraphs.

Entitlement

6   You will be entitled to parental leave if your child was born after 15th December 1999 or have adopted a child after that date.

7   You must have completed one year's service before you will be entitled to parental leave.

Time off

8   You are entitled to 13 weeks' leave for each child. In the case of twins being born you will be entitled to 26 weeks off work.

9   You may take this leave at any time over a period of five years from the date that your child was born and you must take this leave in blocks of seven days.

Notice

10   You must give a minimum of four weeks' notice or twice the number of weeks' notice in relation to the amount of time that you intend to take off. You must advise the Company of the date when the period of leave is to begin and to end.

11   A father who is awaiting the birth or adoption of his child may give 13 weeks' notice of the expected date of birth or adoption and the duration of leave that is required. He will be entitled to take the leave on the birth or adoption of the child.

Deferment of leave

12   Whilst the Company will always seek to accommodate your wishes in relation to taking parental leave there may be certain circumstances where the requirements of the business will mean that the Company will require you not to defer leave. These circumstances will arise where:

1. You are not proposing to take the leave at the time of the birth or adoption of your child.

2. The operation of the Company's business would be seriously prejudiced if you took leave during the period that you had identified.

13 In a case where the Company considers it necessary for you to defer parental leave you will be given written notice and advised of dates within a period of six months on which the Company agrees that you may take parental leave. This notice will be given to you at least as many weeks before the time you are proposing to take off.

Payment

14 You are not entitled to be paid whilst you are taking off parental leave.

Other Provisions Relating to Maternity/Paternity Leave

The provisions set out above contain the obligations that the Company must adhere to in order to comply with the legislation. However, the Company is aware that a stable workforce is one of its assets and there exists the following procedures in order to assist employees who are proposing to take maternity or paternity leave.

1. As soon as possible after you have notified your intention to take maternity/paternity leave it will be arranged that you meet with your Manager or the Personnel Department by way of an informal interview so that the following may be discussed;
   a) your right to maternity or paternity leave including the notice requirements as are applicable;
   b) your rights to return to work — in appropriate cases there may be discussion as to whether you wish to return to work on a different basis (*i.e.* part time or flexible working) and whether the Company can so accommodate you;
   c) any entitlements to payment will be clarified.

2. Where it is necessary to cover your work then prior to commencement of maternity or paternity leave you will be informed of the arrangements for covering your work and you will be involved as far as possible in relation to the provision of a replacement.

3. Where you wish to return to work after maternity leave on a different basis than your original job the following may be considered:

    a) opportunities for flexible or part time working which the Company will make every effort to accommodate;

    b) the possibility of job sharing which will involve appropriately adjusted terms and conditions of employment;

    c) where no such alternatives are available at the time of return to work you will be encouraged to work on a full time basis and we will continue to review the position to seek to accommodate your wishes.

COMMENTARY ON K:
ABSENCES FROM WORK DUE TO MATERNITY OR PATERNITY LEAVE

The Policy on Maternity and Paternity Leave is intended to implement the provisions of the Maternity and Paternal Leave *etc.* Regulations 1999 (SI 1999/3312) which came into force on 15th December 1999. The policy goes slightly beyond the provisions the scope of the Regulations where it refers to 'Other provisions relating to Maternity/Paternity Leave'. The procedures set out in the Regulations are as follows:

MATERNITY LEAVE
There are three stages of maternity leave that are applicable:

1. Compulsory Maternity Leave
By Regulation 8 there is a prohibition against an employee working during compulsory maternity leave. This period is of two weeks from the date that childbirth occurs.

2. Ordinary Maternity Leave
By Regulation 4 entitlement to Ordinary Maternity Leave is available to all employees whose babies were born after 30th April 2000. The entitlement is to 18 weeks' leave (as set out in Regulation 7). The procedure in relation to taking such leave is as follows:

- At least 21 days before the date on which it is intended to take ordinary maternity leave (or as soon as reasonably practicable if 21 days is not reasonably practicable) the employee should notify the employer of (1) her pregnancy (2) the expected week of childbirth and (3) the date on which she intends her Ordinary Maternity Leave to start.

- The employer may request a certificate from a registered medical practitioner or a registered midwife stating the expected week of childbirth (Reg 4(1)(b)).

- The employer may also require the date on which the employee intends to start Ordinary Maternity Leave to be in writing and such notification shall not specify a date earlier than the beginning of the eleventh week before the expected week of childbirth (Reg 4(2)).

However, maternity leave may be triggered earlier for a number of reasons.

- Where childbirth occurs before the maternity leave period would otherwise commence. Regulation 4(4) modifies the notification provision so that the employee must notify as soon as reasonably practicable after the birth that she has given birth and be in writing if so requested.

- Where the employee is absent from work wholly or partly because of pregnancy or childbirth after the beginning of the sixth week before the expected week of confinement. Regulation 4(3) modifies the position so that notification must be given as soon as reasonably practicable and be in writing if so requested.

Whilst the period of Ordinary Maternity Leave is 18 weeks this may be extended where any requirement imposed by or under any relevant statutory provision prohibits the employee from working for any period after the end of the ordinary maternity period (Regulation 7(2)).

3. Additional Maternity Leave

An employee is entitled to additional maternity leave where:

- she is entitled to ordinary maternity leave; and

- she has, at the beginning of the eleventh week before the expected week of childbirth, been continuously employed for a period of not less than a year.

Additional maternity leave commences on the day after the last day of ordinary maternity leave. Additional maternity leave continues until the end of the period of 29 weeks beginning with the week of childbirth (Regulation 7(4)).

Return to work

At the end of the 18 week period of Ordinary Maternity Leave the employee merely has to present herself for work and is entitled to return. She may, however, wish to return earlier, in which case the provisions set out below apply.

Where the employee has taken additional maternity leave Regulation 12 provides that, if requested by the employer, then not earlier than 21 days before the end of the Ordinary Maternity Leave the employee must notify the employer of the date on which childbirth occurred and whether she intends to return to work at the end of her additional maternity leave period The employer's request must be in writing and must be accompanied by a written statement explaining how the employee may determine the date on which her additional maternity leave period will end and warning of the consequences of failing to respond to the employer's request within 21 days.

It should however be noted that the consequences of failure to give notice are not stated but Regulation 12(2) makes it clear that the employer may stipulate what the implications of failure to give notice may entail. The draconian approach of the old Regulations that the right to return may be lost thus no longer exist.

Where the employee wishes to return to work early Regulation 11 provides that 21 days' notice may be given by the employee and the employer is entitled to postpone any return to a date where it has 21 days' notice of such return. Such postponement cannot, however, go beyond the relevant maternity leave period. Moreover, a woman who returns early in the situation where the employer has postponed her period of return is not entitled to remuneration (Regulation 11(4)) which is a clear disincentive to returning in such circumstances!

Dismissal whilst on Maternity Leave

If dismissal takes place during ordinary or additional maternity leave the leave ends at the date of the dismissal (Regulation 7(5)). Where there is a redundancy situation, Regulation 10 provides that:

- if there is a suitable vacancy the employee is entitled to be offered (before the end of her employment under her existing contract) alternative employment with the employer or successor or associated employer under a new contract of employment, to take effect immediately on the ending of her employment under the previous contract; which

- contract is such that the work to be done is suitable to the employee and appropriate for her to do in the circumstances and that the contract of employment's provisions as to capacity and place in which she is to be employed, and as to other terms and conditions of her employment, are not substantially less favourable to her than if she had continued to be employed under the previous contract.

PARENTAL LEAVE

The Government has implemented Council Directive 96/34/EC on the framework agreement on parental leave concluded by UNICE, CEEP and the ETUC by enacting Schedule 4 Part II of the Employment Relations Act 1999, which in turn permits Regulations to be promulgated to cover the detail of parental leave. Those Regulations are now contained in Part III of the Maternity and Parental Leave etc Regulations 1999, and provide as follows:

- where the employee has been continuously employed for a period of not less than one year; and
- has or expects to have responsibility for a child.

The employee will be entitled to be absent from work on parental leave for the purpose of caring for the child (Regulation 13(1).

By Regulation 13(2), the employee has responsibility for the child if:

- the parent and named on the birth certificate of a child born after 15th December 1999 who is under five years old;
- the employee has parental responsibilities in relation to a child born on or a 14th December 1999 who is under five years old; or
- has adopted a child on or after 15th December 1999 who is under the age of eighteen.

Regulations 14 and 15 set out the extent of the entitlement on the part of an employee:

- an employee is entitled to thirteen weeks' leave in respect of any individual child;
- the number of hours for a week's leave is calculated by dividing the total of the periods for which the employee is normally required to work by 52 where there are some weeks that the employee would not otherwise be required to work;
- both parents are entitled to parental leave;
- the entitlement lasts until the date of the child's fifth birthday unless the child is disabled, in which case it lasts until the 18th birthday, or

where a child has been adopted, in which case it lasts for five years after placement up to the child being 18 years of age.

There is provision for the employer and employee to conclude their own agreement and the above provisions may be less favourable if concluded through a collective or workforce agreement. In the absence of any agreement, employees can only take parental leave on the basis that

- 21 days' notice is given to the employer;
- the leave can only be taken in blocks of one or more full weeks;
- four weeks leave can only be taken in any one year;
- the employer may postpone notice for up to six months where the business would be disrupted, save where leave is sought after a child is born or adopted.

TERMS AND CONDITIONS DURING ABSENCE

By Regulation 17, where additional maternity leave or parental lave is taken the employee is entitled to:

- the benefit of the employer's implied obligation of trust and confidence;
- any implied conditions relating to notice of the termination of the employment contract by the employer;
- compensation in the event of redundancy;
- the benefit of any disciplinary or grievance procedure.

The employee is also bound by the implied obligation of good faith and any terms and conditions relating to:

- notice of termination of the employment contract by the employee;
- the disclosure of confidential information;
- the acceptance of gifts or other benefits;
- the employee's participation in any other business.

UNFAIR DISMISSAL AND DETRIMENT

Readers are referred to Chapter 18 of *Unfair Dismissal, Law Practice and Guidance*, in relation to the unfair dismissal provisions of the Regulations.

- By Regulation 19 the employee is protected from being subjected to any detriment because the employee has took or sought to exercise any rights under the Regulations.

- By Regulation 20 a dismissal will be unfair if the reason or principal reason is that the employee sought to exercise any rights under this Act or is due to pregnancy or the birth of a child.

The Precedent

Precedent **K1** seeks to encapsulate the provisions of the Regulations as described above and, as such, is self explanatory.

PART L: ABSENCE FOR OTHER REASONS

Precedent L1: Dependants

Under the Employment Rights Act 1996 you are entitled to time off to care for dependants and the Company will comply with the provisions of the legislation. The following provisions are applicable in relation to time such time off.

1. A dependant will be your spouse, child or parent or someone who lives in the same household as yourself otherwise than by being lodger, boarder or tenant, or who you can show is a person who reasonably relies on your assistance to make arrangements for the provision of care when that person falls ill or is injured or assaulted.

2. You will be entitled to a reasonable amount of time off in order to take action that is necessary:
   a)   to provide assistance when your dependant is ill, injured or assaulted;
   b)   to make arrangements for the provision of care when your dependant is ill, injured or assaulted;
   c)   in consequence of the death of a dependant;
   d)   because of the unexpected disruption or termination of arrangements for the care of a dependant;
   e)   to deal with any incident that involves your child and has occurred unexpectedly in a period when he is in an educational establishment that is responsible for him or her.

3. You must tell the Company of the reason for your absence as soon as reasonably possible including how long you think you will be absent.

Precedent L2: Other Special Leave Arrangements

The Company is always prepared to consider requests for leave because of special circumstances. You should make any request to your manager who will consider whether it should be granted and whether it should be paid or unpaid.

Precedent L3: Marriage

You are entitled to_____ days' paid leave in addition to your holiday entitlement from the date when you marry.

Precedent L4: Public Duties

If you are carrying out public duties you will may have a statutory right to reasonable time off in order to fulfil these duties. You must first notify the Company who will then consider whether you are entitled to time off for such duties and whether your time off should be paid or unpaid.

Precedent L5: Jury Service

You are entitled to time off from the Company for jury service. You will be paid for such time off. You must produce the Summons to the Company to confirm that you have been called for jury service.

Precedent L6: Religious Holidays

The Company recognises that religious beliefs may mean that you need to take time off at certain times and it will seek to allow time off to observe religious holidays. These holidays will form part of your holiday entitlement.

Precedent L7: Other Absences

> Any absences for domestic reasons such as house moving,
> deliveries of furniture or such similar reason must be taken
> as part of your holiday entitlement.

COMMENTARY ON L:
ABSENCE FOR OTHER REASONS

At common law there is generally no implied term that an employee would
be allowed reasonable time off in an emergency. Though it may be implied
into contracts of employment for employees working for very large
organisations this is unlikely to be the case with a small employer (**Warner
v Barbers Stores** [1978] IRLR 109). In the *Warner* case a small employer had
refused an employee time off to look after her son who was a diabetic. The
EAT stated:

> " It seems to us that whereas it is true that in these days there is either an
> express or implied term in many contracts of employment that there
> should be reasonable time off in an emergency, there is certainly no
> authority, nor do we think it would be right, nor do we think it would
> be common sense, to extend such an implied term over the whole realm
> of employer/employee relationship. It seems to us that this is the sort of
> situation in which every case has to be looked at on its own and quite
> separately from any general principle. On the facts of this case we could
> not persuade ourselves that such an implied term ought to be read into
> this contract. That means that, as the Industrial Tribunal found in this
> very sad case — and one has a great deal of sympathy with this lady —
> she has no implied term in her contract on which to rely. The employer
> was entitled to say 'You must come in.' That was a matter which might
> perhaps have been more closely and helpfully discussed. It may well be
> that somehow or other they would have managed on the Saturday;
> perhaps they did. But unfortunately the lady damaged irreparably and
> permanently her case by not turning up for work on the Monday."

However, there are a number of areas where by statute an employee is
entitled to time off or where discrimination law may have some impact.
Precedents L1 to L7 cover the most common areas where an employer may
seek to take time off work.

Precedent L1: Dependants

The Employment Relations Act 1999 introduced a new right for employees to take time off to look after dependants. Council Directive 96/34/EC requires member states to make provision for unpaid leave on grounds of *force majeure,* for urgent family reasons in cases of sickness, or accident making the immediate presence of the worker indispensable (clause 3.1). The 1999 Act has inserted sections 57A and 57B into the Employment Rights Act 1996 to cover the situation. By section 57A(1) an employee is entitled to be permitted to take a reasonable time off during the employee's working hours in order to take action which is necessary:

(a) to provide assistance on an occasion when a dependant falls ill, gives birth or is injured or assaulted;

(b) to make arrangements for the provision of care for a dependant who is ill or injured;

(c) in consequence of the death of a dependant;

(d) because of the unexpected disruption or termination of arrangements for the care of a dependant;

(e) to deal with an incident which involves a child of the employee and which occurs unexpectedly in a period during which an educational establishment which the child attends is responsible for him.

The section only applies where the employee tells the employer as soon as reasonably practicable of the reason for absence and how long the employee expects to be absent (section 57A(2)). There is no express limit on the amount of time off that may be taken.

For the purposes of (a) to (e), a dependant means:

- a spouse;
- a child;
- a parent;
- a person who lives in the same household as the employee otherwise than by reason of being his employee, tenant, lodger or boarder.

For the purposes of (a) and (b), a dependant also includes any person who reasonably relies on the employee:

- for assistance on an occasion when the person falls ill or is injured or assaulted; or
- to make arrangements for the provision of care in the event of illness or injury.

For the purposes of (d), dependant also includes any person who reasonably relies on the employee to make arrangements for the provision of care.

By section 57B the employee may make a complaint to a tribunal that the employer has unreasonably refused time off under section 57A.

Precedent L1 is intended to implement the provisions of section 57A.

Precedent L2: Other Special Leave Arrangements

Although there is no express or implied right to have time off for compassionate or other leave arrangements the reasonable employer may wish to include a clause which states that it will consider time off, whilst reserving the discretion to actually grant time off to itself.

Precedent L3: Marriage

It is also quite common for there to be a provision that the employee may be granted additional time off upon marriage, in order to take a honeymoon. Such provision can only be conducive to good relations with the workforce!

Precedent L4: Public Duties

Section 50 of the Employment Rights Act 1996 gives employees the right to take time off work to perform public duties where the employee is:

- a justice of the peace;
- a member of a local authority, a statutory tribunal, a police authority, the Service Authority of the National Crime Intelligence Service or the Service Authority for the National Crime Squad, a board of prison visitors or a prison visiting committee, a relevance health body, a relevant education authority or the Environmental Agency or the Scottish Environmental Protection Agency. In the case of these employees the employee can take time off work to attend at meetings of the body or any of its committee or sub-committees and for the doing of anything approved by the body or anything of a class so approved for the purposes of the discharge of the functions of the body or committee or sub-committees.

Sections 50(5) to 50(9) contain further elaboration of the definitions of the relevant bodies and reference should be made to these subsections.

By section 50(4) the amount of time off which an employee is to be permitted to take and the occasions on which, and any conditions subject to which, time off may be taken are those that are reasonable to the circumstances having regard to:

- how much time off is required for the performance of the duties of the office or as a member of the body in question, and how much time off is required for the performance of the particular duty;

- how much time off the employee has already been permitted under sections 168 or 170 of the Trade Union and Labour Relations (Consolidation) Act 1992 — time off for trade union duties and activities;
- the circumstances of the employer's business and the effect of the employee's absence on the running of the businesses.

It is clear that the circumstances of the employer must be taken into account. As was stated in **Borders Regional Council v Maule** [1993] IRLR 199:

"It would normally be expected that, where an employee is undertaking duties of the kind to which s.[50] applies, there would be discussion between employer and employee in order to establish, by agreement, a pattern for the absences from work required by the duties; indeed, it does appear that attempts were made in the present case to agree such a pattern, although they may not have been wholly successful. It is also, we think, legitimate to observe that an employee who is undertaking a variety of public and other duties may have some responsibility to plan the absences from work, and to scale the level of commitment which such public duties involve so as to produce a pattern which can be regarded as reasonable in all the circumstances. The statute requires the Industrial Tribunal to consider the whole circumstances, and those circumstances must include the number and frequency of similar absences which have been permitted by the employer. In order to show that they have performed their statutory function, it is, in our view, necessary for the Industrial Tribunal to explain what considerations have been taken into account, and make some attempt to explain how those considerations have been balanced, before reaching the conclusion that the employer has acted unreasonably. That is perhaps particularly important in a case such as this, where the Industrial Tribunal is considering a single refusal of time off in the context of a previous history which is said to have been reasonable. In the present case, the Industrial Tribunal have, in our opinion, failed to make clear that they did take all relevant considerations into account or to explain how the various considerations were balanced. The reasons, so far as they go, indicate that they concentrated on one consideration, to the exclusion of others, when they came to their actual decision."

The draft precedent is deliberately open ended so that the employer can consider what is reasonable in the circumstances.

Other areas where there is a statutory right to time off cover:
- Time off for trade union activities (section 170 TULRCA 1992);
- Time off for trade union officials (section 178 TULRCA 1992);

- Time off to look for work on notification of redundancy (section 52 ERA 1996);
- Time off for safety representatives;
- Time off for ante-natal care;
- Time off for Occupational Pension Trustees (sections 58-60 ERA 1996);
- Time off for employee representatives (section 61 ERA 1996).

Precedent L5: Jury Service

Whilst there is no express provision that permits time off for jury service, the employer who refused permission will probably be in contempt of court. Precedent L5 adopts the pragmatic and sensible approach that time off will be given.

Precedent L6: Religious Holidays

There is no statutory entitlement to time off for religious holidays. However, there may be two grounds on which it is sensible for the employer to permit time off but to make it clear that this forms part of holiday entitlement:

Discrimination

A refusal to allow an employee time off for religious observance may possibly amount to indirect racial discrimination where it can be argued that the requirement or condition to attend work has a disproportionate effect upon the racial group of the employee and cannot be justified. However, it must be related to race and not to religion for the Race Relations Act 1976 to apply (for the distinction; see **Seide v Gillette Industries** [1980] IRLR 427). It may thus be difficult to argue that there is actionable discrimination under the terms of the Act.

The Human Rights Act

The Human Rights Act 1998, which came into force on 2nd October, incorporates the European Convention for the Protection of Human Rights and Fundamental Freedoms. Under Article 9 of the Act individuals have the right to hold religious beliefs, to change their religious beliefs and to "freedom to manifest his religion or belief, in worship, teaching, practice and observance." By Article 9.2, this is subject to

> "such limitations as are prescribed by law and necessary in a democratic society in the interests of public safety, for the protection of public order, health or morals, or for the protection of the rights and freedoms of others."

However, the European Court of Human Rights has tended to apply this Article restrictively. In **Ahmad v UK** [1982] 4 EHRR 126 an employee resigned from a teaching post because he was refused permission to attend worship at his mosque each Friday. The European Commission on Human Rights decided that the terms of his contract had been clearly known to him at the time that he started employment. A claim was rejected in **Stedman v UK** [1997] 23 EHRR 23 where the employee refused to work on Sundays because of her religious beliefs. It was held that she had been dismissed because she had refused to respect working hours and not because of her religious beliefs. It thus remains to be seen what impact the Convention will have upon this area.

Precedent L7: Other Absences

This precedent makes it clear that time off for certain domestic matters will not entail a right to time of but must be taken as holiday. During the debates on the dependancy provisions it was questioned whether the provisions would entail a right to time off when a washing machine needed repairing — a domestic emergency! As we have seen the provisions of section 57A are severely curtailed and employees will have to rely upon their holiday entitlement for such matters.

PART M: CONDUCT AND STANDARD OF BEHAVIOUR AT WORK

Precedent M1: Standard of Work

You must at all times carry out your duties to the best of your ability and you shall obey all lawful and reasonable orders given to you. You must keep the Company informed of your conduct in relation to the Company's business and provide explanations for any conduct as your Manager considers appropriate.

Precedent M2: Non Smoking Policy

It is the Company policy that smoking will not be allowed in the workplace. Smoking poses risks to health both in relation to the smoker and others who are otherwise forced to passively smoke. The Company has therefore imposed a ban on smoking in the Company premises [other than in designated areas]. Smoking on the premises or in an area that is not designated for smoking is a disciplinary offence under the Company's disciplinary procedure.

The Company will have regard to complaints by any member of staff that this policy is being ignored and will ensure that any person making such a complaint does not suffer any detriment by reason of such complaint. It will be a disciplinary offence to abuse or otherwise maltreat any person who has made a complaint.

Precedent M3: Alcohol and Drugs

The Company distinguishes between the use of alcohol and drugs in the workplace which will be regarded as a disciplinary offence and treated appropriately and sickness arising out of alcohol or drug problems. However, you should be aware that abuse of alcohol or drugs in the workplace is likely to lead to dismissal. The following rules apply:

1. If you are found consuming alcohol or taking drugs on the Company's premises or are under the influence of alcohol or drugs in the workplace then this will be treated as gross misconduct under the Company's disciplinary procedure. The possession of drugs for any reason other than medical is forbidden. You must inform your Manager if you are taking drugs for medical reasons and in particular if they are likely to affect your ability to work.

2. You may be required to undergo a medical examination in order to ascertain whether there is a problem in relation to drink or drugs which is affecting your ability to work. You may be suspended from work until the problem has been resolved. The Company will decide whether to require you to undergo a programme of rehabilitation or whether abuse of alcohol or drugs should be treated as a disciplinary matter.

3. If you are offered a programme of rehabilitation and do not comply with the programme this may be treated as a disciplinary matter.

4. You should be aware that the Company will not hesitate to inform the police if it believes that there has been an abuse of controlled drugs for which criminal sanctions are appropriate.

Precedent M4: Personal Telephone Calls from Work

It is the Company policy that you may not generally use the Company telephones to make personal calls from work. The Company recognises that there may be an occasional necessity to make such a call from work and permission should first be sought from your manager. Similar considerations apply in relation to other office equipment such as photocopying and stationery.

Mobile or car telephones must be used for business telephone calls only and you will be required to reimburse any private calls. You must immediately report the loss or theft of your mobile phone so that steps can be taken to disconnect it.

Precedent M5: E-Mail Policy

The Company has an e-mail system which is intended to promote the Company's business by making communication more effective. The Company may be liable if the system is misused by, for example, defamatory messages being sent to third parties through the e-mail system. The e-mail system is not meant for personal messages and they should be avoided so far as is possible. The following rules are applicable.

1. The language and content of any messages must be of an appropriate standard and should be succinct and to the point.
2. Inappropriate language which may include malicious gossip or messages that may amount to a breach of the Company's equal opportunity policies or be otherwise inappropriate will be treated as a disciplinary offence.
3. Confidential information must not be sent by e-mail.
4. E-mail sent through the Company shall remain the property of the Company and the Company shall have the right to retrieve all e-mails for such reasons as it considers appropriate.
5. If you receive an e-mail for which you were not the intended recipient you should immediately notify the sender. If you, yourself, receive an e-mail that is not considered to contain appropriate matter you should notify your Manager.
6. Deliberate or knowing misuse of the e-mail system may constitute gross misconduct and the Company will not tolerate the sending of e-mails that are malicious, untrue, obscene or defamatory. The Company will operate its disciplinary procedures in respect of any such misuse.

7. You should not open unsolicited e-mail if you do not know its source because it may contain a virus. You must immediately report receipt of such e-mail to [. . . . . . .].

Precedent M6:Computers and Data Protection

The Company will comply with all laws that regulate the use of computers, data protection and confidentiality and you are expected to assist in ensuring that the law is complied with. The following rules are applicable.

1. You are not permitted to use the Company's computer for personal use unless you have been given express permission.
2. You should only use your computer for the purpose of your job and should not use the computer system or information for any other purpose.
3. You are responsible for maintaining your computer equipment and software and where you have access to confidential information you must ensure that it remains secure.
4. If you have a password you must make sure that it is kept confidential and you must not give any other person access to your password.
5. You are not permitted to make copies of any software where this will amount to a breach of copyright or in any way make or distribute copies of software.
6. Breach of the above may result in disciplinary action.

COMMENTARY TO M:
CONDUCT AND STANDARD OF BEHAVIOUR AT WORK

This section covers various miscellaneous matters where the employee may feel it is important to have a specific policy. Indeed, in relation to telephone calls, e-mail and data protection, the Data Protection Act 1998, the Regulation of Investigatory Powers Act 2000 and the Telecommunications (Lawful Business Practice) (Interception of Communications) Regulations 2000 [SI 2000 No 2699] have a fundamental impact upon employer's rights and powers. Detailed consideration of these very detailed provisions are outside the scope of the Book but a summary is given below. It should also be noted that the Data Protection Commissioner has issued a draft Code of Practice that contains a very useful summary of the law, entitled *The Use of Personal Data in Employer/Employee Relationships*.

M1: Conduct and Standard of behaviour at work

It is sensible to include in a manual a statement that employees must obey all lawful instructions, though the reality is that this is likely to be implied by law. However, in **Diggle v Ogston Motor Company** [84 LJKB 2165; 112 LR 1029] there was a provision that an employer could terminate the contract in the event of the employee not performing to the satisfaction of the employer. It was held that such provision meant it was for the employer to judge the quality of the employee's work provided it did not act dishonestly or capriciously. The case was of course, long before the right to claim unfair dismissal came about. However, where a skilled worker is taken on there will be a warranty that he can carry out the work to be undertaken with reasonable competence (**Harmer v Cornelious** [1858] 5 CB 236).

M2: Non Smoking Policy

Of increasing concern over recent years have been health issues relating to smoking at work which has lead to many employees imposing smoke free environments. Particular issues may arise in relation to passive smoking with employees arguing that there health is being affected, and this has been addressed in case law and in legislation. Under Regulation 25 of the Workplace (Health, Safety and Welfare) Regulations 1992 an employer is obliged to make arrangements so that employees are protected from discomfort caused by tobacco smoke.

Implied terms

It is was held in **Dryden v Greater Glasgow Health Board** [1992] IRLR 469 by the Court of Session that, although it could not be said that it was impossible to have an implied term based on custom and practice that allowed smoking, in a case where there had been full consultation about a non smoking policy, the employer was entitled to replace this policy with a permission to smoke in various areas that had hitherto existed. The employee left twelve days after a total smoking ban was introduced because of the discomfort she suffered. The Court of Session rejected the argument that the ban was in breach of an implied term that the employer must not do anything that frustrates the employee's ability to carry out the contract and damaged the duty of mutual trust and confidence. Lord Coulsfield said:

"There can, in our view, be no doubt that an employer is entitled to make rules for the conduct of employees in their place of work, as he is entitled to give lawful orders, within the scope of the contract; nor can there be any doubt, in our view, that once it is has been held that there is no implied term in the contract which entitled the employee to facilities for smoking, a rule against smoking is, in itself a lawful rule."

The opposite side of the coin was considered in **Waltons & Morse v Dorrington** [1997] IRLR 488, in which an employee claimed that the smoking of fellow employees was adversely affecting her health. The EAT held that it is was an implied term that employers will, so far as is reasonably practicable, provide and monitor a working environment that is not injurious for their health and the starting point is section 2(2)(e) of the Health and Safety at Work Act 1974 which requires a working environment that is reasonably safe.

"In one sense, the right of an employee not to be required to sit in a smoke-filled atmosphere affects the welfare of employees at work, even if it is not something which directly is concerned with their health or can be proved to be a risk to health."

The employer did have steps it could take in that it could indicate to smokers that, as there were no adequate ventilation facilities within the building, they would not be allowed to smoke.

Precedent M2 sets out a clear policy that smoking will not be allowed in the workplace.

M3: Alchohol and Drugs

In certain circumstances the use of alcohol and drugs may be treated as a disciplinary issue. However, it is apparent from the case law that the abuse of alcohol and drugs may be a sickness or capability issue and be approached in this way by the employer. The cases on this area are considered in detail in Duggan on *Unfair Dismissal, Law, Practice and Guidance* at pages 145 and 193 to 197). In summary:

- the employer will need to consider whether the use of alcohol or drugs is a sickness or a conduct matter. If there are clear disciplinary rules that relate to the consumption of alcohol then it may be treated as a disciplinary matter (**Strathclyde Regional Council v Syme** [EAT 223/79]).
- Where performance or safety is affected or the consumption of alcohol results in unacceptable behaviour then this may justify treating the matter as a disciplinary one (**Weir v Stephen Allen Jewellers** [EAT 550/97]).

- A full and proper investigation should be carried out — see the cases cited at page 194 of *Unfair Dismissal* and factors such as consistency, the content of any rules and the gravity of the offence, taking into account mitigation be considered.

In **Angus Council v Edgley** [*IDS Brief* 647; EAT 289/99] a failure to apply a policy on alcohol abuse where the employee had a long standing problem was held to make a dismissal unfair. The employee had been employed for 28 years and had been subject to a final warning in 1991. He denied that he had an alcohol problem for which the employer could have offered assistance under its policy. He was given a final warning in 1995 in relation to travel and subsistence claims and this warning was to remain permanently on his file and further warning in 1997 relating to abuse of the flexible working hours scheme. A further disciplinary hearing was held on 4th June 1998 relating to him clocking out and visiting a public house. The employer took the view that this was a one off occasion to which the policy did not apply and he was dismissed in accordance with the disciplinary procedure. This was despite the fact that he produced a letter from his G.P. stating that he had been treated for an alcohol problem for years. The tribunal and EAT took the view that this was clearly a case where the employee had an alcohol problem so that the disciplinary procedure on misuse of alcohol should not have been applied. The alcohol policy stated that the employee would be given an opportunity to seek diagnosis and specialist help where the employee had an alcohol problem. The policy should have been applied as it was clear that the employee had a long standing problem.

Policy
The policy should make it clear that:

- The use of prescribed or illegal drugs is banned and will normally be regarded as a disciplinary offence;
- Employees may not drink at work or be under the influence of alcohol whilst at work. This is particularly important where there are safety issues.

Precedent M4 seeks to implement such a policy.

M4: Telephone Calls

There is nothing unlawful in a provision that an employee may not make personal telephone calls from work or that they may be on a limited basis. However, in order to supervise the use of telephones the employer may wish to monitor telephone calls. This may be to ensure that they are not abused or to monitor performance or transactions. However, monitoring calls may give rise to a number of difficulties (See *IDS Brief* 645 page 15 'Telephone

Monitoring at Work' and *Brief 672* 'Monitoring e-mails and telephone calls'). Such monitoring is now subject to the specific provisions of the Data Protection Act 1998, the Regulation of Investigatory Powers Act 2000 and the Telecommunications (Lawful Business Practice) (Interception of Communications) Regulations 2000 [SI 2000 No 2699]. The following points should be noted.

- Where there is a licence arrangement for a private telephone system (Self Provision Licences or Telecommunications Service Licences) it may be a provision of the licence that the licensee informs parties to telephone conversations that the call is being monitored.
- The right to privacy under Article 8 of the European Convention on Human Rights may make it illegal to intercept calls unless the defence under Article 8(2) that the interference takes place in accordance with the law and is:

  "necessary in a democratic society in the interests of national security, public safety or the economic well being of the country, for the prevention of disorder or crime, for the protection of health or morals, or for the protection of the rights and freedom of others".

  It was held in **Halford v United Kingdom** [1997] IRLR 471 that the Article had been infringed where the Merseyside police had monitored Mrs Halford's internal calls without her knowledge in circumstances where she had a reasonable expectation of privacy since there was a phone for private use in her office. Since there was no legal regulation of private telephone calls the Article 8(2) defence could not be applicable. The use of the Convention is also limited to employees of the State or to a claim that the United Kingdom is in breach by not providing any effective remedy and necessitates a petition to Strasbourg.
- The Human Rights Act 1998, however, will provide a more effective remedy since it is incorporates Article 8 and the courts and tribunals are to act in a manner that is compatible with the Convention or to make a declaration of incompatibility.
- In the light of the *Halford* case the Government issued Circular HOC 15/1999 which notes that a legitimate expectation of privacy may not exist where the employee has been warned that telephone calls may be monitored though this may not, in itself be sufficient, since:

  "It is not reasonable to expect that employees will never be contacted on a domestic matter in work time, or that the employee will never have reason to make personal calls from the office."

  OFTEL has also issued Guidance which makes it clear that warnings in themselves may not be sufficient and that employees should have access to a private telephone to make personal calls. The Guidance also states that employers should have a clear policy in relation to private telephone calls.

- The Government Consultation Paper (Cm 4368) proposes a system whereby employers will be required to notify that calls will be monitored and there will then be no reasonable expectation of privacy.
- Article 5 of the EU telecommunications Data Protection Directive (97/66) provides that the interception or monitoring of communication on public or non public networks may only take place if legally authorised. The Government was under a duty to implement this by October 2000 and has done so in the Regulations set out below.
- The Data Protection Act 1998 came into force on 1st March 2000. (See Bainbridge, *Data Protection*, CLT 2000.)
  See also below under M6.
- The Regulation of Investigatory Powers Act 2000 provided a framework to ensure that any investigatory powers are used in accordance with human rights. Section 1 provides that it is unlawful for a person, without lawful authority, to intercept a communication in the course of its transmission by way of a public or private telecommunications system. Section 4(2) provides that the Secretary of State has the power to issue regulations to authorise any such conduct described in the relations as appear to constitute a legitimate practice reasonably required for the purpose, in connection with the carrying on of any business, of monitoring or keeping a record of:
  (a) communications by means of which transactions are entered into in the course of that business; or
  (b) other communications relating to that business or taking place in the course of its being carried on.
  Section 4(3) makes it clear that only communications using apparatus or services provided by or to the person carrying on the business for use wholly or partly in connection with that business will be authorised.
- The Lawful Business Practice Regulations, by Regulation 3, authorise businesses to monitor or record communications without consent where the purpose is:
  — to establish the existence of facts relevant to the business *i.e.* records of transactions where it is necessary to know the contents of conversations;
  — to ascertain compliance with regulatory or self regulatory practices or procedures;

— to ascertain or demonstrate standards that ought to be achieved by the person using the system;

— to prevent or detect crime;

— to investigate or detect the authorised use of telecommunications systems, *i.e.* abuse of e-mail or the Internet;

— to ensure the effective operation of the system.

- In addition it is possible to monitor, but not record, for the purpose of determining whether or not the communications are relevant to the business and for the purpose of monitoring calls to a confidential anonymous counselling or support helpline.

- The employer may also be in breach of the implied term of trust and confidence where calls are monitored without informing the employee.

Policy

The policy should make it clear which calls are permitted, in particular where the calls are made from the employer's own telephones. It should state when calls may be made (*e.g.* premium rates may be regarded as unacceptable because of cost and there may be times when it is essential that the telephone lines are clear for business calls). It is may be that the employer wishes to stipulate that the employee bears the cost of certain calls. In addition, it is important that any disciplinary sanctions for abuse of telephones are made clear.

M5: E-Mail Policy

There are two issues in relation to e-mail policy:

- the monitoring of e-mails by employers for the purpose of the business, as to which see the commentary on telephone calls.

- the sanctions that may be applicable in cases of abuse of the e-mail system or the Internet. Precedent M5 makes it clear that deliberate abuse of the e-mail system is a disciplinary matter. There are three particular areas of concern:

  1. Matters posted through the Internet may be defamatory and in **Godfrey v Demon Internet Limited** (26.3.1999) the High Court held that an Internet service provider was liable for a defamatory e-mail even though it was not the publisher of the statement. Employers may therefore be at risk if employees post defamatory e-mails.

  2. Downloading of pornography may lead to complaints of sexual harassment by women staff (see **Morse v Future Reality Limited** [London North ET] cited at *IDS Brief* 637 and the other cases there cited about when dismissal will be appropriate.

3. Unauthorised access may in itself be a disciplinary matter (but see **British Telecommunications Plc v Rodrigues** [EAT 854/92]).

Any policy should therefore set out very clearly what will amount to a disciplinary matter and the possible sanctions.

M6: Computers and Data Protection

The Data Protection Act 1998 came into force on 1st March 2000. It contains detailed provision for the regulation and management of data. The Data Protection Commissioner has issued a detailed Code for consideration entitled *The Use of Personal Data in Employer/Employee Relationships* which covers every stage of the employment relationship from recruitment, employee records, monitoring, medical testing to discipline and dismissal and reference should be made to that Code for the principles which are wide ranging and beyond the scope of this book. Precedent M6 is intended to set out in general terms what computer misuse will not be tolerated.

PART N: STAFF DEVELOPMENT AND APPRAISAL

Precedent N1: Provision of Staff Training and Development

The Company believes that the skills and expertise of its workforce are of paramount importance in ensuring that it can provide the best possible service and product to its customers. A well motivated and highly trained workforce can only improve the business of the Company. The Company has therefore devised a policy of staff development and appraisal. The general terms of the policy are set out below and you will have received further details in your Letter of Appointment or at your interview for your post.

1. **Induction training** You will have received induction training at the outset of your employment in order that you are made fully aware of the needs of the job and Company procedures. If you have any queries you should raise them with your Manager.

2. **Appraisals** You will be subject to an annual appraisal at which your performance will be discussed and any ongoing training to assist you in your job will be considered. The purpose of the appraisal is to assist you in your job rather than because of any disciplinary reason. The Company will also make available to you a programme of in house training as it considers appropriate which will be discussed with you.

3. **Leave** You may be given paid leave in order to attend classes and to sit examinations. You may also be given leave to revise at the discretion of the Company. However, it is expected that your studies will take place in your own time.

4. **Fees** The Company may pay tuition fees and other costs related to your studies or agree to reimburse the same to you if it considers appropriate.

5. **Professional subscriptions** The Company will reimburse annual subscriptions to the appropriate professional bodies as it considers appropriate.

6. **Repayment of subscriptions** If you do not complete your course of study or leave the employment of the Company before you have completed your studies the Company reserves the right to require that the monies be reimbursed.

COMMENTARY TO N:
STAFF DEVELOPMENT AND APPRAISAL

There will be an implied term in the contracts of employment of probationary employees that the employer takes reasonable steps to appraise and to give instruction, guidance and warning during the period of probation. In **White v London Transport Executive** [1981] IRLR 261 a number of complaints were made about Ms White after she had been promoted to manager on a probationary basis so that she was transferred back to her previous job at another site. She claimed constructive dismissal. The claim was rejected on the facts. The EAT stated:

> "For ourselves we consider that in relation to probation the law would be ill-advised to imply detailed contractual rights relating to the rights of a probationer. We think that the right term to imply is that which the industrial tribunal took in this case, namely an obligation on the employer to take reasonable steps to maintain an appraisal of a probationer during a trial period, giving guidance by advice or warning where necessary."

The precedent contained in the manual is deliberately written in general terms so as to give employers a general discretion as to the training that it will provide. One point that an employer will wish to consider is the issue of repayment of subscriptions or training costs should the employee leave prematurely.

PART 0: EMPLOYEE REPRESENTATION

Precedent 01: Trade Union Representation

1 The Company recognises the _____ union for the purpose of collective bargaining and the terms of any collective agreement with the union are incorporated into your contract of employment.

2 You have the right to belong to an independent trade union. You are entitled to participate in the activities of the union and to become an officer, official or steward of the union.

3 The have the right to decide not to join a trade union and the Company will respect your wishes if you elect not to be a trade union member.

4 You are entitled to time off in order to carry out trade union activities if you are a trade union representative and you may be entitled to paid time off as agreed in order to carry out official duties as a trade union official.

Precedent 02: Staff Association Representation

There is a staff association which the Company communicates with for the purpose of dealing with matters that are of mutual interest and importance to the Company and employees. Staff representatives are elected onto a committee on an annual basis. You are entitled to stand for election to the committee as and when there are vacancies or when the posts come up for election. All staff may vote in any election. The matters which the staff association and the Company discuss include:

1. Company activities including sales, business plans, productivity of the Company and proposals to improve the profitability of the Company.
2. The terms and conditions of employment of staff including salary reviews and other benefits to which staff may be entitled.
3. Health and safety matters.
4. Recreational and social activities.
5. Any other matters as may be agreed between the Company and the Staff Association from time to time as being relevant.

COMMENTARY TO O:
STAFF ASSOCIATION REPRESENTATION

The Employment Rights Act 1996 has introduced significant new rights to recognition by trade unions and the relationship between the employer and trade union representatives or employee representatives are likely to be covered by detailed provisions of a collective or other agreement. Precedents O1 and O2 are merely meant to be general statements of the existence of a trade union or staff representation and should be included in the Manual to make it clear that these rights exist.

PART P: PUBLIC INTEREST DISCLOSURE

Precedent P1: Public Interest Disclosure Policy

The Company operates a strict policy in relation to wrongdoing (which will be regarded as a disciplinary offence) and will not tolerate actions which may amount to a criminal offence or breaches of legal obligations, a miscarriage of justice, danger to health or safety or which may damage the environment ('wrongdoing'). All employees are expected to maintain the highest of standards of integrity and good faith. Under Part 1VA of the Employment Rights Act 1996 employees who report wrongdoing to certain parties are protected. However, it is the policy of the Company that any wronging that has occurred should be reported to the Company. Accordingly, the Company has devised the following policy in order to encourage you to report any matters that you believe are of concern to the Company and to reassure you that you will be protected in respect of any such disclosures.

1 You may be concerned about the repercussions to you in reporting matters that are of concern. The Company assures you that you will be protected and will not be subjected to any detriment because you have reported a matter that you believe in good faith to amount to wrongdoing or potential wrongdoing.

2 However, you must note that if you make any allegation which you do not believe or which is made maliciously or for some ulterior motive (*i.e.* a grudge against a fellow worker) then this may be treated as a disciplinary matter and the Company may invoke the disciplinary procedure.

Reporting wrongdoing

3 In the first instance you may wish to raise the matter with your Manager on an informal basis and discuss with him what steps should be taken to report the matter to more senior management.

4 You may at any time raise the matter formally with your Manager, whether orally or in writing and he pass on the matter to the appropriate level of management.

5 If your concern is about your Manager or someone at a higher level of management then you should feel free to raise the matter with whatever you consider to be the appropriate level of management.

6 At all stages all statements that you make will remain confidential unless you express a contrary wish or it becomes necessary to divulge such statements during the course of an investigation.

Investigations

7 You must recognise that a complaint about wrongdoing may lead to the Company wishing to carry out an investigation into the allegations of wrongdoing. In these circumstances you will be informed before any of the matters that you have raised are put to the alleged wrongdoer and you will be protected by the Company who will ensure that you work environment is not affected because you disclosed the matter to the Company.

8 You will be informed of the outcome of any investigation and what action has been taken.

9 If you have any concern or complaint about the manner in which you feel you are being treated because you made the disclosure, whether by the alleged wrongdoer or any co-employees you should raise this with whatever level of management you consider to be appropriate and this may be dealt with as a disciplinary matter in relation to such individuals.

10 If you are unhappy about the manner in which your disclosure was treated by the person to whom it was reported or you consider that it is not being properly investigated then you should report the matter to whatever level of management you consider appropriate which may include a Director of the Board of Directors. You will not suffer any detriment by making such a report unless point 2 above applies.

At all times the intention of the Company will be to resolve the allegations that have been made and to ensure that wrongdoing has not occurred or, if it has occurred, it is dealt with appropriately. However, the Company will not hesitate to report wrongdoing to the appropriate body if it considers that this is the correct approach to adopt in the circumstances.

COMMENTARY TO P:
CONDUCT OF EMPLOYEE/OTHER EMPLOYEES & PUBLIC INTEREST DISCLOSURE

It is necessary to consider, briefly, the common law position and then to consider the protection afforded by the Public Interest Disclosure Act 1998, which incorporates Part 1VA of the Employment Rights Act 1996, to employees who choose to 'whistleblow'.

Implied Terms: parties' duty to inform the other of breaches
There is no general duty on the part of an employer to inform its employees that it has committed a breach of contract so that a compromise agreement will remain binding even if the employer has been guilty of fraud (**Bank of Credit and Commerce International SA (in liquidation) v Ali** [1999] IRLR 226:

"The current law as generally understood may be stated as follows that (1) (subject to one exception) neither party to a contract is obliged to disclose facts material to the decision of the other party whether to enter into that contract; (2) the exception is limited to contracts which are *uberrimae fidei*; (3) neither contracts of employment or contracts of compromise (unless by way of family arrangement) fall within this exceptional category; and (4) neither the employer nor the employee, once in contractual relations, are under a duty as such to disclose to each other their own breaches of contract."

It was held in **Macmillan Inc v Bishopgate Investment Trust PLC** [1993] ICR 385; IRLR 393 that there is no general duty on the part of an employee to disclose information which it is in the employer's interests to know, regardless of how it is has been obtained. The information must have been obtained "in the course of employment" so that where an employee gave evidence to a liquidator about the insolvency of a third party company it could not be said that the employer had any power over the transcripts of the interview which the employee held.

It has been clear ever since **Bell v Lever Bros Limited** [1932] AC 161 that an employee is under no duty to disclose his own misconduct. As Lord Atkin said in his speech:

"I agree that the duty in the servant to protect his master's property may involve the duty to report a fellow servant whom he knows to be wrongfully dealing with that property. The servant owes a duty not to steal, but having stolen, is there superadded a duty to confess that he has stolen? I am satisfied that to imply such a duty would be a departure from the well established usage of mankind and would be to create obligations entirely outside the normal contemplation of the parties concerned."

(See also **Fletcher v Krell** [1873] 28 LT 105; **Healey v Societe Anonyme Francaise Rubastic** [1917] 1 KB 946; **Hands v Simpson Fawcett & Co** [1928] 44 TLR 295).

There is also no general duty to report the wrongdoing of fellow employees by way of any implied term. In **Sybron Corporation v Rochem Limited** [1983] IRLR 253; ICR 801 a Mr Roques, European Zone Manager for a subsidiary of Sybron, was involved in setting up rival companies in competition, together with subordinates, and he concealed this from his employer. After retirement the matters came to light and the company sought to recover a lump sum it had paid under his pension scheme. The Court of Appeal dismissed an appeal that he must repay such monies. He had been in a senior executive position and there was a continuing fraud or which he was well aware. Fox LJ cited the *dicta* of Greene LJ in **Swain v West (Butchers) Limited** [1936] 3 All ER 261that:

"The plaintiff was responsible for the management of the business and was responsible for seeing that the business was conducted honestly and efficiently by all who came under its control. If the dishonesty of a fellow servant came to his notice, he should tell the board."

This was so, notwithstanding that it would reveal his own dishonesty. Thus, it depends upon the status of the employee as to whether or not there will be such an implied term. If there is an express term on the contract this difficulty will, of course, not arise.

Public Interest Disclosure

Part IVA of the 1996 contains a number of provisions whereby the employee will be protected if he makes a disclosure for one of several reasons. It is necessary to consider:

- The definition of a qualifying disclosure;
- Those circumstances where a disclosure will be protected (this section largely follows the format of Chapter 19 of *Unfair Dismissal*).

Qualifying Disclosure

By section 43B a qualifying disclosure means any disclosure of information which, in the reasonable belief of the worker making the disclosure, tends to show:

1. that a criminal offence has been committed, is being committed or is likely to be committed;
2. that a person has failed, is failing or is likely to fail to comply with any legal obligation to which he is subject;
3. that a miscarriage of justice has occurred, is occurring or is likely to occur;
4. that the health or safety of any individual has been, is being or is likely to be endangered;
5. that the environment has been, is being or is likely to be damaged;
6. that information tending to show any of the five matters set out before has been or is likely to be deliberately concealed.

A disclosure of such information will not be a qualifying disclosure if a criminal offence is committed by disclosing such information (43B(3)) or if it relates to information that was disclosed in the course of taking legal advice (43B(4)).

The six circumstances and the requirements are as follows:

1. Disclosure to employee or other responsible person
By section 43C a qualifying disclosure is made where:

- the worker makes the disclosure in good faith
  - to his employer; or
  - to another person where he believes that the failure relates solely or mainly to the conduct of a person other than the employer or a matter for which a person other than the employer has legal responsibility.

2. Disclosure to legal adviser

By section 43D a disclosure qualifies if it is made in the course of taking legal advice.

3. Disclosure to Minister of the Crown

A disclosure will qualify if made to a Minister of the Crown in circumstances where the employer is an individual or a body appointed by a Minister of the Crown.

4. Disclosure to a prescribed person

The requirements of this section are:

- the disclosure must be made in good faith;
- the disclosure must be made to a person prescribed by an order made by the Secretary of State for the purposes of the section;
- the worker must reasonably believe that the failure falls within any description of matters in relation to which the person is so prescribed;
- the worker must believe that the information disclosed and any allegation are substantially true.

The Public Interest Disclosure (Prescribed Persons) Order 1999 (SI 1999/1549) sets out in detail the prescribed persons to whom complaints should be made.

5. Disclosure in other cases

A qualifying disclosure is made in accordance with section 43G where:

- the worker makes the disclosure in good faith;
- the worker reasonably believes that the information disclosed and any allegation are substantially true;
- the worker does not make the disclosure for personal gain;
- it is reasonable for him to make the disclosure, taking into account those matters set out in section 43F(3), being:
  - (a) the identify of the person to whom the disclosure is made;
  - (b) the seriousness of the relevant failure;
  - (c) whether the failure is continuing or likely to continue in the future;
  - (d) whether the disclosure is made in breach of a duty of confidentiality;
  - (e) what action was taken or could reasonably be expected to have been taken in relation to previous disclosures;
  - (f) whether the worker complied with procedure in relation to previous disclosures made to the employer;

and one of the following conditions is met:

1. at the time that the disclosure is made the worker believes that he will be subjected to a detriment by his employer if he makes the disclosure to the employer or to a prescribed person in accordance with section 43F;

2. where no person is prescribed under section 43F the worker reasonably believes that it is likely that the evidence relating to the relevant failure will be concealed or destroyed if he makes disclosure to the employer;

3. that the worker has previously made a disclosure of substantially the same information to his employer or a prescribed person under section 43F (which may include information about action taken or not taken by any person as a result of the previous disclosure (43G(4)).

6. *Disclosure of exceptionally serious failure*
A qualifying disclosure is made in accordance with section 43H where:

- the worker makes the disclosure in good faith;
- the worker reasonably believes that the information disclosed and any allegation are substantially true;
- the worker does not make the disclosure for personal gain;
- the relevant failure is of an exceptionally serious nature;
- it was reasonable in all the circumstances for him to make the disclosure and, in this respect, regard is to be had to the identify of the person to whom the disclosure was made (43H(2)).

The Precedent seeks to set out policy that is both fair to the employee making the complaint but also protects the rights of others should the complaint be malicious or untrue. It makes it clear that the employee will not be victimised but will be given a fair opportunity to state his case and will be protected. Note that the policy cannot prevent a complaint being made to an outside body where that is appropriate and any attempt to stop the worker is likely to amount to a detriment under the Act or a potentially automatically unfair dismissal if the worker resigns or is dismissed.

PART Q: RESTRICTIONS DURING AND AFTER EMPLOYMENT

Precedent Q1: Employment that Conflicts with your Duties

It is the Company's policy that you will work exclusively upon the Company's business. You are not allowed to undertake any other paid employment during the time that you are employed by the Company without the express agreement in writing of the Company. If you wish to take up any outside appointment you must have the express written permission of _____ in the Company. You will not, in any event, be able to take up any employment that may amount to a conflict of interest between your work with the Company and you should not have any interest, whether directly or indirectly, in a business that may place you in conflict of interest. You must inform the Company if you are involved or become involved in such a businesses.

Precedent Q2: Confidential Information

The Company operates a very strict policy with regard to confidential information. You will appreciate that the nature of the business of the Company is such that its continued success is dependant upon information remaining confidential and any disclosure of such information may be harmful to the Company's business. This information includes, but is not limited to:

[SET OUT LIST OF INFORMATION THAT IT TO BE REGARDED AS CONFIDENTIAL *e.g.*

- Marketing and sales policies.
- Pricing information.
- Customer information and details.]

By the same token the affairs of the Company's clients are private and any information that you obtain about clients or customers during the period that you are employed must be regarded as confidential. The Company will regard any breach of confidentiality as a disciplinary offence and any breaches may lead to dismissal.

Accordingly, you agree that during and after your employment you will not disclose any confidential information that has come to your attention during the course of your employment. You will at all times protect and maintain the confidentiality of the Company's information and that of its clients and may only disclose such information as required by law or as is necessary during the course of your duties with the Company. You understand that this oblation will continue at all times both during and after the termination of your employment unless and until the information has come into the public domain.

You may have been required to sign a confidentiality undertaking when you signed your letter of appointment. You must abide by the terms of that confidentiality undertaking at all times and it will be regarded as an act of gross misconduct if you breach the terms of that undertaking, which may lead to disciplinary proceedings and possible dismissal.

Precedent Q3: Undertaking as to Confidentiality

As part of your continued employment you agree that you will give the following undertakings as to confidentiality in order to protect the business of the Company and the confidential information of the Company's clients or customers.

1   You recognise and agree that you have had access to confidential information belonging to the Company [and its clients/customers] and that you will keep secret and ensure that you do not divulge such information to any third party save for the purposes of your employment or as is required by law.

2   For the avoidance of doubt you agree that you will not divulge such information, whether directly or indirectly, to any third party whether it be a person, company, partnership or any other entity and whether such disclosure is for profit or otherwise.

3   You agree that the confidential information referred to includes all information that is secret or confidential to the Company and is not in the public domain. This information shall include:
   • business plans and forecasts;
   • financial information relating to the Company that is not in the public domain;
   • intellectual property details which are not in the public domain;
   • marketing information;
   • plans, designs, or formulae that are not in the public domain;
   • research that it being carried on by the Company into its products and which is not in the public domain;
   • technical information relating to the Company or its clients.

4   You accept that the Company's ongoing business will mean that from time to time you will be in receipt of information that is regarded as confidential by the Company and you will ensure that you will not disclose such information to any party save as set out in [1] above.

5   If information comes into the public domain other than by way of an unauthorised disclosure by you or any other party then the obligations of confidentiality may no longer apply but you are advised to check with the Company before you make use of any such information.

6 You will at all times during your employment be in a position to make use of information in the performance of your duties. However, if you have any concerns as to whether or not it is appropriate for you to use such information you must draw it to the attention of your Manager who will give appropriate advice, if necessary referring it to a higher level of management.

7 You may disclose any information if the Company has authorised you to do so.

8 The Company expressly acknowledges that there may be circumstances in which you will be required to disclose information as a matter of law and also that you should be entitled to disclose information pursuant to the Public Interest Disclosure Act 1998. In these circumstances (subject to the Company's disclosure policy) at _____ no steps will be taken by the Company if such information is disclosed.

9 You understand that wrongful disclosure of any confidential information may be a disciplinary offence which may invoke the Company's disciplinary procedures.

10 Where your employment involves access to confidential information the Company will at all times be prepared to assist you if you are not sure about which information is regarded as confidential and you should speak to your manager about this matter.

Precedent Q4: Protection of Intellectual Property

If you were employed by the Company to carry out any functions that involve making new inventions or improving original inventions or that relate to the use of confidential information or creating material that it subject to copyright or in applying designs, manufacturing methods, plans, processes or techniques that are new or have been improved then you must have signed an agreement that relates to the protection of all such material ('the Intellectual Property'). You agree that you will keep confidential all such information and will promptly disclose to the Company all such Intellectual Property whether made by yourself or in conjunction with others during the course of, or arising out of, your employment. You will hold in trust for the Company all such intellectual property and will take whatever lawful steps the Company requires to assign the Intellectual Property to the Company and ensure that it is lawfully vested in the Company. Where it is necessary to secure a patent to protect the Intellectual Property or to take any other steps you will render all assistance and do everything that it necessary to assist the Company in obtaining such protection. The use of the Intellectual Property is at the absolute discretion of the Company.

In any event by signing your Statement of Written Terms and Conditions you agree to be bound by the terms of the Agreement, which is described as the 'Intellectual Property Agreement'. For the avoidance of doubt about its contents the terms of that Agreement are set out hereafter.

INTELLECTUAL PROPERTY AGREEMENT

1   You agree that during the course of your employment your job functions may require you to assist, participate or otherwise be involved in the creation or improvement of designs, plans, manufacturing methods, plans, processes or techniques in relation to new or improved inventions relating to the Company's business. For the purposes of this Agreement the term 'Intellectual Property' shall mean every design, development, discovery, formula, improvement or process ('the inventions') and every work or design in which copyright may exist, including moral rights as defined in the Copyright Designs and Patents Act 1988.

2   Should you make an invention in the course of the normal duties of your employment or in relation to duties that have been specifically assigned to you but would not otherwise have been your normal duties or where the invention was made in the furtherance of the Company's undertaking then all such inventions will belong to the Company and all Intellectual Property made during the

course of your duties will so vest in the Company to the absolute extent that is permitted by law.

3   You agree that you will forthwith notify to the Company all Intellectual Property which you may make during your employment, whether made by yourself or with other persons and you will keep the Company appraised at all times of the stage that has been reached in relation to any improvement or creation of such intellectual property.

4   You agree that you will take all steps and carry out all acts that may be necessary to ensure that the Intellectual Property is lawfully vested in the Company, including signing all applications and any other documents that may be necessary to apply for any Patent rights or any other form of application in the United Kingdom and Worldwide and to transfer the entire rights and interests in the Intellectual Property to the Company and you will carry out such acts and steps with expedition on the instructions of the Company, in particular, where the filing of any claim to such Intellectual Property right may give the Company priority.

5   You will not be entitled to payment in respect of any Intellectual Property other than your normal provisions for remuneration. However, if you are entitled to additional compensation by section 40 of the Patents Act 1977 the Company will pay this to you and your rights under sections 39 to 43 of the Patents Act 1977 are recognised. The Company will incur any expenses to enable you to comply with the provisions of clause 4 herein.

6   These provisions remain in force with regard to Intellectual Property notwithstanding the termination of your employment.

Precedent Q5: Model Restrictive Covenants

Acknowledgements

1. In entering into employment with the Company the Employee recognises and acknowledges that:

    (1) The Company [and each Company in the Group] possesses Confidential Information that is important to the business of the Company [Group].

    (2) The Company will give the Employee access to such confidential information in order that he may carry out his duties.

    (3) The Employee has a duty to act at all times in the best interest of the Company and owes duties of fidelity and trust and confidence to the Company.

    (4) The Employee will directly benefit from access to the Confidential information as it will enable him to carry out his duties or to make sales and to earn commissions thereon.

    (5) Other employees are required to accept restrictions which are similar to those set out herein or are appropriate to the employees and which are for the mutual protection of the Company and of the Employee's position.

    (6) Disclosure of Confidential information to any Customer, Supplier or actual or potential competitor is likely to place the Company or Group at a competitive disadvantage or otherwise cause immeasurable financial or other harm to the business of the Company or Group.

    (7) That if the Employee were to take up or hold a position with any Competitor of the Company or Group this would be likely to likely to place the Company or Group at a competitive disadvantage or otherwise cause immeasurable financial or other harm to the business of the Company or Group.

Confidentiality

Precedents Q2 and Q3 should be incorporated.

Non Poaching of Employees

The Employee will not at any time during his employment

and for a period of [.....] months after the termination of his employment seek to entice, persuade, solicit or employ, or provide any work, whether directly or indirectly, through any company firm, person or other entity, or for the benefit thereof, or agree to provide any such work to any person who was for the period of [.....] months employed or engaged by the Company and who by reason of his employment is likely to be a position to solicit or deal with Customers or Suppliers of the Company or to cause harm to the Company or Group if he should accept work from any business which is in competition with the Company or Group.

Post Termination Restrictions

The Employee shall not, whether directly or indirectly, and whether through any company, from person or other entity, and whether as Employer, servant or agent or otherwise, howsoever:

1. For a period of [.....] months after the termination of his employment, in relation to any business that which is or is likely to be wholly or partly in competition with the business of the Employer [or Group]:

1.1. the Employee shall not hold any position as director, officer, employee, consultant, partner, principal or agent, which is the same as or similar to the position that he held when he was an employee of the Company [or Group], or which will or may involve him using Confidential Information in order to fulfill the duties of that position;

1.2. the Employee shall not have any direct or indirect control or ownership of any shares or debentures, whether jointly or alone in any such business, save for investment purpose or not more than [....]% of the issued ordinary shares of any Company;

1.3. the Employee shall not give financial assistance whether directly or indirectly to any such business.

2. For a period of [.....] months after the termination of his employment, in relation to any business that which is or is likely to be wholly or partly in competition with the business of the Employer [or Group] the Employee shall not shall not hold any position as director, officer,

employee, consultant, partner, principal or agent, which is the same as or similar to the position that he held when he was an employee of the Company [or Group] where that position requires or might reasonably thought by the Employer to require him to disclose or make use of any Confidential Information belonging to the Employer in order to carry out his duties or to promote or further such business. For this purpose Confidential Information shall mean [LIST].

3. For a period of [....] months after the termination of his employment the Employee shall not, whether directly or indirectly, or as servant, agent or otherwise howsoever:

3.1. Solicit, canvass, procure orders from or otherwise seek to obtain business from customers or clients who were customers or clients of the Employer at any time during the period of [.....] months prior to the termination of the Employee's employment and with whom the Employee dealt or had contact during that period.

3.2. Solicit from or place orders with or otherwise seek to obtain business from suppliers who were suppliers of the Employer at any time during the period of [.....] months prior to the termination of the Employee's employment and with whom the Employee dealt or had contact during that period.

3.3. Seek any business, orders or custom in relation to any products or services provided by the Employer with which the Employee was concerned during the time he was employed by the Employer.

3.4. Deal with or otherwise accept business from customers or clients who were customers or clients of the Employer at any time during the period of [.....] months prior to the termination of the Employee's employment and with whom the Employee dealt or had contact during that period.

3.5. Deal with, or otherwise have contact with, suppliers who were suppliers of the Employer, in relation to products supplied or to be supplied to the Employer, at any time during the period of [.....] months prior to the termination of the Employee's employment and with whom the Employee dealt or had contact during that period.

3.6. Accept business from customers or clients who were customers or clients of the Employer at any time during the period of [.....] months prior to the termination of the Employee's employment and with whom the Employee dealt or had contact during that period.

3.7. Induce or attempt to persuade, procure or otherwise facilitate employees of the Employer to leave their employment or to accept employment with any business that is wholly or partly in competition with the Employer.

4. The Employee shall not:

4.1. At any time after the termination of his employment represent or hold himself out as being in any way connected with the Employer or any Group Company.

4.2. At any time after the termination of his employment disclose to any person, firm, or company or otherwise howsoever any Confidential Information belonging to the Employer.

5. For the purpose of the above covenants Confidential Information shall mean [LIST] ... **provided** that the Employee is able to use his own personal expertise and information that has come into the public domain.

6. Each of the above clauses are independent and severable and shall be regarded as separately enforceable. If any provisions are unenforceable but would be enforceable if any parts were deleted then the parties agree that such words must be deleted in order to make them enforceable.

COMMENTARY TO Q:
RESTRICTIONS DURING AND AFTER EMPLOYMENT

The employer will want to protect his business during the period that the employee is employed and, so far as he can, for some time after the termination of the employment of the individual employee. It is vital that the employer has in place covenants that are clearly enforceable by the courts. Where the covenants are dubious at first instance then interim relief may be refused and the employer limited to his remedy in damages (see **Wincanton Limited v Cranny** [2000] IRLR 716 for a recent example of where this happened). The nature of the interest to be protected must be sufficiently clearly defined. The Precedents in Q cover each stage of the employment relations and thereafter, as well as taking into account matters such as confidential information and intellectual property rights. These comprise:

Q1: Working exclusively for the Employer whilst the employment relationship is ongoing;

Q2/3: Protection of Confidential Information;

Q4: Protection of Intellectual Property Rights;

Q5: A detailed restrictive covenant relating to non-poaching, confidentially and non-competition after employment has terminated.

Precedent Q1: Employment that conflicts with your duties

There will be an implied term between the employer and employee whereby the employee owes a duty of fidelity. This will mean that competing with an employee whilst the employment relationship subsists will be a breach of duty (**Thomas Marshall (Exports) Limited v Guinle** [1978] ICR 905) and this will be so even if the activities are carried out in the employee's spare time where they affect the business of the employer (**Hivac Limited v Park Royal Scientific Instruments Limited** [1946] Ch 169; **Lancashire Fires Limited v S A Lyons & Co Limited** [1996] FSR 629). Precedent Q1 makes it clear that the employee will not be permitted to act in any way that does create a conflict but must devote his whole duties to the employer.

Precedent Q2/3: Confidential Information

An employer is entitled to protect information that is confidential to itself. It is a matter of law as to whether the information is in truth confidential. A mere assertion that it is confidential may not make it so. The leading case is **Faccenda Chicken Limited v Fowler** [1986] ICR 297. In that case the test was laid down as follows:

"The relevant principles of law to be applied to the use by an employee of information acquired during his employment can be stated as follows:

(1) Where the parties are, or have been, linked by a contract of employment, the obligations of the employee are to be determined by the contract between him and his employer.

(2) In the absence of any express term, the obligations of the employee in respect of the use and disclosure of information are the subject of implied terms.

(3) While the employee remains in the employment of the employer the obligations are included in the implied term which imposes a duty of good faith or fidelity on the employee.

(4) The implied term which imposes an obligation on the employee as to his conduct after the determination of the employment is more restricted in its scope than that which imposes a general duty of good faith. The obligation not to use or disclose information may cover secret processes or manufacture such as chemical formulae, or designs or special methods of construction, and other information which is of a sufficiently high degree of confidentiality as to amount to a trade secret. The obligation does not extend, however, to cover all information which is given to or acquired by the employee while in his employment, and in particular may not cover information which is only "confidential" in the sense that an unauthorised disclosure of such information to a third party while the employment subsisted would be a clear breach of the duty of good faith.

(5) In order to determine whether any particular item of information falls within the implied term so as to prevent its use or disclosure by an employee after his employment has ceased, it is necessary to consider all the circumstances of the case. The following matters are among those to which attention must be paid:

(a) The nature of the employment. Thus employment in a capacity where "confidential" material is habitually handled may impose a high obligation of confidentiality because the employee can be expected to realise its sensitive nature to a greater extent than if he were employed in a capacity where such material reaches him only occasionally or incidentally.

(b) The nature of the information itself. Information will only be protected if it can properly be classed as a trade secret or as material which, while not properly to be described as a trade secret, is in all the circumstances of such a highly confidential nature as to require the same protection as a trade secret eo nomine. Therefore, the court could not accept the suggestion by the judge below that an employer can protect, by means of a restrictive covenant, the use of confidential information which has become part of the employee's own skill and knowledge, even though it does not include either a trade secret or its equivalent. Restrictive covenant cases demonstrate that a covenant will not be upheld on the basis of the status of the information which might be disclosed by the former employee if he is not restricted, unless it can be regarded as a trade secret or the equivalent of a trade secret. It is impossible to provide a list of matters which will qualify as trade secrets or their equivalent. Secret processes of manufacture provide obvious examples, but innumerable other pieces of information are capable of being trade secrets, though the secrecy of some information may be only short-lived. In addition, the fact that the circulation of certain information is restricted to a limited number of individuals may throw light on the status of the information and its degree of confidentiality.

(c) Whether the employer impressed on the employee the confidentiality of the information. Thus, though an employer cannot prevent the use or disclosure merely by telling the employee that certain information is confidential, the attitude of the employer towards the information provides evidence which may assist in determining whether or not the information can properly be regarded as a trade secret.

(d) Whether the relevant information can be easily isolated from other information which the employee is free to use or disclose. The separability of the information in question is not conclusive, but the fact that the alleged "confidential" information is part of a package and that the remainder of the package is not confidential is likely to throw light on whether the information in question is really a trade secret.

In the present case, neither the sales information as a whole which the defendants had acquired while in the employ of the Claimants — the names and addresses of customers, the most convenient routes to be taken to reach individual customers, the usual requirements of individual customers, the days of the week and times of day when deliveries were made to individual customers, and the prices charged to individual customers — nor their knowledge of the prices charged to individual customers looked at by itself, fell within the class of confidential information which an employee is bound by an implied term of his contract of employment or otherwise not to use or disclose after his employment has come to an end. The argument on behalf of the Claimants that any information about the prices charged to individual customers was confidential, and that, as this information formed part of the package of sales information, the package taken as a whole was confidential too could not be accepted. Although in certain circumstances information about prices can be invested with a sufficient degree of confidentiality to render that information a trade secret or its equivalent, in the present case the following factors led to the conclusion that neither the information about prices nor the sales information as a whole had the degree of confidentiality necessary to support the Claimants' case: the sales information contained some material which the Claimants conceded was not confidential if looked at in isolation; the information about the prices was not clearly severable from the rest of the sales information; neither the sales information in general, nor the information about prices in particular, though of some value to a competitor, could reasonably be regarded as plainly secret or sensitive; the sales information, including the information about prices, was necessarily acquired by the defendants in order that they could do their work and each salesman could quickly commit the whole of the sales information relating to his own area to memory; the sales information was generally known among the van drivers who were employees, as were the secretaries, at quite a junior level, so that this was not a case where the relevant information was restricted to senior management or to confidential staff; there is no evidence that the Claimants had ever given any express instructions that the sales information or the information about prices was to be treated as confidential."

The above passage is worth citing in full, since it contains a clear and comprehensive statement of the law in this area (see also **Lock International PLC v Beswick** [1989] 1 IRLR 1268; **Wallace Bogan v Cove** [1997] IRLR 453 and **Brooks v Oyslager OMS (UK) Limited** [1998] IRLR 590 in each case where the information was found not to be really confidential).

The precedents aim to set out clearly what the employer may or may not do. However, it should be noted that the second precedent which consists of a separate undertaking must be carefully tailor made to the employer's confidential information as it is much more strident in its content.

Q4: Protection of Intellectual Property

It is outside the scope of this book to consider the law relating to intellectual property rights but, in order to explain why Precedent Q4 is necessary it is worth considering section 39 of the Patents Act 1977 and a case arising therefrom which is a good illustration.

Under section 39 of the Patents Act 1977 an invention will be taken as belong to the employer where:

- it is made in the course of the employee's normal duties or of duties specially assigned to him, in circumstances such that the invention might reasonably be expected to result from the carrying out of those duties; or

- it was made in the course of the employee's duties and, at the time, (because of the nature of his duties and the particular responsibilities arising out of them) there was a special obligation to further the employer's undertaking.

The employee may, in certain circumstances, be awarded compensation where the invention was of outstanding benefit to the employer (sections 40 and 41).

In **Reiss Engineering Co Limited v Harris** [1985] IRLR 232 the employee was taken on as a fitter by a company that sold valves and was eventually promoted to sales manager. It had no research and design facilities and had never designed, modified or improved any valve. If there were problems it would refer to its supplier. Mr Harris was given notice of redundancy and during this period he invented and designed a new kind of valve that was an improvement on the valves sold by the employer. The employer claimed that the invention belonged to them under section 39 of the Patents Act 1997. Falconer J rejected the claim. He held that the invention was not made in the course of the employee's normal duties such that an invention might reasonably be expected to result from the carrying out of the duties (section 39(1)(a)) and that there was no special obligation to further the employer's interests within the meaning of section 39(1)(b). Mr Harris had never been employed to design or invent and his duty was to sell valves and to deal with after sales service. He had no special duty beyond this to further the interests of the employer.

Precedent Q4 sets out clearly when the employee is to be under the duties contained in section 39 and seeks to protect the employer's position.

Precedent Q5: Model Restrictive Covenants
Precedent Q5 is intended to be a model restrictive covenant that provides for all eventualities upon termination of employment, and as such it contains restrictions relating to:

- Confidentiality;
- Non poaching of employees;
- Non competition by having an interest in a competing business;
- Non solicitation;
- Non dealing.

Each of these will be considered in turn. However, it must be noted that the starting point is that such covenants are *prima facie* in restraint of trade and will only be enforced if they are regarded as reasonable. There is a vast amount of case law on this area and a summary can only be provided in the space of this book (see Brearly and Block QC, *Employment Covenants and Confidential Information* [2nd Edition] which runs to some 378 pages).

The covenant must be carefully tailor made to the employee's position and there are a number of general factors which will be taken into account in considering this:

- The nature of the employee's work and whether it gives him access to confidential information or contact with customers;
- The class of customers: if customers include those who have not dealt with the employer for some time or with whom the employee has not contact this may be unreasonable (**Marley Tile Co Limited v Johnson** [1982] IRLR 75 and see **International Consulting Services UK Limited v Hart** [2000] IRLR 227);
- The period of restriction;
- Which activities are covered: if the employee worked in one particular area he should not be prevented from working across the whole spectrum of the employer's business (see *Wincanton*).

Acknowledgements

It is sensible to contain an acknowledgement as to the fact that confidential information is bring provided as this brings the situation clearly to the attention of the employee.

Confidentiality

See Q2/3.

Non-Poaching of employees

Although a covenant of this nature was struck down in **Hanover Insurance Brokers Limited v Shapiro** [1994] IRLR 82 another division of the Court of Appeal upheld the covenant in **Ingham v ABC Contract Services Limited** [12.11.1993] and such a clause is likely to be upheld provided that it is not too generalised. It appears to be now settled by **Dawnay Day & Co v de Braconier d'Alphen** [1997] IRLR 442 that this is an interest that can be protected.

Non-Competition

Clauses 1 and 2 of the Post Termination Restrictions seek to prevent the employee from holding an interest in a competing business and, in the case of clause 2, where he may use confidential information. The former is a dubious clause as it may go to pure competition but where there is a risk of confidential information being used or customers are not readily identifiable so that it is difficult to police a non-dealing or solicitation clause then such a clause may be valid (see **Lansing Linde Limited v Kerr** [1991] ICR 428; **Dawnay Day & Co Limited v de Braconier d'Alphen** [1997] IRLR 442).

Non-solicitation

Clauses 3.1. to 3.3. are aimed at preventing non-solicitation of customers and suppliers. There covenants are more likely to be upheld where they relate to those with whom the employee had dealings for a limited time before termination of employment (see **G W Plowman & Son v Ash** [1964] 1 WLR 568; **Dentmaster (UK) Limited v Kent** [1997] IRLR 636 and **International Consulting Services (UK) Limited v Hart** [2000] IRLR 227 for examples).

Non-dealing

Clauses 3.4. to 3.6. contain non-dealing covenants. Non-dealing covenants are likely to be upheld where it is difficult to police a non-solicitation covenant (see **John Michael Design PLC v Cooke** [1987] 21 All ER 332; **Marley Tile Co Limited v Johnson** [1982] IRLR 75).

Blue Pencilling

Note that there is a clause at the end of the precedent whereby the covenants can be severed if any part is too wide. The courts will be prepared to blue pencil or sever covenants provided that the independent part left still has meaning, hence the reason that the clauses are broken down in the way they have been drafted (see **Rex Stewart Jeffries Parker Ginsberg Limited v Parker** [1988] IRLR 483).

PART R: DISCIPLINARY PROCEDURES

Precedent R1: Short Form Disciplinary Procedure

1 The following procedure is designed to be fair to all and to ensure that everyone has a chance to put her/his side of the case where a disciplinary matter arises. Its intention is to resolve problems as far as possible without resort to formal sanctions. It applies to all employees.

2 Any breach of the duties set out herein, of the Company's regulations or any other serious breach of contract, misconduct, inefficiency or neglect by you whilst carrying out your duties may be treated as a disciplinary matter. Conduct outside working hours which, in the opinion of the Company, affects the performance of your duties or may bring the Company into disrepute or adversely affect it may also be considered a reason for implementing the procedure set out herein.

Informal stage

3 If your work or conduct is considered unsatisfactory at the discretion of your Manager an informal meeting may be arranged to explain any short comings and suggest ways of correcting them in the future. This is not part of the formal procedure set out hereafter but ensures that, normally, matters are not raised through the procedure unless they have first of all been discussed informally. If any conduct or breach is considered sufficiently serious the Company in its absolute discretion may move on to the formal procedure set out below.

4 When your Manger raises something with you which she/he feels may lead to the formal procedure being implemented, she/he will write to you confirming the nature of the problem, agreed objectives to remedy it and the time scale within which any breaches must be rectified. These informal warnings may be kept on your file as a record for a period of six months and any further breaches may lead to the formal procedure being implemented.

Formal procedure

5 This will be initiated by the Company if the informal stage fails to result in the desired improvement or in the case of any matter that is considered sufficiently serious. Your Manager will produce a formal written statement setting out the nature of the complaint or breach. This statement will be forwarded to a Director of the Company for his/her consideration. A copy will be given to you in good time for you to consider the contents prior to the meeting referred to below.

6 Following production of such a statement the Director will, as soon as reasonably practicable, arrange a meeting with you and with such other persons as he/she may consider necessary. You are entitled as a matter of law to be accompanied by a fellow employee. If the date or time arranged for the meeting is unsuitable you may suggest another date or time within five working days from the hearing date that has been proposed. You may be entitled to call witnesses at such meeting but must first give the Director reasonable notice of the witnesses that you intend to call as it may be necessary to make arrangements to cover the duties of witnesses if they are employed by the Company.

7 After investigating the complaint and taking submissions and evidence from you, any witnesses that you have called and from any other source as necessary the Director shall decide what action should be taken, and may:

- decide that you are not in breach of your contract of employment;
- consider that there has been a breach which warrants giving you an oral warning that such a breach must not recur;

- in more serous cases issue a formal written warning that any repetition of the breach will result in your employment being terminated;
- Terminate the employment on notice.
- Terminate the employment without notice where your breach of contract is considered sufficiently serious to warrant summary dismissal.

8 The decision will be communicated to you and confirmed in writing. Any warning will indicate the breaches of your employment contract and what steps you must take to prevent a repetition of such breach. If you are dissatisfied with that decision you may appeal against it to the Managing Director. Such appeal must be made in writing to the Managing Director within three working days of receiving written confirmation of the decision, and set out your reasons or other submissions you may wish to make. The Managing Director may require such submissions to be supplemented orally or in writing as he considers appropriate.

9 On receipt of notice of your appeal the Managing Director shall be entitled to seek such other submissions, orally or in writing, from you or such other persons as he may think fit, and shall then either confirm the decision or substitute it by such decision that is considered appropriate.

10 In considering whether termination of your contract of employment is appropriate the following matters will be taken into account:

You will not normally be dismissed for breach unless it is of a serious nature. Examples of serious misconduct which is likely to lead to your contract being terminated:

- violence or verbal abuse towards fellow employees;
- giving information about the Company to third parties without permission or otherwise disclosing or assisting in the disclosure of information gained or overheard in the course of your employment where the information is likely to harm the interests of the Company;

- serious insubordination;
- sexual, racial or other harassment;
- deliberate damage to the Company's property;
- inability or physical incapability of carrying out your duties due to the influence of drugs or alcohol;
- conduct likely to bring the Company into disrepute (either inside or outside working hours);
- dishonesty.

It must be stressed that this is not an exhaustive list and summary dismissal may follow where the gravity of the offence is considered to warrant this sanction.

11   The following are examples of misconduct that may lead to a warning and, unless rectified, could lead to dismissal:
- unauthorised absence from work;
- lateness;
- inappropriate standard of dress;
- smoking on the Company's premises otherwise than in accordance with this manual;
- time wasting;
- use of the Company's telephones or photocopiers other than in accordance with this manual.

If your performance remains unsatisfactory after written notice of breach and of the improvements required and the period of time within which it is expected that they should be achieved, or if further breaches occur you will be dismissed. The Company reserves the right, however, to dismiss without warning where the breaches of your contract of employment are considered sufficiently grave or irredeemable but will not do so until you have had an opportunity to make representations as set out in this procedure document.

Precedent R2: Alternative Disciplinary Procedure

1 You recognise that it is necessary for the Company to maintain a standard of discipline conversant with good industrial relations practice and that the appropriate standard of work is maintained in relation to your employment. The Company has separate disciplinary policies in relation to alcohol and drug abuse, equal opportunities, sexual harassment and public interest disclosure but the procedures set out in this section may be implemented should it be considered that you may be guilty of any act of misconduct (including matters relating to the other procedures) or your standard or work or attendance become unacceptable. The procedures contained in this document are not to be regarded as contractual though they are the procedures that the Company will normally follow in disciplinary matters.

2 The primary objective of the procedures contained herein are to correct rather than to punish you and to encourage you to maintain the standards of attendance, behaviour and performance that are commensurate with your position. The Company is always there to assist you in your job should you have any difficulties and you should refer to _____ who will discuss any problems and counsel you in respect of any assistance that may be appropriate. The Company regards it of importance that the procedures contained herein are applied fairly and consistently in accordance with good industrial relations practice. It must however, be noted by you that in certain cases your conduct may warrant disciplinary action in which case the Company with follow the enclosed procedures wherever possible.

Misconduct

3 If your performance falls below standard or your attendance or behaviour becomes unacceptable, then, after receiving warnings as set out in this procedure you may be liable to dismissal. The decision as to whether or not your performance, attendance or behaviour is unacceptable will be made by the Company acting as a reasonable employer.

4 The following is a non-exhaustive list of examples of offences which amount to misconduct falling short of gross misconduct:

  a) Absence from work that is unauthorised. For this purpose absence from work will be regarded as unauthorised if you have not complied with the Company absence policy;

  b) Behaviour that is disruptive or which amounts to time wasting or may cause minor loss to the Company;

  c) Breach of safety regulations that is minor;

  d) Lateness for work without good excuse. For this purpose persistent lateness which is minor may amount to misconduct;

  e) Standard of work performance that falls below the expected standard of your post;

  f) Standard or appearance or dress that is not appropriate to the workplace;

  g) Smoking on company premises or in zones where smoking is prohibited. Smoking may in certain circumstances however be regarded as gross misconduct if it brings the Company into disrepute or you have already been warned about smoking on the Company's premises and the procedure in relation to gross misconduct may then be operated.

Gross Misconduct

5 If the Company reasonably forms the view that you are guilty of gross misconduct you may be summarily dismissed.

6 The following is a non-exhaustive list of examples of offences which the Company will regard as amounting to gross misconduct:

  a) Accepting any bribes or any gifts which could be construed as bribes. In the case of any gifts from clients or customers that are of a minor or inconsequential nature this must nevertheless still be cleared with your Manager before you may accept such a gift;

  b) Attendance at work whilst intoxicated or influenced by drugs that have not been prescribed to you by a medical practitioner. You must be aware of the Company's policy in relation to alcohol or drug abuse;

c) Being abusive or rude to clients or customers;

d) Breach of rules and regulations relating to health and safety matters that may constitute a danger to the health and safety of yourself, your fellow workers or anyone visiting the premises on Company business;

e) Bringing the Company into disrepute by conduct whether at work or outside;

f) Conviction for any offence that is incompatible with your employment, which may place the Company in disrepute or which causes the Company to lose trust and confidence in you;

g) Damaging company property or the property of any employee with deliberate intent;

h) Discrimination against any fellow workers or clients or customers on the grounds of sex, race, sexual orientation or disability. You must be aware of the Company's policy on discrimination;

I) Dishonesty at work whether or not it will cause the Company loss;

j) Dishonesty outside work that may bring the Company into disrepute or is incompatible with your employment;

l) Failing to adhere to any statutory or regulatory requirements where such failure is wilful or amounts to gross negligence or incapability;

m) Failing to correctly fill out your application or any documents relating to your employment which may affect your qualifications for the job, your ability to carry out the job or may affect the Company's trust and confidence in you;

n) Falling asleep whilst on duty;

o) Falsification of any Company documents whether or not they give you a pecuniary advantage or whether it is likely to cause the Company loss;

p) Harassment on the grounds of sex, race, sexual orientation, disability or for any other reason. You must be aware of the Company's policy on harassment and comply with it at all times;

q) Insubordination to your superiors which is incompatible with your position. Insubordination will be regarded as incompatible if it occurs before fellow workers and you must follow the grievance or public interest disclosure procedure if you have a complaint;

r) Misuse of your Company vehicle. It will be a dismissable offence if you drive your vehicle whilst intoxicated. It may be a dismissable offence if damage is caused to your vehicle by reckless or negligent conduct on your part;

s) Negligence behaviour which may be gross or which may affect the Company's trust and confidence in your ability to carry on your job;

t) Use of any confidential information belonging to the Company or of information which the Company considers may cause the Company harm or bring it into disrepute. The Company has a policy on public interest disclosure and encourages its workers to disclose wrongdoing under the terms of its policy. However, use or disclosure of any commercial or other information belonging to the Company is prohibited;

u) Violent behaviour towards fellow workers of clients or customers. This will include physical or verbal behaviour or conduct or words that may be regarded as intimidating.

Right to be Accompanied at a Disciplinary Hearing

7   You have the right to be accompanied to a disciplinary hearing where you have been required or invited by the Company to attend a disciplinary hearing and you reasonably request to be accompanied to the hearing. A hearing will be regarded as a disciplinary hearing if it could result in a formal warning or some other action on the part of the Company or confirmation of a warning or other action.

8   If you make such a request the Company will permit you to have a single companion at the hearing who is employed as a trade union official and is an official who has reasonably been certified as having experience of training in acting as a companion at disciplinary proceedings or who is another worker of the Company.

9   Your companion may be permitted to address the disciplinary panel but will not be permitted to answer

questions on your behalf and will be permitted to confer with you during the hearing.

10 If your companion is not available at the time that the Company has proposed for the disciplinary hearing you may propose an alternative time for the hearing provided it is a reasonable time and is no further away than five working days after the day that the Company had proposed for the disciplinary hearing, excluding Saturdays. Sundays, Christmas Day, Good Friday or Bank Holidays.

11 If your Companion is a Company worker he may have time off to accompany you to the hearing.

Investigation

12 If there is a concern about your conduct the Company will investigate and for this purpose may, at its discretion, nominate an investigating officer who was not involved in the allegations relating to the disciplinary matters. Where the Company considers it appropriate because of the nature of the offence it may, at its absolute discretion, suspend you from work in which case you will be paid your basic remuneration. This suspension may last as long as any investigation and disciplinary process is continuing.

13 The nature and scope of the investigation will be appropriate to the allegation that is being investigated and the Company, in its discretion may:

1. Require you to attend investigatory hearings for the purpose of being questioned about the allegation(s). Refusal to answer appropriate questions may in itself be regarded as a disciplinary matter.
2. Take witness statements from other individuals that were involved in relation to the allegations or who may assist.
3. Take time to collate documentary or other evidence that may be relevant to the allegations.

14 The Company will ensure that the investigation is carried out as quickly as possible but you will in any event be kept informed of the stage that the investigation has reached and if you have any queries you should address them to [*YOUR MANAGER/ THE INVESTIGATING OFFICER*].

15 Once the investigation has been carried out a decision will be made as to whether you will be informed in writing of the results of the investigation as soon as possible but there are no time limits relating to the length of the investigation or the time in which you will be so informed.

16 The above procedure is not contractual and may be amended by the Company in its absolute discretion.

The 'Charges'

17 If the Company considers that you may have committed a disciplinary offence you will be informed in writing of the allegations against you. [You may be sent witness statements if they have been produced depending on the nature of the allegations.] [You will be given an opportunity to see any witness statements prior to the disciplinary hearing.] [You will be given details of the evidence against you.]

18 You will be given a reasonable opportunity to consider the charges against you before any disciplinary hearing takes place and the date of any hearing will be confirmed to you in writing.

The Disciplinary Hearing

19 The nature and format of the disciplinary hearing will be dependant upon the charges that have been made and are subject to the absolute discretion of the disciplinary panel. However, the following procedures may be adopted:
   1. At the outset of the hearing the charges will be read to you and it will be confirmed whether or not you wish to have a companion present. If you wish to have a companion present then he or she will be entitled to address the disciplinary panel.
   2. You will be informed of the gist of the evidence against you. If there is an investigating officer then he may outline the allegations that have been made against you.
   3. You will be permitted to make whatever representations you wish in relation to the allegations.

4. Where witnesses are called you, but not your companion, may be allowed to ask questions that are appropriate.

5. Your attention will be drawn to relevant documentary evidence.

6. Where there is an investigating officer he will normally make closing submissions.

7. You may be permitted to make closing submissions to the panel.

8. The panel will then retire to see if it can reach a decision immediately. However, where the allegations are such that the panel considers it to be appropriate to take further time the hearing may be adjourned pending the decision of the panel.

20 You will be informed as soon as possible of the decision of the panel and in any event within [.....] days.

The Disciplinary Sanctions

21 Where the panel decides that your conduct did not amount to gross misconduct you may be subject to the following sanctions:

1. Where the disciplinary offence is minor or your conduct amounts to a failure to attain satisfactory standards you may be issued with a formal verbal warning. This will be administered to you by [your Manager].

2. Where the disciplinary offence or failure to perform satisfactory is regarded as serious or there have been persistent minor disciplinary breaches a warning in writing may be given to you. This will be administered by [your Manager/Head of Department].

3. Further repetition of disciplinary offences or continued failure to perform satisfactorily may result in a further warning or, if sufficiently serious, a final written warning. You may receive a final written warning before any other warnings if the disciplinary offence is sufficiently serious. The warning will be issue by [your Manager].

4. The warnings will remain on your personnel file as follows:

   • verbal warning: six months in the absence of any other disciplinary offence

- first (or in it is considered appropriated to issue a second warning that is not final) written warning: 12 months in the absence of any other disciplinary offence
  - Final written warning: 12 months.
5. These warnings will not be taken into account once they have expired unless they relate to a disciplinary matter that has become repetitive (*i.e.* alcohol or drug abuse or rudeness to customers or clients).

22 Where you are guilty of gross misconduct or have committed a further disciplinary offence after receiving a final written warning you are liable to be dismissed without notice. In the event of such dismissal you will not receive any pay in lieu of notice and will not be paid any accrued holiday pay.

Appeals

23 If you do not agree with the result of any disciplinary decision you will have the right of appeal provided it is made in writing within [...] days of you being notified. You must set out in full the grounds on which you are appealing the decision, stating whether it is because you disagree with the findings of misconduct or the sanction that was imposed.

24 The appeal will be to [.....]. [It will be by way of review of the decision and not a full rehearing.] [The appeal will consist of a full rehearing.]

25 [You only have the right to appeal in writing and there will not be hearing.] [You have the right to a hearing before [.....] and have the right to have a companion present at the hearing as you did with the disciplinary hearing.]

26 Where you have been dismissed the date of your dismissal will stand if the appeal is rejected and the date of the termination of your employment will not be the date that your appeal was rejected.

[POTENTIAL SIX MANAGERIAL AVENUES OF DISCIPLINE
It may be sensible to set out the different level at which
matters will be heard.]*

27 The following levels of management will deal with
disciplinary matters:
- Misconduct/Verbal warnings: Manager
- Misconduct/Written or final written warnings: Manager
- Gross Misconduct: Appeal panel consisting of Appeals:
  [Director, etc.]

COMMENTARY ON R:
DISCIPLINARY PROCEDURES

There is a vast amount of case law relating to disciplinary offences and these
are fully considered in Duggan *Unfair Dismissal: Law Practice and Guidance* at
Chapter 6 pages 149 to 230. This section will summarise the procedures that
should be followed in order for there to be a fair and reasonable disciplinary
process. The two precedents that have been provided are intended to provide
comprehensive procedures in this respect. *The precedents should be considered
along with the new ACAS Code on Disciplinary and Grievance Procedures now in
force.* A fair procedure will encompass the following:

A clear statement of offences that are likely to amount to misconduct or gross misconduct

The employee should know what sanctions certain breaches of discipline will
attract so that he is aware of circumstances in which he may be dismissed for
gross misconduct. Figure to specify that a matter amounts to gross
misconduct may make any dismissal unfair; see **Aberdein v Robert L
Fleming** [EAT 1277/97] and Duggan on *Unfair Dismissal* at page 159. The
two precedents contain lists of offences that may attract different sanctions.

A statement of the right to be accompanied to any disciplinary hearing

The Employment Rights Act 1999 now provides for the right to be
accompanied at a hearing and the ACAS Code takes this into account. Full
consideration is given to this new right at Duggan on *Unfair Dismissal* pages
172-174.

The procedure that will be followed if an investigation is to be carried out before any 'charges' are laid

The following should be borne in mind in considering the nature of any investigation to be carried out:

- Any breach of discipline should be dealt with speedily but no disciplinary action should be taken until the case has been fully investigated (see **RSPCA v Cruden** [1986] ICR 205; *Unfair Dismissal* at page 162-3);
- Where police investigations are being carried out there is no absolute rule that an investigation cannot take place but the employee may feel inhibited. He may be given an opportunity to state whether he wishes to make any comment (*Unfair Dismissal* at 197-199);
- Where evidence from informants is to be relied upon the safeguards set out in **Linford Cash & Carry Limited v Thomson** [1989] ICR 518 should be followed (see *Unfair Dismissal* at pages 164-165);
- Any investigating officer should be independent and the manner in which the investigation is to be carried out be made clear to the employee;
- Consider whether witness statements will be taken and provided to the employee;
- Is the investigating officer to provide a report with recommendations?

The nature of the charges that may be made

Once the investigation has been carried out and a decision is made to conduct a disciplinary hearing, the employee should be made aware of the charges with sufficient certainty that he knows the allegations he has to meet and be informed in good time (*Unfair Dismissal* at pages 167-169 and the cases there cited).

The Disciplinary Hearing

The Disciplinary Hearing must be conducted with scrupulous fairness and this will mean:

- The employee must be given every opportunity to challenge the evidence and state his or her own case (*Unfair Dismissal* at pages 169-171 and the cases there cited);
- Representation is now a statutory requirement;
- The panel will need to consider whether it is necessary for witnesses to be called and cross examined (see **Ulsterbus Limited v Henderson** [1989] IRLR 151);
- The panel must avoid any appearance of bias (*Unfair Dismissal* at page 174);

- The panel should consider how it will come to and deliver its decision.

The sanctions for breach of an disciplinary matter

Once the panel has decided that there has been a breach on the part of the employee they will consider the sanction to be imposed. There are a wide range of factors that can be taken into account, which are considered exhaustively in *Unfair Dismissal* at pages 177 to 182 and in relation to specific areas of misconduct at pages 187-230.

The right to appeal

The Disciplinary procedure will provide for a right of appeal and consideration must be made as to whether this is a complete rehearing or a review. Again this is covered exhaustively in *Unfair Dismissal* at pages 183-187 and in relation to the specific misconduct at 187-230.

PART S: GRIEVANCE PROCEDURES

Precedent S1: Grievance Procedure

1   This grievance procedure is designed to ensure that you are able to raise any grievance that you have about your employment or your working environment. You should read this grievance procedure in conjunction with the Company's procedures and policies relating to discipline, public interest disclosure, the equal opportunity policy and the policy on sexual harassment.

2   The Company regards it as important that you are able to air any grievances that you have about your employment or working environment without feeling worried about making a grievance. You will not be prejudiced by making a grievance and any grievance will be dealt with as soon as possible.

3   In the first instance any grievance should be communicated to your immediate supervisor or manager. If the complaint is about your immediate supervisor or manager then you should communicate the grievance to the next level of management. Where the grievance is of a serious nature then you should communicate the grievance to senior management or director level as is appropriate. You may in any event at all times bring your grievance to the attention of the Human Resources Department.

4   Any grievance you have will be dealt with in the following stages, at the Company's absolute discretion:

1.   Your grievance may be raised on an informal basis at the first stage, which will normally entail a verbal discussion with your manager or supervisor. You may,

however, submit a grievance in writing on an informal basis if you so wish.

2) You may submit a formal grievance after stage one, or move straight on to submitting a formal grievance. This should be in writing. You must be aware that once you have submitted a formal grievance the Company may wish to investigate it even if you decide that you do not want to pursue it, depending on the nature of the grievance.

3) Your formal grievance will normally be considered in writing. However, if you wish you may request a meeting in order for the grievance to be considered.

4) You will be informed of the decision in respect of your formal grievance as soon as possible which will normally be within [. . .] days but may be sooner if the grievance is urgent or take longer if the grievance is complicated.

5) If you are not satisfied with the result of your grievance or consider that it is taking too long to resolve you may refer it to the next level of management. In the case of being dissatisfied with the result of your grievance you have [. . .] days to refer it to the next level. A decision will be given in [. . .] days.

6) If you remain dissatisfied you may refer your grievence to a director who has been nominated to deal with grievances.

7) At every stage the person dealing with your grievance may decide to deal with it by way of a hearing or you may request a hearing. If you request a hearing it will be at the discretion of the person dealing with the grievance.

8) Given that the Company wish to ensure that your grievance is investigated as fully as possible this may entail speaking to other individuals. Any hearing will not take place until the person dealing with your grievance is satisfied that he or she has the necessary information to properly understand your complaints.

9) You are referred to the rights of representation contained in the disciplinary procedure. You have the same rights of representation in circumstances where your grievance relates to the performance of the Company of any duty that relates to your employment.

10) The decision of the director who has been nominated to hear the last stage of the grievance procedure will be final.

COMMENTARY ON S:
GRIEVANCE PROCEDURES

It is apparent that the reasonable employer will wish to have in place grievance procedures to deal with the position where the employee has a grievance about his workplace. This has been encouraged by the Employment Relations Act 1999 and the provisions of the revised ACAS Code on Disciplinary and Grievance Procedures. The philosophy behind the provisions are stated in the Code:

"in any organisation workers may have problems or concerns about their work, working environment or working relationships that they wish to raise and have addressed. A grievance procedure provides a mechanism for these to be dealt with fairly and speedily, before they develop into major problems and potentially collective disputes."

A failure to investigate an employee's grievance may amount to a breach of an implied term that the employers will reasonably and promptly afford a reasonably opportunity to their employees to obtain redress of any grievance that they may have. In **W A Goold (Pearmark) Limited v McConnell** [1995] IRLR 516 two salesmen suffered a substantial loss of salary as a result of a re-organisation. Although they raised this on a number of occasions nothing was done. There was no written grievance procedure. It was held that they had been constructively dismissed. The right to have a grievance dealt with was a fundamental one.

Where the employee does not utilise any grievance procedure in circumstances where there has been a fundamental breach of contract on the part of the employer the fact it is has not been implemented will not affect the issue of breach of contract (**Fruscher v Mycalex Motors Limited** [EAT 182/80]).

By section 3 of the Employment Rights Act 1996 an employer, who employed over 20 employees at the time the individual entered into employment, must provide a note specifying (by description or otherwise) a person to whom that employee can apply for the purpose of seeking redress of any grievance and the manner in which any application should be made.

The duty is limited to identifying the person and, if there are any, setting out the procedures.

The ACAS Code suggests that grievance procedures should be there for employees to address issues with management about their work or their employers, clients or fellow workers' actions that affect them. Some examples are listed:

- terms and conditions of employment;
- health and safety;
- relationships at work;
- new working practices;
- organisational change and equal opportunities.

Precedent S sets out a grievance procedure which is intended to emulate the suggestions in the ACAS Code. The approach that is adopted is as follows:

First Stage
The emphasis is on a speedy procedure. Employees should be able to put their grievance to their line manager and it should be dealt with speedily. Where the grievance is against the line manager it should go to the next level of management. If matters cannot be resolved informally the first stage is that the employee should preferably put the grievance in writing and, if it is contested, be able to attend a hearing to discuss it. He should be informed of his right to be accompanied. The manager should respond in writing within a time period or, if it is not possible to do that, tell the employee when he can expect a response.

Second Stage
If the matter cannot be resolved at that stage it should go to a further stage with a more senior manager and there should be a hearing within a fixed period of time. Again there is a right to be accompanied. The manager should respond within a set time.

Third Stage
If the matter still cannot be resolved the worker should be able to raise his or her grievance with a higher level, perhaps a director depending on the organisation. They should be able to respond at a hearing, be represented and given a response within a period of time.

In some cases external assistance may be appropriate.

Reference should be made to Part R for the right to be accompanied at a hearing.

PART T: EQUAL OPPORTUNITIES

Precedent T1: Equal Opportunities Policy

1   The Company is an equal opportunities employer and is committed to opposing all forms of discrimination in the workplace. The Company will not tolerate discrimination based upon [ADD AGE IF DESIRED] disability, marital status, race (which means colour, race, nationality, ethnic or national origins), sex discrimination or sexual orientation. The aim of this policy is that all members of staff know that they are able to work in an environment that is free from discrimination and you are able to achieve your full potential in your job. The Company will make decisions without reference to discriminatory critera. All members of staff must be aware of this equal opportunites policy and should abide by its terms at all times.

The definition of discrimination

2   In a number of areas the law protects employees and discriminatory conduct or omissions are prescribed by Government legislation. There are specific concepts of discrimination which make it clear what is unlawful.

Direct Discrimination

3   The first area, which has become known as direct discrimination, occurs when an individual is treated less favourably than another person on the grounds of their disability, marital status, sex or race. Whilst the law does not recognise discrimination based upon sexual orientation or age, unless it is based upon one of the recognised reasons, the Company will treat less favourable treatment on these grounds as a disciplinary offence. It does not matter that you may believe you are acting in the interests of the individual or the employee if your less

favourable treatment is on one of these grounds. This is because if you would not have treated a person who did not possess that characteristic in the same way this is direct discrimination.

Indirect Discrimination

4   Indirect discrimination occurs when a requirement or condition is applied to an employee that the employee finds he/she is not able to meet because of one of marital status, sex or race and which cannot be shown to be objectively justified. This means that if the requirement or condition has a disproportionate effect on the particular group it will be indirect discrimination; that is a considerably smaller proportion of one sex, those who are married or of one race can comply when compared to the other sex, single people or other racial groups.

5   Whilst this concept may appear technical it is of importance since the Company may incur liability if you, in the scope of the duties entrusted to you, apply requirements or conditions that are discriminatory against a particular group.

Reasonable adjustments

6   Disability discrimination does not have a concept of indirect discrimination because it has a concept that goes further and requires the Company to make a reasonable adjustment to seek to take away the disadvantage a disabled person may have in the workplace because of the disability. This means that the Company will consider alternative means by which a disabled person may be able to carry out the job or alternatively whether other steps may be possible.

Victimisation

7   Victimisation occurs where an individual is treated less favourably by fellow workers for asserting the above rights or the individual and this would not have happened if these rights had not been asserted.

COMPANY POLICY STATEMENT

The Company will not tolerate discrimination on any grounds and operates an active equal opportunity policy. However, it cannot operate to stamp out discrimination unless it is made aware that this is happening. Discrimination may be treated as part of the disciplinary procedure, grievance procedure or sexual harassment depending upon its nature. The equal opportunities policy will apply at all stages from recruitment, throughout employment to issues of termination of employment.

8 All recruitment procedures followed by the Company will be on the basis of fair and objectively justified criteria that do not apply any requirements or conditions that are not necessary for the needs of the post or the business. Where job applicants have a disability the position of the Applicant will be reviewed and all possible steps will be taken to ensure that the Applicant does not suffer from any disadvantage in the recruitment process.

9 Throughout your employment you are expected to conduct yourself in a manner that is not discriminatory and the Company will take all possible steps to ensure that equal opportunity is maintained. This will include:
1. Ensuring that job specifications relate to the requirements for the performance of the job.
2. Providing equal opportunity training as the Company considers it is appropriate to enable you and other staff to implement equal opportunities. Where you consider that it is appropriate for you to receive equal opportunities training then you may contact the Personnel Department to discuss this matter.
3. Monitoring the ethnic and gender composition of the workforce. This will be done in accordance with accepted practice as recommended by Equal Opportunities bodies or good human resources practice. All monitoring will be used only for the purpose of equal opportunity monitoring and will be anonymous.
4. In the case of disability, considering what steps may be taken to enable disabled individuals are not disadvantaged in the Company's workplace.

Precedent T2: Company Policy against Harrassment

POLICY STATEMENT

The Company is an Equal Opportunities Employer and does not permit any form of harassment in its workplace, whether it be based upon sex, race, disability, sexual orientation, age or personality. Harassment will be regarded most seriously and will be treated as gross misconduct under the Company's Disciplinary Procedure. The following Policy sets out the steps that you may take if you feel that you are the victim of harassment and the steps that the Company will take in relation to complaints of harassment.

The Definition of harassment

1   There is no legal definition of harassment and legislation does not, at the moment, provide separately for harassment though it is likely to amount to discrimination and the Equal Opportunity Policy should be borne in mind. The Company will regard harassment as being any of the following.

1. Unwanted conduct whether verbal or not, which is of a sexual or racial nature or is based upon age or sexual orientation, or other behaviour that is based on race, gender, sexual orientation or age which affects the dignity of the individual in the workplace. By way of example:

- sexual or racial banter may amount to harassment and should be avoided;
- the Company will not tolerate the display of any material that has sexual or racist connotation;
- Verbal or non-verbal conduct or other behaviour that is directed to someone because of their disability and which could affect the dignity of the individual in the workplace. By way of example:
  — comments about an individual's ability to carry out the job because of disability may amount to harassment.

2. Any form of verbal or non verbal conduct which could be regarded as bullying or intimidatory behaviour. By way of example:

— comments made to junior staff that demean them in the workplace may amount to harassment.

2 It should be noted that:

- Any of the above committed outside the workplace or outside working hours will be regarded by the Company as harassment if it affects the working environment;
- A single act or incident can amount to harassment;
- The issue is whether the recipient of the conduct said to amount to harassment could take the view that he or she was being harassed; it does not make any difference if you consider your conduct to be acceptable where the recipient does not.

HARASSMENT PROCEDURE

1 Stage 1: Informal procedures

In the first instance, the recipient of conduct that is considered by the employee to amount to harassment may seek to resolve the complaint on an informal basis. This may involve three stages:

1. If you consider that you are the recipient of such conduct you may prefer to resolve the matter by speaking to the individual concerned and pointing out that the conduct is not acceptable because it is unwanted and is interfering with the working environment. This is acceptable to the Company but you should not feel that this step must be taken if you feel uncomfortable about speaking to the harasser.

2. You may seek confidential advice from [Human Resources/Counselling etc]. Any staff from whom advice is sought have been fully trained to assist and will give advice about how a re-occurrence of the conduct may be prevented. Any advice will be confidential and will not be reported to anyone in the Company without your consent.

3. You may take the matter up with [SET OUT WHO] if you prefer and an informal meeting can be arranged between yourself and the individual about whom you

have a complaint at which an attempt may be made to resolve matters. Alternatively, the individual may be approached and informal discussions held if you request.

4. No disciplinary action will arise at this stage as this is intended to be an informal procedure which will enable you to resolve the matter without any further action by the Company.

5. However, if you consider that a criminal offence has been committed (i.e. assault or a sexual offence) you may seek the assistance of [....] to make a formal complaint to the police. Where a serious criminal offence is alleged [.....] will discuss with you whether reconsideration should be given to a report to the police.

6. *You may be offered compassionate paid leave in certain circumstances or, if you feel that you need such leave, you should not hesitate to request it.*

2   Stage 2: Formal Stages

If you have not been able to resolve maters on an informal basis or you consider the outcome to be unsatisfactory, you are entitled to make a formal complaint. The procedure that will be adopted is as follows:

1. You should make your formal complaint in the first instance to [SET OUT]. This may initially be oral but you will be asked to put your complaint in writing so that the nature of the complaint is clear. It is recognise that complaints may be sensitive and difficult to formulate and you may seek assistance from [SET OUT] in formulating such complaint.

Investigation

2. The next stage will involve the investigation of your complaint. This will be carried out with sensitivity and with respect to you and the person against whom the complaint is made. The investigation will remain confidential and everyone who is interviewed will be told that they are not to discuss the matter with anyone and that breach of confidentiality is a disciplinary matter. The investigation will be carried out as follows:

1) The investigation will be carried out as expeditiously as possible. It will be conducted by someone who is not connected with any of the allegations and who is at least a grade above the person against whom the complaint is made;

2) The investigator will carry out the investigation as he considers most appropriate. This is likely to involve interviewing all concerned. Anyone who is interviewed will be permitted to be accompanied by a friend, colleague or trade union representative;

3) Notes will be taken of the interviews and those interviewed will receive copies to ensure that they agree with the notes. The investigator will concentrate on the facts of the complaint and will avoid, wherever, possible, embarrassing or intimate details. The complainant and harasser's witness statements will not be provided to any other party;

4) At all stages you will be kept informed of the progress of the investigation and are entitled to ask how the investigation is progressing.

3. During the investigation consideration will be given, wherever possible, to the complainant and harasser being kept apart at work. You will not be moved to any position that is detrimental to you or if you object to being moved. You are entitled to ask for compassionate leave but this will not be required of you.

The decision

4. Once the investigating officer has carried out his investigation he will prepare a report. This will be submitted to [.......] who will decide whether the complaint has been made out. [.......] may wish to make further inquiries or hold a meeting in order to come to his conclusion. A decision will normally be issued within [....] days of receipt of the investigator's report.

The sanctions

5. If the complaint is upheld, consideration will be given to the wishes of the complainant as to what should be done. This may involve:

- Moving the harasser to another post. It should be noted that the question of disciplinary action against the harasser is separate matter.
- If the complainant so wishes, moving him/her to a different place or post. The complainant will not be required to move if this is not acceptable.
- The complainant may be offered counselling and will be given leave of financial assistance to enable the complainant to recover from the effect of the harassment.

6. If the complaint is not upheld, because there is insufficient evidence and the parties cannot work together consideration may still be given to any steps that can be taken to resolve the situation.

7. Complaints that are malicious, known by the complainant to be unfounded or made in bad faith may result in disciplinary action.

As an Equal Opportunities Employer, the Company monitors and keeps records of any complaints to ensure that harassment is being dealt with effectively and eradicated from the workplace.

COMMENTARY ON T:
EQUAL OPPORTUNITIES

Precedent T1: Equal Opportunities

Precedent T1 contains a model Equal Opportunities Policy and is largely self explanatory. It sets out the definitions of discrimination and the approach that will be taken by the employer if there is discrimination in the workplace. It contains a company policy statement and makes it clear the positive steps that will be taken by the employer to promote good relations. The employer should ensure that employees are aware of the statement and that active steps are taken to promote and implement equal opportunities.

Precedent T2: Harrassment

The issue of harassment in the workplace has come to the fore in recent years. There is, generally speaking, an implied term that an employer will give its employees reasonable support so that they can carry out their duties without harassment or disruption from other workers. In **Wigan Borough Council v Davies** [1979] IRLR 127; ICR 411 Ms Davies received 'cold shoulder' treatment from fellow employees arising out of a dispute where she had sided with management and, despite giving an undertaking to support her, her employer did nothing when she made a number of complaints. The ET and EAT held that the employer was in breach of the express undertaking and in breach of an implied term that the employer would give reasonable support. The onus of showing that there was nothing that could be done was on the employer. This may be compared with **McCabe v Chicpack Limited** [1976] IRLR 38 where there was nothing further an employer could do other than make it is clear to employees that conduct was not acceptable in circumstances where a disabled employee had been bullied but refused to name the culprits.

Sexual Harassment

Sexual harassment is not defined in the Sex Discrimination Act 1975 but is defined in the Recommendation on the Protection of the Dignity of Men and Women at Work (91/131) as an " unwanted conduct of a sexual nature, or other conduct based on sex affecting the dignity of men and women at work. This may include unwelcome physical, verbal or non verbal conduct". Sexual harassment includes behaviour that is "unwanted, unreasonable and offensive to the recipient" and which is regarded at creating "an intimidating, hostile or humiliating work environment for the recipient". In **Insitu Cleaning Co Limited v Heads** [1995] IRLR 4 the EAT held that a one off act may be discriminatory and that it will be obvious in certain circumstances that conduct is unwanted. The lay members also gave guidance as to the procedure that an employer should follow:

"1. The appellants [should] adopt a separate procedure which deals exclusively with complaints of sexual harassment.
2. Such a procedure should contain an informal first step which will enable complaints to be dealt with sympathetically before matters get out of hand. The experience of the lay members is that many women just want the harassment to stop and are not concerned to have the offender disciplined.
3. Any complaint should be dealt with 'from the perception of the person aggrieved'."

It was held in **Reed & Bull Information Systems Limited v Stedman** [1999] IRLR 299 that such conduct is unwanted if it is unwanted to the recipient regardless of what the harasser thought. General guidance was also given on the way that harassment cases should be approached:

"For the sake of brevity only, we will take the more usual case where a woman makes a complaint of sexual harassment against a man, whilst accepting that there may be cases where a man complains of a woman's conduct towards him. The sort of questions which appear to have been of concern may be summarised thus:

1. If a woman regards as a harassment of a sexual nature words or conduct to which many women would not take exception or regard as a harassment, has her claim been made out?
2. If a man does not appreciate that his words or conduct are unwelcome, has her claim been proved?
3. Is a 'one-off' act (words or conduct) sufficient to constitute harassment?

It seems to us important to stress at the outset that 'sexual harassment' is not defined by statute. It is a colloquial expression which describes one form of discrimination in the workplace made unlawful by section 6 of the Sex Discrimination Act 1975. Because it is not a precise or defined phrase, its use, without regard to section 6, can lead to confusion. Under section 6 it is unlawful to subject a person to a 'detriment' on the grounds of their sex. Sexual harassment is a shorthand for describing a type of detriment. The word detriment is not further defined and its scope is to be defined by the fact-finding tribunal on a commonsense basis by reference to the facts of each particular case. The question in each case is whether the alleged victim has been subjected to a detriment and, second, was it is on the grounds of sex. Motive and intention of the alleged discriminator is not an essential ingredient, as in any other direct discrimination case, although it is will often be a relevant factor to take into account. Lack of intent is not a defence.

The second question must always be asked, but in a sexual harassment case, the answer will usually be quite clear without resort to a comparator, actual or hypothetical.

The essential characteristic of sexual harassment is that it is words or conduct which are unwelcome to the recipient and it is for the recipient to decide for themselves what is acceptable to them and what they regard as offensive. A characteristic of sexual harassment is that it is undermines the victim's dignity at work. It is creates an 'offensive' or 'hostile' environment for the victim and an arbitrary barrier to sexual equality in the workplace.

Because it is for each individual to determine what they find unwelcome or offensive, there may be cases where there is a gap between what a tribunal would regard as acceptable and what the individual in question was prepared to tolerate. It does not follow that because the tribunal would not have regarded the acts complained of as unacceptable, the complaint must be dismissed. It is seems to us that there will be a range of factual situations which may arise, in relation to which there may be difficult problems of proof. It is particularly important in cases of alleged sexual harassment that the fact-finding tribunal should not carve up the case into a series of specific incidents and try and measure the harm or detriment in relation to each. As it is has been put in a USA Federal Appeal Court decision (eighth circuit) (**USA v Gail Knapp** [1992] 955 Federal Reporter, 2nd series at p.564):

'Under the totality of the circumstances analysis, the district court [the fact-finding tribunal] should not carve the work environment into a series of incidents and then measure the harm occurring in each episode. Instead, the trier of fact must keep in mind that "each successive episode has its predecessors, that the impact of the separate incidents may accumulate, and that the work environment created may exceed the sum of the individual episodes."'

Thus, for example, as here, a blatant act of a sexual nature, such as the deliberate looking up of the victim's skirt whilst she was sitting down, may well make other incidents, such as asking to be shown personal photographs, which the victim was looking at in work, take on a different colour and significance. Once unwelcome sexual interest in a female employee has been shown by a man, she may well feel bothered about his attentions which, in a different context, would appear quite unobjectionable.

As to whether the conduct is unwelcome, there may well be difficult factual issues to resolve. In general terms, some conduct, if not expressly invited, could properly be described as unwelcome. A woman does not, for example, have to make it clear in advance that she does not want to be touched in a sexual manner. At the lower end of the scale, a woman may appear, objectively, to be unduly sensitive to what might otherwise be regarded as unexceptional behaviour. But because it is for each person to define their own levels of acceptance, the question would then be whether by words or conduct she had made it is clear that she found such conduct unwelcome. It is not necessary for a woman to make a public fuss to indicate her disapproval; walking out of the room might be sufficient. Tribunals will be sensitive to the problems that victims may face in dealing with a man, perhaps in a senior position to herself, who will be likely to deny that he was doing anything untoward and whose defence may often be that the victim was being over-sensitive. Provided that any reasonable person would understand her to be rejecting the conduct of which she was complaining, continuation of the conduct would, generally, be regarded as harassment. But at all times, the tribunal should not lose sight of the question at issue: was the applicant subjected to a detriment on the grounds of her sex? The answer to that question does not depend upon the number of incidents. A one-off act may be sufficient to damage her working environment and constitute a barrier to sexual equality in the workplace, which would constitute a detriment."

In **Driskell v Peninsula Business Services Limited** [2000] IRLR 151 the EAT stated:

"the tribunal's approach should be as follows:

(a) The tribunal hears the evidence and finds the facts. As has already been pointed out, it is desirable not to include in this exercise judgments as to the discriminatory significance, if any, of individual incidents — judgment thus far should be limited to the finding of all facts that are *prima facie* relevant. If *ad hoc* assessments 'discrimination or no' are made the result is a fragmented and discursive judgment; more importantly, there is the potential noted in *Reed and Bull* for ignoring the impact of totality of successive incidents, individually trivial.

(b) The tribunal then makes a judgment as to whether the facts as found disclose apparent treatment of the female applicant by the respondents as employers in one or more of the respects identified in section 6(2)(a) and (b) that was less favourable than their treatment, actual or potential, of a male employee.

(c) The tribunal further considers any explanation put forward on behalf of the respondent employers. In the light of any such explanation is the discrimination so far potentially identified real or illusory?

(d) In making judgments under (b) and (c) above (and in practice these two stages may elide together) the following guidance is applicable:

1. Sexual harassment is helpfully categorised in *Reed and Bull, op cit.* At 302:
It seems to us important at the outset that "sexual harassment" is not defined by statute. It is a colloquial expression which describes one form of discrimination in the workplace made unlawful by section 6 of the Sex Discrimination Act 1975. Because it is not a precise or defined phrase, its use, without regard to section 6, can lead to confusion. Under section 6 it is

unlawful to subject a person to a "detriment" on the grounds of their sex. Sexual harassment is a shorthand for describing a type of detriment. The word detriment is not further defined and its scope is to be defined by the fact-finding tribunal on a common-sense basis by reference to the facts of each particular case. The question in each case is whether the alleged victim has been subjected to a detriment and, second, was it is on the grounds of sex.'

2. The finding of less favourable treatment leading to 'detriment' is one of fact and degree so that a single act may legitimately found a complaint, c.f. *Insitu Cleaning Co Ltd, op cit.*

3. The ultimate judgment, sexual discrimination or no, reflects an objective assessment by the tribunal of all the facts. That said, amongst the factors to be considered are the applicant's subjective perception of that which is the subject of complaint and the understanding, motive and intention of the alleged discriminator. Thus, the act complained of may be so obviously detrimental, that is, disadvantageous (see *Insitu, op cit*) to the applicant as a woman by intimidating her or undermining her dignity at work, that the lack of any contemporaneous complaint by her is of little or no significance. By contrast she may complain of one or more matters which if taken individually may not objectively signify much, if anything, in terms of detriment. Then a contemporaneous indication of sensitivity on her part becomes obviously material as does the evidence of the alleged discriminator as to his perception. That which in isolation may not amount to discriminatory detriment may become such if persisted in notwithstanding objection, vocal or apparent. The passage cited from the judgment of the US Federal Appeal Court is germane. By contrast the facts may simply disclose hypersensitivity on the part of the applicant to conduct which was reasonably not perceived by the alleged discriminator as a being to her detriment — no finding of discrimination can then follow.

4. In making its judgment a tribunal should not lose sight of the significance in this context of the sex of not just the complainant but also that of the alleged discriminator. Sexual badinage of a heterosexual male by another such cannot be completely equated with like badinage by him of a woman. Prima facie the treatment is not equal: in the latter circumstance it is the sex of the alleged discriminator that potentially adds a material element absent as between two heterosexual men.

5. Throughout the tribunal should remain conscious of the burden and standard of proof. That said, the notion that discrimination may well be covert and is not readily admitted is as applicable in the context of sex as in the context of race. The passage cited from **King v Great Britain China Centre**, *op cit*, consistently proves authoritative guidance on these aspects."

Precedent T2 seeks to implement the approach recommended in these cases.

PART U: HEALTH AND SAFETY

Precedent U1: Health and Safety at Work Policy Statement in Accordance with the Health and Safety at Work etc Act 1974

The Company is committed to providing a safe working environment and to care for the health and safety of its employees. The Company has a strict policy that it will comply with the provisions of the Health and Safety at Work Act 1974 and all associated regulations and codes of practice that are made and may come into force under it from time to time. The Company co-operates with the Health and Safety Executive and takes into account all recommendations that it may make. The Company will comply with what is regarded as best practice in relation to the work that it carries out.

The following is a general policy statement. Detailed matters relating to Health and Safety can be found in [*SET OUT*].

COMPANY RESPONSIBILITY

1. The Directors have ultimate responsibility for Health and Safety matters and are committed to ensuring that standards are upheld and that sufficient funding and training is made available.

2. At all times the Company will conduct its activities in such manner as to ensure that the health and safety of its employees are not affected and that they are not exposed to risk to heath and safety. The nature of the industry means that there may be risks and where they exist the Company will do everything that is reasonable to reduce these risks. In this respect there are two broad areas that the Company will seek to ensure mean that the health and safety of its employees will be placed first.

Lines of Responsibility

3. It is important that there is clear recognition of the lines of responsibility in relation to health and safety matters so that areas of health and safety are not ignored or neglected. In this respect the general lines are:

1 Overall and final responsibility for health and safety policy rests with [. . . . .] [A DIRECTOR].

2. Overall responsibility for the day to day implementation of health and safety policy rests with [. . . . .].

3. The Company takes its duties of consultation very seriously and responsibility for consultation with employees on health and safety issues rests with [. . . .]. Where appropriate this consultation will take place through trade unions or staff representatives.

4. On a day to day basis, managers have responsibility for implementing health and safety policies and employees must ensure that they comply with all rules, regulations, instructions or other measures to ensure health and safety at work and they must co-operate with their managers in this respect.

5. On a day to day basis there are set procedures should an accident occur and employees should be fully acquainted with these procedures, which can be found [. . . . .]. There are also rigorous reporting procedures in relation to accidents, which can be found [. . . . .]. The person to whom any queries should be directed in relation any accident you may have at work is [. . . . .].

The Company's responsibilities

4. The Company carries out the following in order to ensure that health and safety standards are complied with:

1. Assessment of risks in the workplace to the health and safety of employees and identification of measures that need to be implemented to comply with all health and safety obligations. Periodic risk assessments are carried out for this purpose.

2. The provision of:
    a) a safe place of work by ensuring that all equipment, machinery and safety devices thereon, locations and

means of access and egress to the workplace are such that the environment is safe;

b) all necessary safety equipment and clothing;

c) instruction and training to ensure safety standards are complied with.

3. The establishment of clear emergency procedures.

4. Regular consultation with the workforce to ensure that they are fully aware of safety matters, are able to air their concerns and that there is full co-operation between the Company and the workforce.

5. The establishment of appropriate committees for consultation.

THE EMPLOYEE'S RESPONSIBILITIES

5. In order to assist the Company in ensuring safety standards are met the employee has a responsibility to ensure that he is fully conversant with all requisite standards and any failure to comply with health and safety standards may amount to a disciplinary offence. As part of this duty the employee should:

1. Actively co-operate with the Company to ensure that this health and safety policy is met by complying with all safety instructions or directions that are issued, ensuring that the health and safety of other persons are taken into account by complying with all health and safety requirements and by using all safety equipment or clothing that has been provided.

2. Ensure that any equipment or machinery is used in accordance with safety instructions and immediately report any malfunction or other difficulty with machinery or equipment that could be a risk or health hazard.

3. Report any accidents that occur and co-operate in any investigation.

This policy is for your own good and must be adhered to. If there are any queries about the policy or training you may contact [. . . . .].

Precedent U2: Fire Policy

You should be fully conversant with this fire policy which is for you own safety.

1. The Workplace

You should make yourself fully aware of your nearest fire exit and alterative exits and you should be aware of the details of the procedures and assembly points in the event of a fire. These are posted on notice boards and you should be familiar with them. A Fire Warden is appointed to [your area][floor] and his name is on your notice board.

Regular drills will be carried out to ensure everyone knows the procedure.

2. If you witness a fire

Operate the nearest fire alarm immediately and make known the location of the fire to reception or to the most appropriate person [*i.e.* Head of Department, *etc.*]

Do not attempt to tackle a fire yourself unless it is very minor and you have been trained and are able to do so. The Company wants Healthy staff not Heroes!

3. In the event of a fire

In the event of a fire the Fire Warden will be responsible for the evacuation of your floor. You should follow the Fire Warden's instructions. You should in any event make your way to the nearest exit. You should leave immediately in a calm and orderly manner and should not stop to collect personal possessions or any other items. Do not use any lifts. Assemble at your assembly point.

Do not go back into the building unless you are instructed that it is safe to do so.

COMMENTARY TO U:
HEALTH AND SAFETY

The two precedents contain model statements of (1) general health and safety policy and (2) a model fire procedure. They are statements of general practice since there is a myriad of statutory provisions that the employer has to comply with in this field and a complete overview of health and safety cannot be achieved in a book of this size. The employer has both common law and statutory duties that are onerous.

At common law there is an implied term that employers will take all reasonable care for the safety of their employees whilst they are carrying out their duties (**Matthews v Kuwait Bechtel Corporation** [1959] 2 QB 57) which will include transferring employees to work that may be detrimental to safety (**Jagdeo v Smiths Industries Limited** [1982] ICR 47). Employers should deal promptly with matters of safety that are drawn to their attention as part of their general duty to take reasonable care for the safety of employees (**BAC v Austin** [1978] IRLR 332).

There is an implied term that employees will not be expected to work in unreasonable working conditions (**Concord Lighting International v Willis** [EAT 343/800] where the employee had to work in a cold draft in winter; **Graham Oxley Tool Steels Limited v Firth** [1980] IRLR 135 — cold temperatures; **Keys v Shoefayre Limited** [1978] IRLR 476 — where the employer failed to do anything about staff safety after armed robberies).

Risk to health

A term in a contract which requires the employee to carry out work that is injurious to health is likely to be unenforceable. The Court of Appeal refused to strike out an action as disclosing no reasonable cause of action in **Johnstone v Bloomsbury Health Authority** [1991] IRLR 118 where a trainee doctor claimed that a requirement he work 48 hours overtime in addition to a 40 hour week was injurious to his health and therefore unlawful.

Where it is known that the employee is suffering from depression, anxiety or other psychological illness as a result of the stressful nature of the job the employer may be in breach of contract by failing to give sufficient support or training (**Walker v Northumberland County Council** [1995] IRLR 36; **Lancaster v Birmingham City Council** (*IDS Brief* 648 page 7 — and see *Workplace Stress*, CLT Publishing). However, in **Morrison v West Lothian College and Lothian Regional Council** [Court of Session 21.7.1999 *IDS*

Brief 655] it was held that the employer will only be liable in relation to a stress related illness, caused by the working environment, where they have a recognised psychiatric illness or disorder and it is reasonably foreseeable to an ordinary bystander that stress or anxiety is likely to be suffered to the extent that it will cause such disorder.

Duties at common law include:
- A duty to provide a safe place of work (**General Cleaning Contractors v Christmas** [1953] AC 180) which cannot be delegated and includes providing a safe means of access.
- A duty to provide a safe system of work (see section 2 of the Health and Safety at Work Act 1974 and *Christmas.*)
- A duty to provide safe equipment plant and materials.
- A duty to ensure that fellow workers do not indulge in dangerous horseplay when it is known that they have such a propensity (**Hudson v Ridge Manufacturing Co Limited** [1957] 2 QB 348).
- A duty to protect from risk of injury.

Notable statutes include:
- The Health and Safety at Work Act 1974 and related statutory instruments;
- The Occupiers Liability Act 1957;
- The Fire Precautions Act 1971 and related statutory instruments;
- The Management of Health and Safety at Work Regulations 1992;
- The COSHH Regulations;
- The Workplace (Health, Safety and Welfare) Regulations 1992.

Reference must be made to specialist health and safety texts for a detailed outline of their effect*.

*See further, *Health and Safety: A Modern Guide*, CLT Professional Publishing, 2001.

PART V: TERMINATION PROVISIONS

Precedent V1: Termination of Employment and Notice

You are entitled to the following notice from the Company:
1. Less than two years' continuous employment: One week
2. After two years' continuous service: One week for every year of such continuous employment up to a maximum of 12 weeks.

You must give four weeks' notice to terminate your employment. Notice, once given by you, cannot be retraced unless the Company agree in writing.

The above notice periods are subject to the Company's right to terminate your employment without notice where it is entitled to do so.

V2: Payments in lieu of notice

Precedent V2.1: The Company may decide in its absolute discretion to pay you salary *in lieu* of the notice period that would otherwise be given by making payments to you during the notice period at the time you would have otherwise been paid your salary. However, during the notice period you will use your best endeavours to obtain other employment and should you obtain such employment you will provide details of all benefits to the Employer who shall be entitled to offset such payments against any salary otherwise due.

Precedent V2.2: Upon notice having been given to terminate by either party the Company reserves the right to make a payment *in lieu* of notice for the whole or any unexpired period (which it may make at any time during the notice period) and such payment shall consists solely of basic salary [*LIST ANY OTHER ITEMS THAT MAY BE INCLUDED*] and shall be subject to such deductions as the Company is required or authorised to make.

Precedent V3: Accrued Holiday Pay on Termination

Your holiday entitlement is as provided for [in the contract of employment]. Upon the termination of your employment:
1. You will not be entitled to any holiday pay for holiday that would otherwise have accrued. [You will be paid accrued holiday pay at your basic rate of salary].
2. If you have taken more days holiday than you entitlement would have been at the date of termination of your employment you will be responsible for re-paying holiday pay that you have already received in respect of this excess and, for this purpose the Employer will be entitled to deduct from your final salary such excess.

Precedent V4: Sick Pay during the Notice Period

During your notice period, given by either party, the Company may withhold payment for sickness absence, other than any statutory entitlement.

Precedent V5: Garden Leave

Upon notice being given by either party the Company shall have the absolute right to require you not to attend work during your period of notice but to remain available for work during normal working hours should you be required. If the Company exercises this right:
1. You must not attend at your workplace or at any Company or group premises unless required.
2. You must not without the written permission of the Company contact or make any attempt to contact any client, customer supplier or employee of the Company or Group and must not make any representation or statement in this regard. You are also not permitted to

contact any professional advisers of the Company or group (such as solicitors and accountants) nor its bankers.

3. The Company may require you to return all Company equipment and other property to it during the notice period.

4. The Company may require you to resign any Company directorships or other positions during your notice period.

5. You will continue to receive your full salary and benefits during your notice period.

Precedent V6: Summary Termination

The Company will be entitled to dismiss you without notice if you commit any of the following acts:

1. You are guilty of conduct set out in the Company's Disciplinary Procedures which warrants dismissal without notice.

2. You commit any act of negligence, neglect of duty which is serious or any act which causes the Company to lose trust and confidence and which justifies dismissal without notice.

3. You are in serious or repudiatory breach of this agreement.

4. You commit any act outside your employment which is liable to bring the Company [or Group] into disrepute.

5. You are declared bankrupt or otherwise enter into any arrangement with creditors.

6. You are convicted of a criminal offence and in the case of a motoring offence this results in disqualification or imprisonment.

7. You suffer from mental disorder which makes it unable to carry out your duties.

8. You are persistently absent from work for a period of [.....] days in any [....] months.

Precedent V7: Retirement

> The normal retirement age is [....] years and your contract will automatically terminate on you [....] birthday. The Company may permit early retirement and may permit you to work after normal retirement age. Enquiries should be made of ....

COMMENTARY TO V:
TERMINATION

Precedent V1: Notice

This precedent sets out the statutory entitlements to notice under section 86 of the Employment Rights Act 1996

Precedent V2: Payment in lieu

Where there is a provision that the employer may give notice to the employee or may make a payment *in lieu* of notice this may have two effects. First, the employer may lawfully bring the contract to an end by summary terminating the employment and making a payment *in lieu* of notice. If the money is not paid then it may be claimed as a debt. Second, there will be no duty to mitigate as the payment may be characterised as liquidated damages.

In **Abrahams v Performing Right Society Limited** [1995] ICR 1028; IRLR 486, Mr Abrahams was employed under a five year fixed term contract which was amended to give two years' notice or an equivalent payment *in lieu* of notice. Shortly before the fixed term was due to expire it was sought to agree a new fixed term but this could not be agreed and on 12th March 1992 it was agreed that two years' notice would be worked out to 31st March 1994. He was summarily dismissed on 14th October 1992. The Court of Appeal held that the employer had brought the contract to an end lawfully by summarily terminating the contract but had neglected to pay money *in lieu* and the claim was for a contractual sum in respect of which no duty to mitigate arose.

In **Morran v Glasgow Council of Tenants Association & Ors** [1998] IRLR 67 the employee was entitled to four weeks' notice and the contract provided that he was not entitled to a notice period if he was summarily dismissed for gross misconduct or if a payment *in lieu* of notice was made. He was dismissed just before the qualifying period for unfair dismissal but was not given any payment *in lieu*. The Court of Session had to decide the sole question of whether or not he was entitled for the loss of the right to bring an unfair dismissal claim. The Court of Session held that the employee was entitled to damages that would put him in the position he would have been if the employer had performed the contract in the least burdensome manner to themselves. If they had done so they could have brought the contract to an end by making a payment *in lieu* and the employee would not then have been employed for two years. The employee was therefore only entitled to payment based upon two years' payment *in lieu* and not to damages for loss of the chance of claiming unfair dismissal.

The Court of Appeal construed a differently worded clause in **Gregory v Wallace & Anor** [1998] IRLR 387. The contract provided that (1) the contract could be terminated by giving two years' written notice (2) in the event of two years' written notice being given the employee was free to take other employment during the period (3) upon the giving of two years' written notice the employer would be entitled to terminate the agreement henceforth ('forthwith') and could at their election pay monthly instalments over a two year period or the aggregate sum discounted to reflect early payment. Administrators were appointed and Mr Gregory was summarily dismissed. The Court of Appeal held that the administrators had not given two years' notice so that the option of paying two years *in lieu* never arose as two years' notice was required to be given before the employer could terminate the employment forthwith. This was the effect of the contract so that there was a breach of contract and the employee's claim was for damages for breach and not liquidated damages. However, the contract entitled the employee to do other full time work in addition to receiving the sums due to him during the notice period so that the employee was entitled to receive the full damages.

In T & K Home Improvements Limited v Skilton [1999] IRLR 375 the employee's contract provided that he failed to achieve his performance target in any quarter he could be dismissed with immediate effect. The EAT held that this did not entitle the employer to dismiss without contractual notice pay. In order for the employer to be entitled to do this the clause must be clear a unambiguous so that the requirement of notice is negated.

The recent case of **Cerebus Software Limited v Rowley** [1999] IRLR 690 highlights the difficulties of drafting clauses relating to payment *in lieu*. The contract provided that the employee was entitled to six months' notice. It also provided that the employer could make a payment *in lieu* of notice to the employee. Mr Rowley was summarily dismissed and not paid *in lieu* of notice with effect from 26th June. He obtained a job at a higher salary from

1st August. An ET held that he had been entitled to six months' salary and was not under any duty to mitigate his losses. In the EAT the employer argued that it had three options: to give notice; to give no notice but to pay money *in lieu* of notice or to give no notice and make no payment. It argued that the third option was a breach of contract so that there was a duty to mitigate. The EAT held that the employee was entitled to full payment as the employee was given the right to notice or to a payment *in lieu* of notice. The employer was in breach of contract by not making the payment so that the employee was entitled to claim the monies without any deduction for mitigation. The same result was achieved whether the claim was regarded as being one under the contract or a claim for damages for breach which put the employee in the position he would have been if the contract had been performed. However, the EAT questioned whether the employee should be entitled to the statutory minimum notice period but considered itself bound by the authorities.

A payment *in lieu* is taxable under Schedule E as an emolument if made pursuant to the express contractual right to bring the contract to an end by making such a payment (**EMI Group Electronics Limited v Coldicutt (Inspector of Taxes)** [1997] British Tax Cases 540).

Precedent V3: Accrued Holiday Pay
This precedent sets out whether or not there is an entitlement to accrued holiday pay on termination of employment. It should be read in conjunction with **Part I** on holidays.

Precedent V4: Sick pay
This further precedent should be read in conjunction with **Part J** on sickness.

Precedent V5: Garden leave
Garden leave clauses are common in contracts with executives and directors and a model is contained at V (see also the contracts for precedents). There may be an implied right to order garden leave or it may be express.

Implied terms
In **William Hill Organisation Limited v Tucker** [1998] IRLR 313 Mr Tucker was employed as a senior dealer in the field of spread betting, which was a specific form of betting pioneering by CI Limited. His contract of employment provided for six months' notice and contained a clause that prevented him from undertaking any employment that conflicted with the interests of the company. He decided to leave and to work for CI Limited. He was told that his six months' notice was required but that he was not

expected to attend work during the notice period, would be paid and that he could not start work elsewhere during this period. There was no express term permitting garden leave and the High Court and Court of Appeal held that the failure to provide work was a breach of contract so that Mr Tucker was entitled to leave forthwith. The Court of Appeal stated that the employer had no express or implied right to insist that the employee stay at home. The Courts have been increasing ready to recognise the importance of work to the employee and of exercising his skills. This was a case where it could be said that the employee's job was unique and the skills necessary for carrying it out required frequent exercise for their preservation and enhancement. The employer was not obliged to provide work if there was none that could be done with profit or to allocate work to the employee in preference to others, but it was not allowed to exclude him from the position. Morritt LJ stated that "..the court should be careful not to grant interlocutory relief to enforce a garden leave clause to any greater extent than would be covered by a justifiable covenant in restraint of trade previously entered into by an employee."

Express terms

In **Evening Standard Co Limited v Henderson** [1987] ICR 588; IRLR 64, Mr Henderson was employed as a production manager. His contract provided that he had to give twelve months' notice and he was not allowed to work anywhere else during the notice period without permission. He was offered a job with a competitor and gave two months' notice. The Court of Appeal held that the balance of convenience was in favour of granting an injunction. It was not possible to quantify the damage to the employer if the employee went to work for a competitor. Lawton LJ stated:

> "The injunction must not force the defendant to work for the plaintiffs and it must not reduce him, certainly, to a condition of starvation or to a condition of idleness, whatever that may mean on the authorities on this topic. But all that, in my judgment, is overcome by the fact that the plaintiffs have made the offer they have. The defendant can go back to work for them. If he elects not to go back...he can receive his salary and full contractual benefits under his contract until such time as his notice would have expired had it been for the proper period."

A different result was reached in **Provident Financial Group PLC v Hayward** [1989] IRLR 84 where there was a twelve months' notice period with a provision that the employee could be required to remain at home on 'garden leave'. On the facts of that case there was no damage to the employer if the employee took up new employment as it was not in competition with the employer and there were no elements of confidential information so that the employer could not be caused any damage.

In **Euro Brokers Limited v Rabdy** [1995] IRLR 206 the employee intended to work for a rival firm in breach of a six months' notice requirement in a case where customer connection was important. He offered to go on garden leave for three months. The High Court held that a six month period was enforceable given that the customer connection had been built up at the employer's expense, even if this meant that he remained idle for a period.

Where the employee is paid *in lieu* of notice this may have the effect of receiving the employee from being required to stay at home on garden leave and enable her to undertake work for another employee. In **Hutchings v Coinseed Limited** [1998] IRLR 190 Miss Hutchings' contract provided that: "During any period of notice the company is under no obligation to provide you with work and may require you to stay at home and do no work for the company or for anyone else." She gave one month's notice on 29th March and was told that she would be paid *in lieu* of notice. On 2 April, Miss Hutchings started work in a new job at a higher basic salary. Soon afterwards, her former employers discovered that the new job was with a competitor and, as a result, they refused to pay her the promised salary. The Court of Appeal held that a district judge had been wrong in holding that she was not entitled to her salary for her notice period on grounds that she had repudiated her contract of employment by starting a new job with a competitor, notwithstanding that she had been told by the defendants that she was not required to work for them during the period of notice. The mere fact that an employee takes another job during the notice period does not necessarily amount to a repudiatory breach entitling the employer to elect to bring the contract to an end, even where the employee goes to work for a "competitor". Whether there is a repudiatory breach depends upon whether taking the new job was wholly inconsistent with the employee's obligations to the employers at that time. In the present case, there was no express obligation that the plaintiff should not take another job and an obligation that she should not do so could not be implied, given that she had been released from further work and told that she would be paid *in lieu* of notice.

Restrictive covenants and garden leave

Where there is a restrictive covenant as well as a garden leave clause, a combination of the two may mean that the employee is kept out of the industry for a lengthy period. The Court of Appeal considered the interrelationship between the two in **Credit Suisse Asset Management Limited v Armstrong** [1996] IRLR 450. Employees were placed on garden leave for a six month period after they resigned. There was a non competition clause for six months after termination of employment in the contracts. The Court of Appeal held that the restrictive covenant, being valid, was enforceable notwithstanding the garden leave clause. The Courts are entitled to exercise their discretion as to the period that it considers a garden leave clause should apply. If the restrictive covenant is valid the employer is entitled to have it enforced but the existence of a garden leave clause at the time the contract is entered into may be taken into account in determining the validity of the garden leave clause. Neill LJ stated that he would "leave open the possibility that in an exceptional case where a long period of garden leave had already elapsed, perhaps substantially in excess of a year, without any curtailment by the court, the court would decline to grant any further protection based on a restrictive covenant."

Duties during garden leave

In **Symbian Limited v Chritensen** (8.5.2000, unreported) it was the view of the Vice Chancellor that the duty of fidelity and fiduciary duties no longer applied when an employee was required to go on garden leave. He stated:

> "There are obligations of good faith and fidelity both ways, as the BCCI employees have succeeded in establishing in the House of Lords. The origin of these obligations is the relationship of employer and employee. What a garden leave notice does, in effect, is to put an end to the contractual relationship. It is expressed to continue only for so long as the notice period terminating the contract continues. But since the garden leave not only requires the employee not to attend for work but forbids him to attend for work, not only absolves him from carrying out employment duties, but forbids him to take any part in the work of his employer or to enter upon his employer's premises, or to approach any of his co-employees, it seems to me that it fundamentally and irretrievably undermines the employment relationship between the parties. The contractual relationship continues but the employment relationship is destroyed as it seems to me, by the garden leave notice. I do not think that thereafter there can subsist any implied obligation of good faith and fidelity between the parties."

The Court of Appeal (24.5.2000, unreported) did not think it necessary to address the point, though Counsel for the employee, Andrew Stafford QC, conceded he would have difficulty in putting forward the proposition. It is submitted that it is wrong and that the duties do continue, otherwise the employee would be free to do what he wanted during the garden leave period. (For a full consideration of garden leave, see Duggan, *Wrongful Dismissal, Law Practice and Precedents*.)

Precedent V6: Summary Termination

These clauses are a variation on the provisions contained in **Part R** and should be read in conjunction with them.

PART W: STRESS POLICIES

Precedent W1: A Model Stress Policy

The company recognises that its staff are its most important asset and it is committed to providing the support to assist its staff to undertake their work and develop their skills in an environment that is as stress free as possible. It is recognised that all staff are subject to stress in their daily lives and that if it reaches debilitating levels then work performance can suffer.

Stress is a matter of legitimate concern, be it physical or mental, and the Company is committed to assisting by providing a support system that will help minimise and alleviate stress within the workforce. Where work suffers because of stress related matters the Company will not normally treat this as a disciplinary matter but may treat it as a capability/sickness issue.

If you feel that your working is suffering because of stress related matters occurring outside the workplace you may raise this informally with your line manager who will do everything in his power to assist. This may include referring the matter to more senior management who will consider what they can do to assist and will handle matters in a sympathetic and helpful way. Remember: if you do not tell the Company that you have a problem, they cannot help you.

The same applies where stress is caused by matters within the working environment. It you consider there to be a problem you may take the same approach as set out above. Alternatively if you think it more appropriate you may invoke the grievance procedure.

The Company will ensure that management have the necessary training in stress awareness.

Where appropriate the Company is prepared to provide professional counselling at its own expense.

COMMENTARY ON W:
STRESS POLICIES

Precedent W contains a general statement about how stress will be dealt with in the workplace. However, the policy will be of no use unless it is actively implemented (to that end see the Management Strategy checklist below). Employers are at risk if they do not provide a safe working environment (see Part U on Health and Safety).

There is potential liability as follows:
- Personal injury claims;
- Constructive and unfair dismissal claims, which may include claims for psychiatric injury;
- Claims under the Disability Discrimination Act 1995;
- Breach of contract claims;
- Claims in negligence.

In **Walker v Northumberland County Council** [1995] IRLR 35; [1995] ICR 702; [1995] 1 All ER 737 the plaintiff claimed damages arising out of stress and anxiety due to increased pressure of work. In 1995 he produced reports stressing the need to alleviate the work pressures of himself and his team. His proposals were not accepted. At the end of November 1986 he suffered a nervous breakdown. He was told that he would be given assistance when he returned to work but, in the event, this only lasted for a month. His stress symptoms returned and on 16th September 1987 he was advised to go on sick leave. He had a second mental breakdown and was dismissed on the grounds of permanent ill health in February 1988. He claimed damages for breach of care in failing to take steps to avoid exposing him to a health endangering environment, contending that the Council ought to have appreciated the effect of the workload given his warnings and his first breakdown. Colman J held that the defendant County Council was in breach of the duty of care it owed to the plaintiff as his employer in respect of the second mental breakdown, which he suffered as a result of stress and anxiety occasioned by his job as Area Social Services Officer responsible for an area with a very heavy workload, including an increasing incidence of child abuse cases.

The judge stated that an employer owes a duty to his employees not to cause them psychiatric damage by the volume or character of the work that they are required to perform. Although the law on the extent of the duty on an employer to provide an employee with a safe system of work and to take reasonable steps to protect him from risks which are reasonably foreseeable had developed almost exclusively in cases involving physical injury to the employee, there was no logical reason why risk of injury to an employee's mental health should be excluded from the scope of the employer's duty. The judge was of the view that the standard of care required for performance of that duty must be measured against the yardstick of reasonable conduct on the part of a person in the employer's position.

He decided that what is reasonable depends upon the nature of the relationship, the magnitude of the risk of injury which was reasonable foreseeable, the seriousness of the consequences for the person to whom the duty is owed of the risk eventuating, and the cost and practicability of preventing the risk. The practicability of remedial measure must take into account the resources and facilities at the disposal of the person or body who owes the duty of care, and the purpose of the activity which has given rise to the risk of injury.

The case is a warning for employers who ignore stress related illness brought on by the working environment. Mr Walker eventually received over £200,000 (cf, **Fraser v The State Hospitals Board for Scotland** [Court of Session 11.7.2000] where there was no liability when the employer could not foresee that the employee would suffer psychiatric illness as a result of disciplinary action).

The employer should have a management strategy for its senior employees, for which the checklist below may prove a starting point.

MANAGEMENT STRATEGY CHECKLIST

AIMS	ACTIONS
Introduce a staff development and review scheme that takes account of stress	• Ensure that all employees are aware of the stress policy • Make clear to employees that stress is not a sign of weakness • Be prepared to discuss stress at appraisals • Ensure stress is taken into account when job descriptions are prepared or altered, including the hours and quantity of work
Ensure that all individuals are aware of the harassment policies	• Make sure there is a harassment policy and it is properly implemented • Make sure employees are aware of the policy

Ensure equal opportunity policies are applied	• Make sure there is an equal opportunities policy and it is properly implemented • Make sure employees are aware of the policy
Be aware of the effect of management styles on employees	• Ensure that management have proper training in relation to stress in the workplace
Ensure health and safety requirements are complied with	• Make sure that proper consideration is given to the working environment, taking into account such matters as accommodation, noise, security and other such matters that may cause stress • Ensure that employees know that they are also responsible for their own well being and that of their co-employees
Regularly review the workload of staff	• Ensure that the workload is not excessive leading to stress
Ensure employees have a current job description and are clear about their roles and responsibilities	• Ensure that employees are clear about what is expected of them and that they can cope
Where roles are changed make sure this is done with proper consultation and sympathetically	• Ensure that there is no uncertainty about roles as this can lead to additional stress
Ensure that employees are aware of the options open to them if they are suffering from stress because of work or no work related matters	• Ensure that all employees are aware of the stress policy • Ensure that employees know that stress is not treated as a sign of weakness • Ensure all employees know the procedures to be followed if they are having problems

SECTION FOUR
DIRECTORS

PRECEDENT:
DIRECTOR'S CONTRACT OF EMPLOYMENT

PRECEDENT 7.1: DIRECTOR'S CONTRACT OF EMPLOYMENT

SERVICE AGREEMENT BETWEEN . . . . ('The Company') and
. . . . ('The Director').

1. Employer and Employee	The Company is . . . . of . . . . Company Registration No . . . . The Employee is . . . . of . . . . The execution of this Service Agreement was approved at a meeting of the Board of Directors on . . . . by a minute number . . . .

2. Definitions	The Board:	The Board of Directors of the Company
	Associated Company:	Any Associated Company as defined in the Employment Rights Act and the Companies Act
	Group:	The Associated Companies and any Holding Company

3. Date employment began, continuous employment and hours of work	The Director's employment as an Employee began on . . . . and the Director's date of continuous employment began on . . . . [The Director's employment began on . . . . and will continue for a [. . . .] year fixed period. The employment may be terminated during the fixed period as provided for hereafter, and, subject to termination as set out hereafter, after the end of the fixed term period by the giving of [. . . .] months' notice.] If the Service Agreement is not terminated earlier it will end automatically on the Director reaching retirement age as defined in the Company [Group] Pension Scheme. *Hours of work* The Director's normal hours of work are . . . . . a.m. to . . . . . p.m. However, the nature of the Director's

3. Date employment began, continuous employment and hours of work (cont.)	position is such that he will be expected to work such hours as are necessary in order that he can fully carry out his duties. There is no additional pay for overtime. The provisions of the Working Time Regulations in relation to hours of work are not applicable.
4. Job title and duties	Director [ADD IN IF MANAGING DIRECTOR, ETC] The Company may change the Director's job title in its absolute discretion and as it considers necessary. It may also appoint a Director to act in a joint capacity. *Description* The Director's job description [was provided with the Letter of Appointment][is appended to this contract]. *Duties and flexibility* During the period of his Employment: 1. The Director will diligently, well and faithfully serve the Company [and Group] and will do all in his powers to promote the interests of the Company [and Group]. 2. The Director will not accept or take up any other employment nor will he accept, whether indirectly or directly, any form of paid or unpaid Consultative or other work whilst employed by the Company [or any Group Company]. 3. The Director agrees that he will carry out such duties as may from time to time be assigned to him by the Board, or instructed by [. . . . . . .], whether or not those duties fall within the job title or description, provided that they are consistent with his status and position with the Company. 4. The Company is part of the Group and the Director agrees that he will carry out duties for other Companies in the Group if so instructed. 5. The Director will endeavour at all times to promote the interests of the Company [and the Group].
5. Remuneration and other benefits	*Salary* 1. The Director will be paid the sum of £ . . . . per annum. 2. The Salary will be calculated and accrue on a daily basis and will be paid by credit transfer on the . . .

3. Date employment began, continuous employment and hours of work	day of each month, provided that the Director acknowledges that the salary may be paid at a later date if, for reasons beyond the control of the Company salary was not paid on the above date and such late payment shall not be regarded as any breach of this Service Agreement. Salary will be paid once the Director has provided details of the bank to which it is to be transferred. 3. The Salary will be reviewed by [the Managing Director/ Board /Remuneration Committee, *etc.*] [on . . . . . /by end of the . . . . . month] each year and a Salary rise may be awarded in the absolute discretion of the [the Managing Director/ Board / Remuneration Committee, *etc.*]. There is no guarantee of any Salary rise [but the Salary will not be adjusted downwards]. *Bonus* 4. The Company may award a bonus at the [set out when]. The bonus is based upon [*SET OUT HOW — e.g.* profitability of the Group, Division, turnover brought in by the Director]. The bonus is paid at the absolute discretion of the Company [and the Director acknowledges that he has no set expectation that he will be paid a bonus]. *Commission* 5. Commission is paid as follows: [*SET OUT HOW IT IS CALCULATED*].
6. Share options	The Company [Group] operates a Share Option Scheme. If the Director is entitled to participate in the Scheme he will have been advised in his Letter of Appointment. The Options are subject to the Rules of the Scheme to which reference should be made.
7. Company car	1. The Director will be provided with a Company car, which shall be not less than [*SET OUT* . . . . . .] [suitable for the Director's duties and status]. The Company will tax, insure, pay for maintenance and repairs [provided they were not caused by the Director's negligence]. 2. The car may be replaced when the Company considers it appropriate. 3. The car may be used for private purposes as well as

7. Company car (cont.)	Company business. The Company will pay for petrol used for business purposes which may be claimed as part of expenses.
	4. The Director warrants that he has a clean driving licence and he will bring to the attention of the Company any matter that may affect his continued ability to drive the car.
	5. The Director agrees that he will not do anything that may invalidate the insurance policy.
	6. Upon termination of this Agreement, for whatever reason, the Director agrees that he will immediately deliver up the car or make it available for collection [and acknowledges that he will no longer be insured to drive the car from the date of termination].
	[*ALTERNATIVELY:* The Company operates a car policy which the Director agrees he has read and signed. **See MANUAL PRECEDENT F10 & COMMENTARY**]
8. Pension	The Director is entitled to join the [Group] Company's Pension Scheme and the terms of the Scheme are incorporated into this Agreement.
	There is [is not a] contracting out certificate in relation to the Pension Scheme.
9. Expenses	The Company will reimburse the Director expenses incurred in the course of his employment which were incurred in the furtherance of his duties. The Director should acquaint himself with the procedure for reclaiming expenses.
10. Holidays and other absences	*Holiday*
	1. The Director is entitled to [. . . . .] days' holiday per year on full salary, in addition to the normal statutory holidays.
	2. The Director must agree holiday in advance with [. . . . .] by giving at least twice the number of working days' notice of the number of days he intends to take on holiday and this will be subject to the Agreement of the Company. The Company may stipulate the days that the Director must take as paid holiday.
	3. Holidays not taken in the calendar year which

| 10. Holidays and other absences (cont.) | runs from [. . .] to [. . .] and cannot be carried over [save with the written agreement of . . . .]. |

4. For the purposes of termination of employment, holidays accrue on a daily basis and the Director will be entitled to any accrued holiday pay on the termination of his employment.

Other absences

The Company operates a maternity and paternity policy to which reference should be made.

[SEE MANUAL PRECEDENT K1 & COMMENTARY]

| 11. Sickness absences and benefits | *Sickness* |

1. Where the Director is absent due to sickness he must, as soon as is possible, inform or cause to be informed [*STIPULATE WHO — E.G. THE BOARD*] of the Company.

2. Self certificates must be provided for periods of up to [. . .] days and medical certificates must be provided for any longer periods.

3. The Company will continue to pay full salary whilst the Director is absent due to sickness for a period of [. . . .] days. However, the Company has the right not to pay salary where:
   (1) The Director is absent for more than [. . . .] days in any one period or [. . . .] days during the calendar year.
   (2) The Director does not provide certificates as required.
   (3) The Director fails to respond to any reasonable request from the Company about his condition and prognosis.
   (4) The Director has repeated spells of short absence that cumulatively amount to [. . . .] days in any six month period.
   (5) The functions of the Director become impossible of performance due to the absence of the Director.

4. The Director will give credit for any statutory or other benefits he receives arising out of his absence due to sickness and which do not arise out of any private insurance taken out by the Director.

| 11. Sickness absences and benefits (cont.) | 5. The Director's employment may be terminated for sickness in the circumstances set out herein. |

Medical examination

The Company may require the Director to undergo a medical examination and refusal to do so may result in non payment of salary or in dismissal.

[SEE MANUAL AT J FOR FURTHER EXAMPLES OF THE ABOVE PRECEDENTS]

Private Health Insurance

The Director [and his family which shall consist of spouse and children] are entitle to membership of the Company's Private Health Insurance Scheme, on the terms that may from time to time exist. If the Director chooses not to join the Scheme he is not entitled to any sums by way alternative.

Third Parties

Where the Director's absences arise out of the action of a third party which entitles him to claim damages the Director agrees that any sums advanced to him by way of salary will be regarded as sums that must be refunded out of any damages recovered for loss of earnings.

[SEE ALSO MANUAL PRECEDENT F11 & COMMENTARY]

| 12. Place of work | The Director's place of work will be as set out above [*OR SET OUT ADDRESS, ETC*]. However, the Director agrees: |

1. Should the Company decide to relocate, he may be required to move to anywhere within the United Kingdom upon such relocation, provided that the Company will pay the reasonable costs of removal and other incidental expenses to be agreed beforehand.

2. The Director will be required, as part of his duties, to travel in the United Kingdom and abroad (for which he confirmed has a valid passport) and the Company [or Group] may so instruct him in the proper furtherance of his duties [*provided* that he will not have to spend time abroad for more than [. . . .] days at any one time without prior mutual

12. Place of work	agreement]. The Director can claim expenses in relation to such travel.
	[FOR AN OVERSEAS CONTRACT SEE 5.10]
	[FOR A RESIDENTIAL REQUIREMENT SEE 5.12]
13. Disciplinary and other procedures	The Director's attention is drawn to the Company's Disciplinary and Grievance Procedures which are applicable with appropriate modifications. They do not form part of this Service Agreement.
	For the purposes of any disciplinary matter, the following persons are responsible:
	• Warnings: . . . .
	• Dismissal: . . . .
	• Appeals against warnings: . . . .
	• Appeals against dismissal: . . . .
	For the purposes of the Grievance procedure, the following individuals:
	• Initial informal Grievance: . . . .
	• Formal Grievance: . . . .
	• Further complaint where not satisfied with outcome: . . . .
	[SEE MANUAL PARTS R AND S FOR FURTHER DETAIL AND COMMENTARY]
14. Standard of work and other duties during employment	The Director acknowledges that his title, position and the nature of his work require a high standard and breach may cause the Company or Group [irremediable] harm. He therefore warrants that he has the requisite qualifications and abilities to perform the full functions of his job and will drawn to the attention of the Company any matter that may affect his ability to carry out his job.
	Because of the nature of his Employment, the Director recognises that, in addition to those matters set out in the Disciplinary Policy as constituting grounds for dismissal, any act of negligence or act that may bring the Company or Group into disrepute or that undermines the trust and confidence of the Company or Group may lead to summary dismissal.
	The Director also expressly acknowledges that he will draw to the attention of the Company any act by Director, employees or third party, that is a breach on

14. Standard of work and other duties during employment	their part or may harm the interests of the Company or Group.

[ALTERNATIVELY:

The Director undertakes that he will disclose to the Company [Board], forthwith upon it coming to his knowledge, any of the following information or matters:

- Any activities on the part of other Directors or employees that may be harmful to the interests of the Company, including but not limited to:
  (1) any plans of employees to leave the Company [or Group] or to join a Competitor or to take any steps to set up or establish a business that is or may be in competition;
  (2) any steps taken by employees to carry out such plans;
  (3) any use of confidential information or other property or assets of the Company [or Group] by Directors or employees for the furtherance of such plans;
  (4) any other matters that may adversely affect the business of the Company.]

15. Scope of duties	*Whole Employment*

The nature of the Director's employment is such that the Director cannot be engaged in any activity that may mean he cannot give his full attention to his duties with the Company [or Group] or which may place him in a position of conflict. The Director therefore agrees that he will not accept or take up any employment whilst employed by the Company nor will he accept, whether indirectly or directly, any form or paid or unpaid Consultative or other work [without the prior permission in writing of the Managing Director Board of the Company, which will not be unreasonably withheld]. The Director may however, purchase shares in [set out the extent of the interests that may be permissible or any other interests].

Implied Duties

The Director further acknowledges that the nature of his employment creates implied fiduciary duties and duties of fidelity and any and all covenants herein are subject to those implied duties where they be wider.

16. Covenants during employment

Directors and Employees

The Director will not at any time during his employment solicit or seek to recruit any current Directors or employees of the Company [or Group] to be engaged to work for the Director or any other person, firm, company or organisation, and will not make any comment, representation or statement that may facilitate, induce, persuade procure, or howsoever cause any Director or employee to leave the employment of the Company [or Group].

[*ALTERNATIVELY:*

The Director shall not at any time during his employment with the Company, whether directly or indirectly, and for his own behalf or that of any company, firm, person or other third party, seek to encourage or entice any employee of the Company [or Group] to leave the employment of the Company [or Group].]

Other activities

The Director will not during the period that he is employed by the Company:

1. take any steps to seek work with any competitor which will be regarded as a breach of his fiduciary obligaitons;

2. canvass solicit or otherwise make any representation or statement to any customer or supplier which may cause harm or adversely affect the Company/Group's business or entertain any offers from customers or suppliers, and in the event of the latter shall immediately inform the Company of any offers.

Secret Profits

The Director agrees that he will not take any money or other benefit from any client of the Company and will immediately advise the Company if any such money or other benefit is offered to the Company and he will not make any benefit from his position other than his agreed remuneration without the prior agreement of the Board.

[SEE ALSO MANUAL PRECEDENT Q5 & COMMENTARY]

17. Intellectual property	*[SHORT FORM CLAUSE]*
	Where the Director's duties will involve him in formulating and dealing with [LIST *e.g.* marketing, *etc.*] these duties will involve the production of designs, manufacturing methods, plans, processes or techniques in which any copyright or other intellectual property rights will subsist. The Director agrees that any such rights vest absolutely in the Company and he will take all steps and carry out all acts that may be necessary to ensure that the intellectual property is lawfully vested in the Company, including signing all applications and any other documents that may be necessary to apply for any Patent rights or other form of application in the United Kingdom and Worldwide, and that this obligation will continue to exist when the Director's employment has ended.
	[ALTERNATIVELY:
	Because of the nature of the employment the Director has signed an Intellectual Property Agreement. [It is a condition of your employment that you sign the Company's Intellectual Property Agreement]]
	[SEE MANUAL PRECEDENT Q4 FOR AN AGREEMENT AND Q5 FOR A FURTHER CLAUSE & COMMENTARY]
18. Confidentiality	The Director agrees that he will not at any time during his Employment and after the termination of his employment without restriction in time communicate, disclose or divulge to any third person or in any way make use of the Company/Group's Confidential Information or Trade Secrets [which, without prejudice to the generality of the foregoing include *[LIST]* relating to the Company, the Group, its customers or Suppliers *provided* that once the Director has left the employment with the Company this restriction shall not apply where such information has been ordered to be disclosed by a Court or otherwise by law and the Director shall not be prevented from using his own skills and experience.
	[FOR MORE DETAILS PROVISIONS SEE MANUAL PRECEDENTS Q2 AND Q5 AND COMMENTARY]

| 19. Post termination covenants: non solicitation, non dealing and non poaching | The Director agrees that for a period of [. . . .] months from the termination of his Employment he will not:

1. Canvass, solicit or otherwise in any way seek to procure, the business or business opportunities from any customer or client of the Company [or Group], where the customer or client of the Company [or Group] has been a customer or client [. . . .] months immediately preceding the termination of employment of the Director and with whom the Director has had, or is aware of, business dealings within the previous [. . . .] months.

2. Canvass, solicit or otherwise in any way seek to procure, orders from any supplier of the Company [or Group] where the supplier has supplied the Company [or Group] within the previous [. . . .] months and the Director has had dealings with the supplier or is aware of any agreement between supplier and the Company [or Group].

3. Deal with any customer or client of the Company [or Group], where the customer or client of the Company has been a customer or client [. . . .] months immediately preceding the termination of employment of the Director and with whom the Director has had business dealings within the previous [. . . .] months.

4. Deal with any supplier of the Company [or Group] where the supplier has supplied the Company [or Group] within the previous [. . . .] months and the Director has had dealings with the supplier or is aware of any agreement between supplier and the Company [or Group].

5. Seek to persuade or solicit or provide work, whether directly or indirectly, or by self employment or consultancy, to any person who was an employee of the Company [or Group] [. . .] years prior to the termination of the Director's employment, or was engaged in any capacity, and who would be in a position to harm the business of the Company [or Group] were he to accept any employment or engagement.

6. Accept, whether through himself or a third party, indirectly or indirectly and whether of his own or a third party's benefit any orders for any products |

19. Post termination covenants: non solicitation, non dealing and non poaching (cont.)	or services with which the Director was concerned whilst he was working for the Company [or Group] or which fell within his responsibilities as a Director and which the Company [or Group] would have been in a position to supply. **[SEE MANUAL PRECEDENT Q5 FOR A MORE DETAILED COVENANT & COMMENTARY]**
20. Post termination: working for competitors	The Director agrees that for a period of [. . . .] months from the termination of his Employment he will not: 1. Hold any material interest in any business which is or is likely to be in competition with the Company [or Group]. 2. Hold any material interest in any business which may require or might reasonably be considered by the Company [or Group] to require the disclosure of Confidential information belonging to the Company [Group] in order to properly discharge his functions in such business. 3. Accept employment or take any engagement, whether self employed or otherwise and whether directly or indirectly, from any competitor of the Company [Group] which is likely to adversely affect the business of the Company [Group]. **[SEE MANUAL PRECEDENT Q5 FOR A MORE DETAILED CLAUSE & COMMENTARY]** **[SEE SALESMAN AT 5.13 FOR A TERRITORIAL COVENANT]**
21. Company's property	Upon the termination of the Director's contract for whatever reason, the Director shall immediately return to the Company all property that belongs to the Company [Group], including: 1. Any computer, printer or other such equipment, and all computer discs and other software. If the Director has a password on any computer, the detail of the password. 2. All documents in whatever form, including any copies or summaries of the same and including the Director's working notes. 3. The Company car and keys.

21. Company's property (cont.)	For the purpose of this Agreement the Director irrevocably gives the Company the right to enter any property where the Company's property is held and remove the same.
22. Directorships	The Director agrees that upon the termination of his employment for whatever reason he will immediately resign all Company directorships in the Company or any Group Company and will sign all necessary forms for such purpose.
23. Severability of covenants	The Director agrees that the each of the covenants contained in this Agreement are reasonable and are necessary for the protection of the Company's business. However, each provision of this Agreement is independent and severable and if any of them should be found by a Court of Law to be unenforceable or ineffective for whatever reason that shall not affect the validity of the separate covenants. If any covenants would become valid if any wording was deleted then the covenant shall be deemed to be applicable with such deletions and shall apply as so amended as to make the same enforceable.
24. Termination of contract	*Notice* Save as set out below, the Company must give the Director [. . . .] months' notice to terminate this Agreement and the Director must give [. . . . .] months' notice. *Payment in lieu* The Company will have the right in its absolute discretion to terminate the Director's employment by paying *in lieu* of notice, on the following terms: 1. The payment will be the basic salary of the Director and no account shall be taken of any bonus, pension contributions or any benefits in kind. 2. The payment shall be subject to deductions for income tax and national insurance contributions. 3. The Director has no right to payment *in lieu* of notice. **[CONSDER THE ISSUE OF MITIGATION — SEE MANUAL AT PART V]**

24. Termination of contract	*Earlier Termination*
	The notice period is subject to the Company's rights to dismiss the Director without notice if:
	1. He is guilty of conduct set out in the Company's Disciplinary Procedures which warrant dismissal without notice.
	2. He commits any act of negligence, neglect of duty which is serious or does any act which causes the Company to lose trust and confidence and which justifies dismissal without notice.
	3. He is in serious or repudiatory breach of this agreement.
	4. He commits any act outside his employment which is liable to bring the Company [or Group] into disrepute.
	5. He is declared bankrupt or otherwise enters into any arrangement with his creditors.
	6. He is convicted of a criminal offence and in the case of a motoring offence this results in disqualification or imprisonment.
	7. He suffers from mental disorder.
	8. He is persistently absent from work for a period of [. . . .] days in any [. . . .] months.
	9. He is guilty of any serious or repudiatory breach of this Agreement.
25. Garden leave	Where notice has been given by either side to this Agreement, or the Director purports to leave the employment in breach of the notice that he is required to give
	The Company:
	1. shall no longer be under any duty to provide work to the Director and the Director shall have no right to carry out any work or services for the Company [but the Director may be required to make himself available during normal working hours should the Company [or Group] require his services];
	2 may direct that the Director cease all contact with any customers or Suppliers or employees of the Company [or Group];

25. Garden leave (cont.)	3. shall be entitled to exclude the Director from the Company [or Group]'s premises; *provided that* 4. the Company shall continue to have the right to suspend the Director in the circumstances provided for in the Disciplinary Policy; 5. during the notice period the Director will continue to receive all his contractual benefits.
26. Whole Agreement	This Agreement forms the Whole Agreement between the parties, save that it is subject to any further terms contained in the Letter of Appointment and the Director acknowledges that he has read the Letter, this Agreement and any Company Policies that are referred to in the Letter of Appointment. *[CONSIDER WHETHER EXPRESS REFERENCE SHOULD BE MADE I.E. TO EQUAL OPPORTUNITY POLICIES, ETC]*
27. Disputes	*[CONSIDER WHETHER AN ARBITRATION/ MEDIATION CLAUSE SHOULD BE INCLUDED — SEE Duggan on Wrongful Dismissal]*
SIGNATURES	*[CONSIDER WHETHER THE DOCUMENT SHOULD BE SIGNED AS A DEED]*

COMMENTARY

This detailed contract of employment contains model clauses that one would expect to find in a Director's Service Agreement and has been cross referenced with many of the earlier parts of this book. A detailed commentary on each clause is not therefore necessary and the checklist in relation to managers (see pages 137-144) is also a useful guide in considering what clauses to include. There are, however, a number of issues that are very specific to directors.

Status of directors

It is possible for a director to have the status of an officer and also be an employee, even if it is a one man company: see Duggan on *Unfair Dismissal* at page 17 for a full discussion. There is a distinction between executive and non-executive directors, the latter usually being an officer but not an employee. Non-Executive Directors will play a part in fixing remuneration for Executive Directors. However, the duties of a director mean that he owes a fiduciary duty to the company and there are also restrictions on the type of contract that may be entered into.

The Service Agreement

The following points may be made about the nature of the Service Agreement of a Director.

- A director cannot be given a fixed term appointment of more than 5 years without the shareholders' approval (section 319, Companies Act 1985).
- In the case of listed companies the Combined Code of the London Stock Exchange recommends that approval should be sought for a fixed contract of more than one year.
- Directors of public companies may not be appointed after the age of 70 unless the shareholders have voted on a resolution of which special notice has been given (section 293, CA 1985).
- Directors may be required to hold shares and if they are not acquired within two months the office will be regarded as vacated (section 291, CA 1985).
- The company must keep a copy of the contract of employment available for inspection by shareholders (section 318, CA 1985).
- The listing rules of the London Stock Exchange have more onerous requirements for inspection. They must be available for inspection by any party and there are a number of requirements of disclosure that must be contained in them, particularly relating to remuneration, profit sharing, commission or compensation on termination.

Fiduciary Duty

The following points may be made.

- Executive Directors owe a fiduciary duty to the company. By section 317 of the CA 1985 they must avoid any conflicts of interest and declare any interests in transactions or contracts discussed by the Board.
- If a director makes a profit from his position he will have to account to the company for all the profits (**Regal (Hastings) Limited v Gulliver** [1942] 1 All ER 378) and he will have to account for any damage caused by activities that were not the company's (**Bishopgate Investment Trust Limited v Maxwell** [1994] 1 All ER 262).

- If a director puts his interests before the company the court will not enforce the transaction (**Wilton Group PLC v Abrams** [1991] BCLC 315).
- A director cannot take part in any discussions about his salary and, in the case of listed companies it is recommended that a remuneration committee be set up, with a majority of non-executive directors to decide terms and conditions.
- A director must disclose his and his family's interests in the shares and debenture holding in the company (section 324, CA 1985).
- He may also not exploit inventions and discoveries made in the course of his employment even if he would have been able to claim copyright were he not a director.
- Any provision that a director will not be liable for negligence or other breaches of duty is void (section 310, CA 1985) but he may be insured against certain liabilities.

Termination

Payment of compensation for loss of office must be approved by the shareholders (section 312 CA 1985). There are a range of grounds on which the director's contracts may be terminated

- by resignation provided proper notice is given (**Glossop v Glossop** [1907] 2 Ch 370;
- by failure to attend, which may be provided for in the Articles of Association and should be considered when drafting the Clauses relating to sickness and sick pay;
- if he is disqualified from holding a directorship;
- if he is removed by ordinary resolution on special notice (section 303 CA 1985). This will not prevent the director from bringing a claim for breach of contract or a claim in the Employment Tribunal (see **Schindler v Northern Raincoat Co. Ltd** [1960] 2 All ER 239; 1 WLR 1038 and Duggan, *Wrongful Dismissal, Law, Practice and Precedents* for a full consideration of the principles);
- upon retirement. The articles may provide for the directors to retire by rotation. A director of a public company must retire at the annual general meeting on his seventieth birthday. He may be reappointed only by a shareholders' special resolution, of which special notice has been given, that states his age (section 293 CA 1985).

INDEX

Precedents or clauses are indicated in bold